UML Diagramming: A Case Study Approach

UML Diagramming
A Case Study Approach

Dr. Suriya Sundaramoorthy

CRC Press
Taylor & Francis Group

AN AUERBACH BOOK

First edition published 2022
by CRC Press
6000 Broken Sound Parkway NW, Suite 300, Boca Raton, FL 33487-2742

and by CRC Press
4 Park Square, Milton Park, Abingdon, Oxon, OX14 4RN

© 2022 Taylor & Francis Group, LLC

CRC Press is an imprint of Taylor & Francis Group, LLC

ISBN: 978-1-032-26129-4 (hbk)
ISBN: 978-1-032-12078-2 (pbk)
ISBN: 978-1-003-28712-4 (ebk)

DOI: 10.1201/9781003287124

Typeset in Garamond
by codeMantra

In the loving memory of my paternal grandfather Mr. S. Shanmugavelayutham (Telecom Employee), who taught me how much important is to educate a girl child in a family.

In the loving memory of my late maternal grandmother Mrs. A. Shenbagalakshmi (School Teacher) and late paternal grandmother Mrs. S. Sethulakshmi (Home Maker), who both taught me that the life of a working mother is actually a life of a warrior.

To my father, Mr. S. Sundaramoorthy (Postal Employee), who always have faith, love and hope on me with a strong belief that he has given enough education to his daughter to make a better tomorrow for herself.

To my mother, Mrs. R. J. Shanthi (BSNL Employee), who motivated me always to break all my hurdles.

To my loving daughters Shriya and Sana Dheepthi.

To my well-wishers and Gurus: Dr. V. C. S. Immanuel, Dr. S. P. Shantharajah and Mr. Ganesh Natrajan

To all my dear students who make me learn every time especially the batches of 2015–2019, 2016–2020, 2017–2021 and 2018–2022 of PSG College of Technology, Coimbatore, India who assisted me in this regard.

Finally, I would like to thank the great Almighty for blessing me with all these wonderful superheroes around me.

Contents

Preface

UML Diagramming: A Case Study Approach is the outcome of efforts of bringing out the role of UML Diagrams in exposing the needs of any innovative idea. It covers 40 chapters focusing on development of UML diagrams to expose the requirements for better understanding of underlying systems. The various case studies taken for discussion are WEBMED – Healthcare Service System Services, Inventory Management System, Business Process Outsourcing (BPO) Management System, E-Ticketing for Buses, Weather Monitoring System, E-Province, DigiDocLocker, Online Marketplace, Product Recommendation System, Advocate Diary, My Helper, COVID-19 Management System, Car Care, E-Rationshop, Textile Management System, National Health ID 2020, Device Handout System Online College Magazine System, Crime Bureau, Smart Traffic Management System, Job Seeker Portal System, AAROGYA SETU – Health Care APP, Online Pharmacy Management System, EQUIHEALTH, an OTT-based System – MINI REEL, E-Med Medical Assistance Tool, Diet Care, Student Counselling Management System, Video Suggestion System, E-Visa Processing and Follow-Up System, Placement Automation System, Farm Management System, Green Rides, Art Gallery Management System, GUIDE – Dropshipping Website, Online Quiz System, Book Bank Management System, Website Development, START-UP MEET and Video Suggestion System.

Author

Dr. Suriya Sundaramoorthy has completed her B.E. degree in the field of Computer Science and Engineering securing the 31st rank among all self-financing Engineering colleges under Anna University in 2004. She is a GATE scorer in GATE 2007. She is a gold medallist at ME CSE from PSG College of Technology, Coimbatore under Anna University in 2008. She was awarded with the BEST PROJECT AWARD for ME CSE stream. She was awarded with the BEST ALL ROUNDER of that batch. Later, she completed doctorate in the field of Information and Communication Engineering under Anna University in 2015. Currently, she is guiding Ph.D. scholars under Anna University. She has 10 years of experience in teaching. She has more than 50 journal and conference publications in the field of Grid Scheduling, Data Mining, Cloud Computing, Artificial Intelligence and Computational Intelligence. She has nearly 10 book chapter publications in CRC Press, Springer and Elsevier.

Chapter 1

Introduction to UML Diagrams and Its Components

1.1 UP Phases

An approach that helps a user to build, deploy and maintain a software is termed as Software Development Process. Such a Software Development Process which is required to build an Object Oriented System is called as 'Unified Process'. Craig Larman states Unified Process as 'The Unified Process (UP) combines commonly accepted best practices, such as an iterative lifecycle and risk-driven development, into a cohesive and well-documented description/process'. There are four phases of the Unified Process, namely Inception, Elaboration, Construction and Transition. The inception phase takes a problem statement from a client as input. It traces answers for the below seven questions to generate a report to decide about the feasibility of developing the software (Figure 1.1).

The elaboration phase takes the report generated by the inception phase as input to perform its processing. It involves three main activities like developing a core architecture for the given system, developing a project schedule and finally sketching a Unified Modeling Language (UML) Usecase diagram (Figure 1.2).

The construction phase involves a set of three activities, namely, coding, testing and feedback. Notable point is that the construction phase involves Alpha testing, i.e. testing a software at the developer site (Figure 1.3).

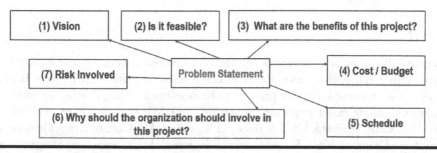

Figure 1.1   Inception phase.

DOI: 10.1201/9781003287124-1

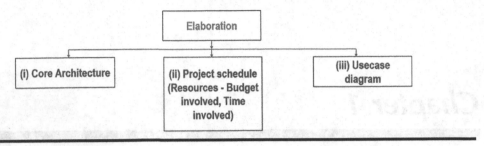

Figure 1.2   Elaboration phase.

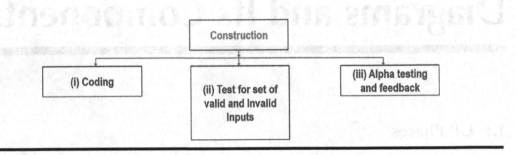

Figure 1.3   Construction phase.

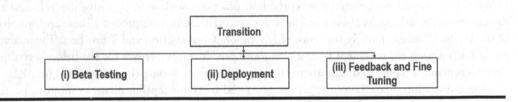

Figure 1.4   Transition phase.

The transition phase involves Beta testing, i.e. testing a software at the client site without the support of developers, followed by deployment, and finally, fine tuning is done based on feedback from the client's side (Figure 1.4).

1.1.1   UML

It is a standard diagrammatic tool for designing. It is a graphical language for specifying, visualizing, constructing and documenting the artefacts of software systems. It helps in better understanding of the software or system or product to be developed among developers and customers. UML diagrams include major important diagrams like UML Usecase Diagram, UML Activity Diagram, UML Class Diagram, UML Sequence Diagram, UML Collaboration Diagram or UML Communication Diagram, UML State Machine Diagram, UML Component Diagram and UML Deployment Diagram (Figure 1.5 and Table 1.1).

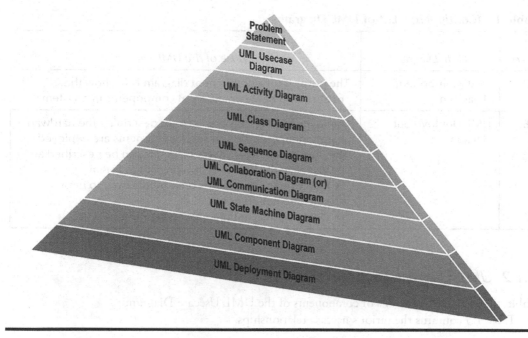

Figure 1.5 Pyramid of UML diagrams.

Table 1.1 List of UML Diagrams

S. No	UML Diagram	Purpose of the UML Diagram
1	UML Usecase Diagram	It focuses on the identification of functional requirements of the system under consideration.
2	UML Activity Diagram	It focuses on sequential and parallel activities involved in each functional requirement of the system.
3	UML Class Diagram	It describes the structure of the system in terms of classes and objects.
4	UML Sequence Diagram	It depicts the objects involved in the scenario and the sequence of messages exchanged between the objects needed to carry out the functionality.
5	UML Collaboration Diagram or UML Communication Diagram	It shows interactions between objects using sequenced messages in a free-form arrangement.
6	UML State Machine Diagram	It describes the life of an object using three main elements: states of an object, transitions between states and events that trigger the transitions.

(Continued)

Table 1.1 (*Continued*)   List of UML Diagrams

S. No	UML Diagram	Purpose of the UML Diagram
7	UML Component Diagram	The purpose of a component diagram is to show the relationship between different components in a system.
8	UML Deployment Diagram	Deployment diagrams are used for describing the hardware components, where software components are deployed. The purpose of deployment diagrams can be described as: • Visualize the hardware topology of a system. • Describe the hardware components used to deploy software components. • Describe the runtime processing nodes.

1.1.2 UML Usecase Diagram

Table 1.2 contains the details of components of the UML Usecase Diagram.

Table 1.3 contains the various usecase relationships.

Table 1.2   Components of UML Usecase Diagram

S. No	Name of the Component	UML Notation	Purpose
1	System Boundary	System	• It represents the scope of the system. • It encapsulates the complete set of functionalities of the system.
2	Actors	**Actor**	• The users that interact with a system. • An actor can be a person, an organization or an outside system that interacts with your application or system. • An actor in a usecase diagram interacts with a usecase. • It is up to the developer to consider what actors make an impact on the functionality that they want to model.
3	Usecases	Usecase	• A usecase is a visual representation of a distinct business functionality in a system. • It ensures that the business process is discrete in nature. • List the discrete business functions in given problem statement. • Identifying usecases is a discovery.

Table 1.3   Usecase Relationships

S. No	Usecase Relationship	UML Notation and Its Functionality
1	Association	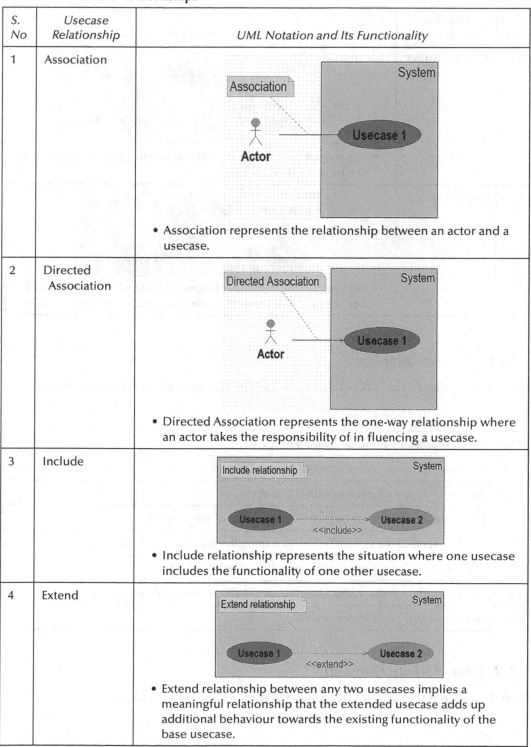 • Association represents the relationship between an actor and a usecase.
2	Directed Association	• Directed Association represents the one-way relationship where an actor takes the responsibility of in fluencing a usecase.
3	Include	• Include relationship represents the situation where one usecase includes the functionality of one other usecase.
4	Extend	• Extend relationship between any two usecases implies a meaningful relationship that the extended usecase adds up additional behaviour towards the existing functionality of the base usecase.

(*Continued*)

Table 1.3 (*Continued*)   Usecase Relationships

S. No	Usecase Relationship	UML Notation and Its Functionality
5	Generalization	 • Generalization is the relationship between a parent usecase and one or more child usecases.
6	Dependency	 • Dependency defines the relationship in which the existence of one usecase is dependent on the existence of another usecase.

1.1.2.1 Usecase Template

Every usecase is explained in detail through a standard template called as usecase template.

Usecase ID – represents a unique ID for a usecase.
Usecase Name – represents a meaningful name of the usecase.
Actors Involved – actors interacting with the usecase.
Description – the brief explanation of the functionality of the usecase.
Preconditions – state of the system before executing this functionality of the usecase.
Main Flow – description of how the functionality is implemented.
Post Conditions – state of the system after executing this functionality of the usecase.
Alternate Flow – other possibilities available.

1.1.3 UML Activity Diagram

Table 1.4 contains the details of components of the UML Activity Diagram.

Table 1.4 Components of UML Activity Diagram

S. No	Name of the Component	UML Notation and the Purpose of the Component
1	Initial state	• It represents the start state of the system under consideration.
2	Final state	• It represents the termination state of the system under consideration.
3	Swimlanes	• A swimlane contains two partitions namely a top partition representing entities like an actor/a usecase/a class, etc. and the second partition focuses on the set of activities involved. • Swimlane is of two types namely vertical swimlane and horizontal swimlane. • Vertical swimlane – represents parallel activities of a particular scenario of the system under consideration. Actor/ Usecase/ Class of the system under consideration Actor/ Usecase/ Class of the system under consideration • Horizontal swimlane – represents sequential activities of a particular scenario of the system under consideration.
4	Action state	• An action state represents an operation or a business activity or a process. Action State

(Continued)

Table 1.4 (*Continued*)   Components of UML Activity Diagram

S. No	Name of the Component	UML Notation and the Purpose of the Component
5	Object	• An entity that carries data between any two action states. [Object]
6	Synchronization	• Synchronization represents two or more activities happening at same time or rate. • It is of two types namely: Fork – divides a single activity flow into two or more concurrent activities and Join – combines two or more concurrent activities into a single flow by ensuring that only one of the activities at a time. Actor/ Usecase/ Class of the system under consideration FORK Action State Concurrent Activity 1 Concurrent Activity 2 Actor/ Usecase/ Class of the system under consideration Concurrent Activity 1 Concurrent Activity 2 JOIN Finally chosen one Activity out of all concurrent activities
7	Decision	• A decision node has one input or two or more outputs depending on the condition for which it is designed. • Each output flow has a condition attached to it. • If a condition is met, the flow proceeds along with the appropriate output. • An 'else' output can be defined along which the flow can proceed if no other condition is met. Actor/ Usecase/ Class of the system under consideration Action State before Condition checking [Condition 1] [Condition 2] Action State 1 Action State 2 DECISION [ELSE Condition] Action State 3

(Continued)

Table 1.4 (*Continued*) Components of UML Activity Diagram

S. No	Name of the Component	UML Notation and the Purpose of the Component
8	Merge	• The purpose is to merge the input flows. • The inputs are not synchronized; if a flow reaches such a node it proceeds at the output without waiting for the arrival of other flows. Actor/ Usecase/ Class of the system under consideration Action State 1 Action State 2 Action State 3 MERGE Action State 4
9	Flow Final	• It represents abnormal termination of a path in an activity diagram that is not considered as a part of the system under development.
10	Transition	• Transition are arrows that represent a movement from the source activity state to the target activity state which gets triggered by the completion of the activity of the source activity state. Source Activity State Target Activity State
11	Self-Transition	• It represents the internal transition to an actions state itself. Activity with Self Transition
12	Signal Send State	• Signals represent how activities can be influenced externally by the system. • They usually appear in pairs of sent and received signals. • Signal Send State represents sending signal action outside of the activity. • The signal sends state does not wait for any responses from the receiver of the signal. • It ends itself and passes the execution control to the next action. • A Signal Send State takes its notation as a convex pentagon. Signal Send State

(*Continued*)

Table 1.4 (*Continued*) Components of UML Activity Diagram

S. No	Name of the Component	UML Notation and the Purpose of the Component
13	Signal Accept State	• An action state whose trigger is a signal event is informally called Signal Accept State. • It corresponds to Signal Send State. • Signal Accept State with incoming edges means that the action starts after the previous action state completes. • Signal Accept State with no incoming edges remains enabled after it accepts an event. • It does not terminate after accepting an event and outputting a value, but continues to wait for other events. Signal Accept State
14	Subactivity	• A subactivity is an action state that can become as another main activity scenario in future. Sub Activity State

1.1.4 UML Sequence Diagram

Table 1.5 contains the details of components of the UML Sequence Diagram.

Table 1.5 Components of UML Sequence Diagram

S. No	Name of the Component	UML Notation and the Purpose of the Component
1	Object	• It represents an entity of the system that gets involved in interaction with other entities of the system via messages. • An object has three related information namely object name, lifeline and focus of control. • The standard syntax of naming an object is Object_name: Class_name. • Lifeline represents the complete existence of a particular object involved in a scenario. • Focus of control represents the active session of the object. OBJECT Object Name : Class Name LIFELINE FOCUS OF CONTROL (OR) ACTIVATION BAR

Table 1.5 (*Continued*) **Components of UML Sequence Diagram**

S. No	Name of the Component	UML Notation and the Purpose of the Component
2	Message & its types	• The communication between objects of any scenario is done through the concept of message passing with the help of transition component. • Messages are numbered over the transition arrows. • Syntax of message is Message_no: Message() • There are five types of messages applicable to any transition between any two objects in a sequence diagram.
2.1	Synchronous Message	• The messages sent from the sender are based on wait semantics. • Wait semantics is a situation where the sender needs an acknowledgement of each message sent from the receiver before transmitting the next successive message. • The notation of a synchronous message is a solid line with a shaded arrow head. Object a : Class A Object b : Class B 1 : Synchronous Message()
2.2	Return Message	• It represents a reply message for a synchronous message. Object a : Class A Object b : Class B 1 : Synchronous Message() 2 : Reply Message
2.3	Asynchronous Message	• These type of messages are sent by the sender to the receiver which does not require an acknowledgement from the receiver. • This feature enables the sender to send any number of messages to the receiver. Object a : Class A Object b : Class B 1 : Asynchronous Message_1 2 : Asynchronous Message_2 3 : Asynchronous Message_3

(Continued)

Table 1.5 (*Continued*)   Components of UML Sequence Diagram

S. No	Name of the Component	UML Notation and the Purpose of the Component
2.4	Create Message	• Create message represents the instantiation of objects in a scenario. • It includes the stereotype called <<create>>. Object a : Class A Object b : Class B 1 : Creating an instance of an object() <<create>>
2.5	Destroy Message	• Destroy message represents the destruction of the lifecycle of an object in a scenario. • It includes the stereotype called <<destroy>>. • Destruction is pictorially represented by a large X pointing at the end of the lifeline of an object. Object a : Class A Object b : Class B 1 : Creating an instance of an object() <<create>> 2 : Destruction of an Object() <<destroy>>
3	Fragments	• Fragments represent a set of conditional messages or looping messages in a scenario. • The most vital fragments are opt, alt, loop. • Each fragment is represented as a rectangular box encapsulating those set of messages with a label in the top left corner representing the fragment type.
3.1	Opt	• This fragment represents a simple IF scenario. • Messages get executed only if the condition defined in the opt fragment remains true. • In case of condition does not get satisfied, the control jumps out of the fragment. • Conditions are technically called as Guard. Object a : Class A Object b : Class B opt [Condition] 1 : Message_1 2 : Message_2

Table 1.5 (*Continued*)   Components of UML Sequence Diagram

S. No	Name of the Component	UML Notation and the Purpose of the Component
3.2	Alt	• This fragment represents IF ELSE scenario. • This fragment has two partitions inside the rectangular area. • Messages in the first compartment get executed only if the condition defined in the first partition of the alt fragment remains true. • Otherwise, the messages in the second partition of the alt fragment get executed.
3.3	Loop	• This fragment represents those set of messages that gets executed repeatedly until the condition defined in the loop fragment remains true. • This fragment has two partitions inside the rectangular area. • Messages in the first compartment get executed only if the condition defined in the first partition of the alt fragment remains true.
4	Nesting of fragments	• Depending on the demand of multiple conditions to get verified or repeated execution of the set of nested conditions, this concept of nesting can be applied to different types of fragments.

1.1.5 UML Collaboration Diagram

Majority of the components are common between UML Sequence Diagram and UML Collaboration Diagram. Table 1.6 contains the details of the unique components of the UML Collaboration Diagram.

Table 1.6   Unique Components of UML Collaboration Diagram

S. No	Name of the Component	UML Notation and the Purpose of the Component
1	Object	• It represents an entity of the system that gets involved in interaction with other entities of the system via messages. • In the case of UML Collaboration diagrams, an object does not have any lifeline or focus of control. Object a : Class A
2	Link	• Link enables the communication between any two objects. • It is represented as a solid line without any arrow heads, so that it represents bidirectional communication. • Any number of bidirectional messages between two objects can be communicated via a same link. Object a . Class A ————— Object b . Class B
3	Self Link	• A self-link connects an object to itself. Object a : Class A
4	Forward stimulus	• It represents messages from sender (first object) to receiver (second object). • It can of any of the five types of messages as discussed in UML Sequence Diagram like Synchronous messages, Return messages, Asynchronous messages, Create messages and Destroy messages. Object a : Class A — 1 : Message → Object b : Class B
5	Reverse stimulus	• It represents response messages from the receiver (second object) to sender (first object). • It can of any of the five types of messages as discussed in UML Sequence Diagram like Synchronous messages, Return messages, Asynchronous messages, Create messages and Destroy messages. 3 : Forward Stimulus Return Message ⋯⋯⟶ 1 : Forward Stimulus Asynchronous Message ⟶ Object a : Class A Object b : Class B ⟵ 2 : Reverse stimulus Synchronous message()

1.1.6   UML State Chart Diagram

Table 1.7 contains the details of components of the UML State Machine Diagram.

Table 1.7   Components of UML State Machine Diagram

S. No	Name of the Component	UML Notation and the Purpose of the Component
1	Initial State	• It represents the start state of a system under consideration.
2	Final State	• It represents the end state of a system under consideration.
3	Flow final	• It represents abnormal termination of a path in a state machine diagram which is not considered as a part of the system under development.

4	State	• It represents the state of the object in the system under consideration.
		 • It is described using the following attributes namely:
		   i. Name – Name of the object.
		   ii. Entry – Action to be done before to enter the system.
		   iii. Do – Action to be done in that state.
		   iv. Exit – Action to be required to exit the system.
		
		 Name of the state
		 entry/EntryAction
		 do/DoAction
		 exit/ExitAction

5	Transition	• Transition are arrows that represent a movement from one state to the other state which gets triggered by the completion of the activity of the source state. Source state — entry/EntryAction, do/DoAction, exit/ExitAction → Target state — entry/EntryAction, do/DoAction, exit/ExitAction
6	Self-Transition	• It represents internal transition to a state itself. State entry/EntryAction do/DoAction exit/ExitAction
7	Junction Point	• The purpose is to merge the input flows from different states • The inputs are not synchronized; if a flow reaches such a state it proceeds at the output without waiting for the arrival of other flows from other states.

(Continued)

Table 1.7 (*Continued*)   Components of UML State Machine Diagram

S. No	Name of the Component	*UML Notation and the Purpose of the Component*
		State entry/EntryAction do/DoAction exit/ExitAction State_3 entry/EntryAction do/DoAction exit/ExitAction **Junction Point** State_1 entry/EntryAction do/DoAction exit/ExitAction State_2 entry/EntryAction do/DoAction exit/ExitAction
8	Choice Point	• A Choice point has one input or two or more outputs depending on the condition for which it is designed. • Each output flow has a condition attached to it. If a condition is met, the flow proceeds along with the appropriate output. State entry/EntryAction do/DoAction exit/ExitAction State_3 entry/EntryAction do/DoAction exit/ExitAction **Choice Point** [Condition_3] [Condition_1] [Condition_2] State_1 entry/EntryAction do/DoAction exit/ExitAction State_2 entry/EntryAction do/DoAction exit/ExitAction
9	Shallow History	• Shallow history of a state is a reference to the most recently visited state on the same hierarchy level. **H**
10	Deep History	• Deep history of a state is a reference to the most recently visited simple state. **H***
11	Submachine state	• A submachine is a state that can become as another main state chart diagram scenario in future. SubmachineState entry/EntryAction do/DoAction exit/ExitAction

1.1.7 UML Class Diagram

Table 1.8 contains the details of components of the UML Class Diagram.

Table 1.8 Components of UML Class Diagram

S. No	Name of the Component	UML Notation and the Purpose of the Component
1	Class	• Each class has three compartments namely: 　i. Top compartment represents the name of class, 　ii. Middle compartment represents structure of the class (attributes) and 　iii. Bottom compartment represents behaviour of the class (operations) **Class_Name** +Attribute +Operation() • Attribute represents properties that describe the state of the object. • Syntax: Visibility Attribute_Name : Data_Type • Examples of data types are: Int, Char, Float, String, Date, Time, Money, Dollars, Colour, City, Country, Postal Code, Address, Boolean, etc. | Visibility Notation	Access Specifier
---	---
+	Public
#	Protected
-	Private	 • Derived attributes are those attributes that are calculated or derived from other attributes denoted by placing slash (/) before name. • Syntax:/Visibility Attribute_Name: Data_Type • Operations represents the actions or functions that a class can perform. • Syntax: Visibility Operation_Name (Input Arg): Data_Type • Input arguments take the syntax of an attribute. • Methods that don't return a value (i.e. void methods) should give a return type of void.
2	Class Relationships	• There are seven types of class relationship namely association, directed association, dependency, aggregation, composition, generalization, realization.
2.1	Association	• When two classes communicate with each other, an association is used to connect those two classes. **Class1** +Attribute — Association Name — **Class 2** +Operation()　　　　　　　　　　+Attribute 　　　　　　　　　　　　　　　　+Operation()

(Continued)

Table 1.8 (*Continued*)   Components of UML Class Diagram

S. No	Name of the Component	UML Notation and the Purpose of the Component
2.2	Directed Association	• When two classes get connected in such way by giving priority to one-way communication, they are connected by directed association. *[diagram: Class1 (+Attribute, +Operation()) — Association Name → Class 2 (+Attribute, +Operation())]*
2.3	Dependency	• When the existence of one class is dependent on the existence of another class, then they are connected using dependency. *[diagram: Class1 (+Attribute, +Operation()) ----→ Class 2 (+Attribute, +Operation())]*
2.4	Aggregation	• It represents a 'part of' relationship. • Many instances of Class1 can be associated with Class2. • Aggregation implies a relationship where the child class can exist independently of the parent class. *[diagram: Class1 (+Attribute, +Operation()) —◇ Class 2 (+Attribute, +Operation())]*
2.5	Composition	• It represents a 'whole' relationship. • Composition implies a relationship where the child class cannot exist independent of the parent class. *[diagram: Class1 (+Attribute, +Operation()) —◆ Class 2 (+Attribute, +Operation())]*
2.6	Generalization	• Generalization represents the concept of inheritance. • It represents the relationship between parent class and its child classes. *[diagram: Parent Class (+Attribute, +Operation()) with two child classes — Child Class 1 (+Attribute, +Operation()) and Child Class 2 (+Attribute, +Operation()) connected by generalization arrows]*

Table 1.8 (*Continued***) Components of UML Class Diagram**

S. No	Name of the Component	UML Notation and the Purpose of the Component
2.7	Interface & role of Realization	• Interfaces can be of two types namely required interfaces and provider interfaces. • Provider interface describes the functionality offered by a class. • Required interfaces describe the functionality needed by another class. • Provided interface is the interface implemented by a class, i.e a class implements an interface. • The required interface would be any use of an interface by a component, i.e if a class defines a method that has the interface as a parameter. Required Interface (Dependency between the class and interface) **Class 1** +Attribute +Operation() Interface 1 **Class 2** +Attribute +Operation() Interface 2 Provider Interface (Realization between the class and interface)
3	Association Class	• An association class is an association that is also a class. • It not only connects a set of classifiers but also defines a set of features that belong to the relationship itself and not any of the classifiers. **Class 1** +Attribute +Operation() **Class 2** +Attribute +Operation() **Association Class** +Attribute +Operation()

1.1.8 UML Component Diagram

Table 1.9 contains the details of components of the UML Component Diagram.

Table 1.9 Components of UML Component Diagram

S. No	Name of the Component	UML Notation and the Purpose of the Component
1	Component	• It is a modular part of a system that encapsulates its contents. • They are the logical elements of a system that plays an essential role during the execution of a system. • A component is a replaceable and executable piece of a system. Component
2	Interface	• There are two types of component interfaces, namely provider interface and required interface. • Provider interface describes the functionality offered by a component. • Required interfaces describe the functionality needed by another component. Component —— **Required Interface** Component 1 —— **Provider Interface**
3	Port	• A port enables better communication between an interface and a component. Component — Port —— **Required Interface** Component 1 — Port1 —— **Provider Interface**
4	Artifact	• Scripting files like PHP, database files, configuration files, rar files, executable files. Component 1 <<artifact>> **Artifact**
5	Association	• It represents the two-way communication between any two components involved in a relationship. Component —— Association Name —— Component 1

1.1.9 UML Deployment Diagram

Table 1.10 contains the details of components of the UML Deployment Diagram.

Table 1.10 Components of UML Deployment Diagram

S. No	Name of the Component	UML Notation and the Purpose of the Component
1	Node	• Any computational resource with memory and processing capability. • There are two types of nodes namely Device node and Execution Environment Node. • A Device node represents a hardware device like Application server, workstations, mobile device, embedded device, etc. • An Execution Environment node represents a software or a program like Operating system, workflow engine, browser, Container, web server, database system, etc. Device Node Execution Environment Node
2	Artifact	• Scripting files like PHP, database files, configuration files, rar files, executable files. Device Node Execution Environment Node <<artifact>> Artifact
3	Port	• Port enables the communication between a device node and an execution environment node. • It also enables the communication between a node and an external environment. Port for communciation with external environment Device Node　　Port Execution Environment Node <<artifact>> Artifact　　Port Port for communication between nodes

(Continued)

Table 1.10 (*Continued*) Components of UML Deployment Diagram

S. No	Name of the Component	UML Notation and the Purpose of the Component
4	Association	• It represents the two-way communication between any two nodes involved in a relationship.
5	Directed Association	• It represents the one-way communication between any two nodes involved in a relationship.
6	Dependency	• It represents how an existence of a node is dependent on another node involved in a relationship.

Chapter 2

Design of UML Diagrams for Webmed – Healthcare Service System Services

2.1 Problem Statement

Healthcare service has huge demand these days as it really helps in managing a hospital or a medical office. The scope of healthcare service systems is increasing by each day and it is true for the entire world. Some of these solutions include improved awareness about healthcare services and health policies. The objective of this system is to provide medical assistance to people instantly with the help of technology. This system eradicates the cultural sensitivity that prevails in many hospitals and improvises the quality of medical assistance. The captivating features of this system are online doctors, medicines at doorstep and bulletin of awareness. The users can also navigate and choose among various insurance schemes that are displayed.

The primary objectives of Webmed healthcare system are to enable all citizens to receive healthcare services whenever needed, and to deliver health services that are cost-effective and meet pre-established standards of quality. The main functions of this system deal with finance, health A–Z, resources, drugs and supplements, news and experts, payment and feedback. Register function allows the patients or the caregivers to register on the website. Login function allows the patients to access the website. Financing focuses on the purchase of insurance. Health A–Z displays all the diseases along with their symptoms. Resources function consists of the sub-functions including symptoms checker, health calculator, find a doctor based on the geographical location of the patient, insurance guide and ambulance providence. Drugs and supplements include online medicine delivery, where people could shop for medicines online. News and experts function is to provide health awareness and threats that are prevailing. This function also gives information regarding counselling programs and blood donation camps. The payment function is to reimburse providers for services delivered. The feedback function collects user reviews for the website.

DOI: 10.1201/9781003287124-2

2.2 Major Functionalities and Its Description

The major functionalities of this system along with their description are as follows:

Register – this functionality acts as a membership functionality that allows the users, patients or caregivers to register into this website to access all the resources. Login – this functionality authenticates the user to provide access permissions. Facilities – this functionality allows us to access all the options available on the website. Logout – this functionality ends the access to the website. Finance – this functionality allows to purchase insurance, or to pay for healthcare services consumed. Health A–Z – this functionality provides details of all the diseases. Resources – this functionality has sub-functions, namely symptoms checker, health calculator, find a doctor, insurance guide and ambulance providence. Drugs and supplements – this functionality provides online delivery of medicines. This functionality takes the doctor's statement for the issue of medicine and the patient's willingness to buy it online. News and experts – this functionality provides health awareness and threats that are prevailing. Payment – this functionality deals with the payment for the services consumed. This functionality is split into two sub-functions namely, payment for doctors, for the services issued and payment for online med-delivery. Feedback – this functionality collects user reviews for this website.

System Architecture: System architecture is the conceptual model that defines the structure, behaviour and more views of a system. An architecture description is a formal description and representation of a system, organized in a way that supports reasoning about the structures and behaviours of the system. This architecture diagram shown in Figure 2.1 includes all the functionalities of the system in an ordered manner based on the sequence of occurrence of these functionalities. It represents the complete data flow starting from the register functionality through which the user could access the system to the logout functionality that ends the access

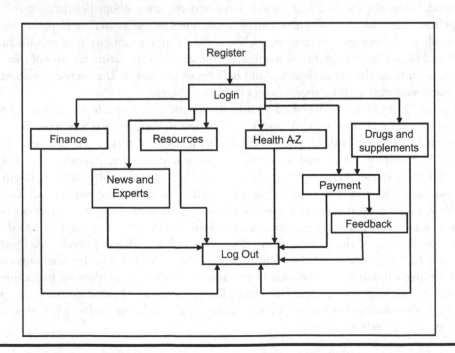

Figure 2.1   System architecture.

of the user to the system. Initially, the user must register onto the system. Once registered, the user would be able to log on to the system and could access all the services offered – finance, news and experts, resources that include finding a doctor, health A–Z that includes health calculator and fitness calculator, drug and supplements, payment and feedback. The payment is done through the insurance for the services consumed. After consuming the services, the user could log out of the system.

2.3 Data-Flow Diagrams

A data-flow diagram (DFD) is a way of representing a flow of a data of a process or a system. The DFD also provides information about the outputs and inputs of each entity and the process itself. A DFD has no control flow; there are no decision rules and no loops. A DFD can dive into progressively more detail by using levels and layers. DFD levels are numbered 0, 1 and 2.

DFD Level 0 is also called a Context Diagram. It is a basic overview of the whole system or process being analyzed or modelled. It is designed to be an at-a-glance view, showing the system as a single high-level process, with its relationship to external entities. This level 0 DFD diagram as shown in Figure 2.2 consists of the healthcare service provider system – Webmed and the actors who affect those systems – the users that is the patients and the service providers who are responsible for the maintenance of the system. This is the basic diagram that could be easily understood by a wide audience. DFD Level 1 as shown in Figure 2.3 provides a more detailed breakout of pieces of the Context Level Diagram. We will highlight the main functions carried out by the system, as you break down the high-level process of the Context Diagram into its sub-processes.

These systems too have the same external entities – patients who require the service and the service providers who offer those services via the system. The Webmed system is broken down into a number of sub-processes. These sub-processes represent the functionalities of the system – register, login, finance, health A–Z, resources, drugs and supplements, news and experts, payment, feedback and logout. Payment is done to find a doctor and the drugs and supplements services provided. The user could also give the feedback for the services available. Table 2.1 describes the comparison between the existing system and the proposed system.

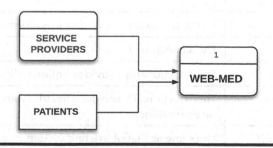

Figure 2.2   Level 0 DFD.

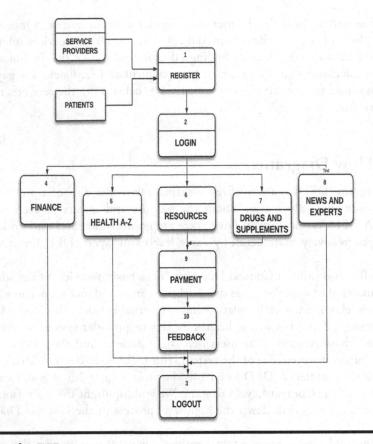

Figure 2.3 Level 1 DFD.

Table 2.1 Comparison of Proposed System and Existing System

Existing System	Additional Features of Proposed System with Reference to Existing System
Register	The same as that of the existing system
Login	
Logout	
Finance	
Health A–Z	It acts as a dictionary of diseases along with their symptoms.
Resources	The same as that of existing system.
Drugs and supplements	This functionality provides online delivery of medicines.
News and experts	This functionality provides health awareness and threats that are prevailing.
Payment	The same as that of existing system.
Feedback	This functionality collects user reviews for this website.

2.4 Proposed Design – UML Diagrams

2.4.1 Usecase Specification for the UML Usecase Diagram Generated Using Star UML Tool

Actor Specification

1. **Patient** – This actor plays the role of a patient who can register on the website and can make use of all the services provided by the website. This actor can also play a role of a caregiver.
2. **Service Provider** – This actor acts as the master of this website who provides certain services. This actor maintains a database of doctors that helps a patient to find a doctor and looks after the finance, insurance and payment requirements. He also gives descriptions regarding various diseases that can be referred by the users. He also provides a facility for the users to purchase drugs and other medicines online and spreads awareness through news regarding the prevailing threats (Figure 2.4).

Usecase Specification

1. **Drugs and Supplements**
   Description: This functionality provides online delivery of medicines.
   Flow of Events
   Basic Flow: It allows the users to search for and purchase drugs and other medical supplies like sringes, bandages and dressing, earloop face masks, etc.

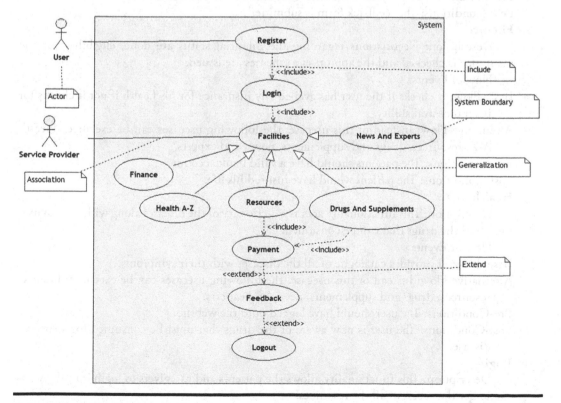

Figure 2.4   UML usecase diagram.

Alternative Flow: Alternate flow for this usecase is: Health A-Z, resources, finance, news, and experts.

Pre-Conditions: The user must have logged on to the website to make use of this functionality.

Post-Conditions: The drugs and medicines database get updated accordingly.

2. **Facilities**

Description: The service provider controls all the facilities on the website through this usecase and the user can utilize these facilities.

Flow of Events

Basic Flow: The user can obtain the services like: Health A–Z, resources, drugs and supplements, news and experts, and finance.

Alternative Flow: The user can provide his feedback for improvement of the website.

Pre-Conditions: The user must have logged on to the website in order to make use of this functionality.

Post-Conditions: By getting into this usecase, the user can make use of the available services.

3. **Feedback**

Description: This Feedback section helps the users to give their honest opinions about the quality of services that have been provided. It also helps them to give their suggestions for further improvements.

Flow of Events

Basic Flow: It verifies whether the feedback is given or not.

Alternative Flow: LOGOUT.

Pre-Conditions: The payment function should have been completed.

Post-Conditions: The feedback form is submitted.

4. **Finance**

Description: Negotiations regarding the financial status are done, eligibility for the insurance is checked and the appropriate schemes are issued.

Flow of Events

Basic Flow: It checks if the user has availed any insurance for his health if not it checks for insurance availability.

Alternative Flow: Instead of this usecase, the following usecases can be executed: Health A-Z, resources, drugs and supplements, news, and experts.

Pre-Conditions: The patients should have a valid bank account.

Post-Conditions: The patient would have insured his life.

5. **Health A–Z**

Description: This functionality acts as a dictionary of the diseases along with their symptoms and the drugs that can be consumed.

Flow of Events

Basic Flow: It provides catalogue of all the diseases with their symptoms.

Alternative Flow: Instead of this usecase, the following usecases can be executed: finance, resources, drugs and supplements, news, and experts.

Pre-Conditions: The user should have logged onto the website.

Post-Conditions: The user is now aware of the drugs that must be consumed for a specific disease.

6. **Login**

Description: This functionality allows the patients and caregivers to login into the website to get the access to all the resources.

Flow of Events

Basic Flow: It allows the user to access all the resources that are available in the website.

Alternative Flow: After this usecase is executed, then the control flows through any one of the following usecases: Finance, health A-Z, resources, drugs and supplements, news, and experts.

Pre-Conditions: The user should have registered into the website.

Post-Conditions: The user is given the complete access to all the resources available on the website.

7. **Logout**

Description: This functionality ends the access to the website. So the user must log in again to access all the resources.

Flow of Events

Basic Flow: It ends the access of the resources by the user.

Alternative Flow: It has no alternate flow.

Pre-Conditions: The user should have logged onto the website.

Post-Conditions: Once this usecase is executed, the user is denied from the resources provided by this website.

8. **News and Experts**

Description: A bulletin of news regarding the latest diseases that prevails in the environment, expert opinions to avoid those communicable and non-communicable diseases, awareness about the diseases will be displayed publicly.

Flow of Events

Basic Flow: The current affairs about the diseases are well received by the users.

Alternative Flow: Instead of this usecase, the following usecases can be executed: Health A-Z, resources, drugs and supplements, and finance.

Pre-Conditions: The user should have logged in.

Post-Conditions: The user is enlightened about the prevalent diseases.

9. **Payment**

Description: This functionality deals with the payment for the services consumed.

Flow of Events

Basic Flow: This functionality involves the payment for the services provided by the doctor.

Alternative Flow: After executing this usecase, the control moves to the usecase feedback.

Pre-Conditions: The user should have consumed the services provided by the doctor or should have purchased medicines online.

Post-Conditions: After executing this usecase, the user has made the payment for the medicines purchased or the service providers have made the payment to the doctors.

10. **Register**

Description: This acts as a membership functionality that allows the patients or caregivers to register into this website to access all the resources

Flow of Events

Basic Flow: It allows the user to register on the website.

Alternative Flow: After the register usecase is executed, the usecase that can be executed is: LOGIN functionality.

Pre-Conditions: This is no precondition as register is the first usecase to be executed.

Post-Conditions: After the register usecase is executed, the user will be given a Webmed membership.

11. **Resources**

Description: The resources such as health calculator, ambulance services, symptoms checker, find a doctor and insurance guidance are unveiled in this segment.

Flow of Events

Basic Flow: Thus the resources are gathered by the users.

Alternative Flow: Instead of this usecase, the usecases that can be executed are: HEALTH A–Z, NEWS AND EXPERTS, DRUGS AND SUPPLEMENTS, and FINANCE.

Pre-Conditions: The availability of the resources should be ensured.

Post-Conditions: The users have enjoyed the privileges of accessing the resources (Figure 2.5).

The two actors, user and the service providers can access the resources on the website. The facilities class consists of the functions like news and experts, health A–Z and health calculator. The finance class checks if the user has health insurance and if not alerts the service provider who buys the insurance for the user. The realization relationship is used to link the user and the service provider with the finance class. The payment class involves the payment by the user for the services consumed. The payment can either be an online payment or through cash on delivery of drugs and other supplements. Thus the generalization relationship is used to represent the cash and online payment of the payment class. The payment class is loosely related to the user class and it is strongly related to the service provider class as the service provider takes care of all the payment procedures. The resources like finding a doctor, which suggests a suitable doctor specialized for a disease and purchase of drugs and supplements are the resources for which the payment is done. So these resources are common to both the facilities class and the payment class. Hence these resources are kept in an association class named as 'utilization' (Figure 2.6).

The activity diagram represents the flow of data through the system. It represents the entire flow of data from the registration of the user, followed by logging on to the website with username and password. Once the user has logged on to the system, the user could access all the resources and can navigate through the resources again until the user wishes to log out the system. The user needs to pay for the services which they acquired. The user could also give the feedback for the system if the user opts it (Figure 2.7).

In this activity diagram, the register is a sub-activity. The register has an individual flow of control that enables the user to enrol them into the system. The activity diagram above illustrates the flow that takes place in the register function. The user is prompted to give all the details. The service provider then generates the random id and receives the password from the user and confirms the password. If the password and confirm password are the same then the user is registered to the system else the user is prompted to give the text for the confirm password field alone (Figures 2.8 and 2.9).

The system first checks if the user is a registered user, if yes the user is prompted to the login state, else the user is asked to register into the system and is prompted to the register state. Once logged into the system, the user could access the facilities based on the choice of the user. Based on the choice of the user, the user is prompted to the required state. In this diagram, the login is a submachine state that consists of many disjoint states. If the user needs to find a doctor or needs to purchase drugs then the user is checked for the availability of insurance. If not the system buys an insurance for the user and is allowed to use the services. The payment is done for the services consumed using the payment state. Once the user has accessed the resources, the user could again loop on all the resources again if required, else the user could log out of the system. Before logging out of the system, the user could also give the feedback for the services provided by the system if the user wishes to do so.

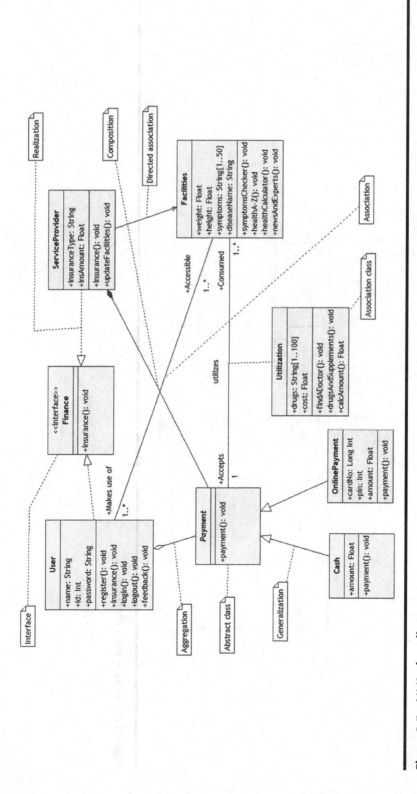

Figure 2.5 UML class diagram.

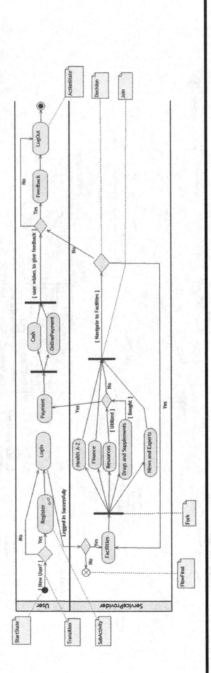

Figure 2.6 UML activity diagram (1).

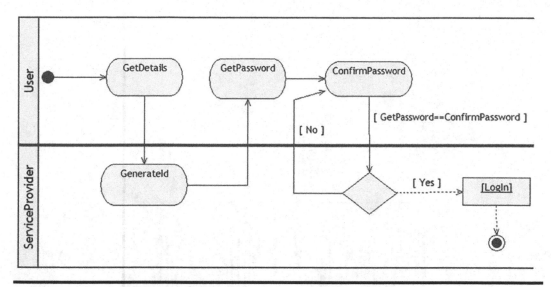

Figure 2.7   UML activity diagram (2).

The interaction between the user and the service provider is clearly depicted in this diagram. The user is checked if the user is already registered to the system or not. If not registered to the system, the register function takes place. If registered, the user can logged in the system with username and password. For this if else case, the alternate fragment is used. After logging on to the system, the user is correctly prompted to the functionality based on the choice of the user. Hence to select the resource, the optional fragment is used. In order to access the find a doctor and the drugs and supplements, the user is checked for the insurance. If not, the service provider buys insurance for the user. This insurance is used for the payment of the resources utilized. The request from the user is sent as a synchronous message as the user needs the response for the request. The response is sent as a reply message. The complete flow of messages from the register to the payment and delivery of the purchased drugs is clearly depicted in the sequence diagram (Figure 2.10).

It focuses on the interaction between the actors in the system same as that of the sequence diagram. The collaboration diagram does not consist of any fragments. Hence the messages are used to represent the conditional and looping statement. The sequence diagram has 34 messages. But the collaboration diagram has 35 messages. This extra one message (23) is used to prevent the overlapping of messages. Since the entire payment function involves overlapping of messages, an extra message is used to indicate the start of the payment function. A component is a replaceable and executable piece of a system whose implementation details are hidden. A component provides the set of interfaces that a component realizes or implements. Components also require interfaces to carry out a function. Components also require interfaces to carry out a function. UML component diagrams are used to represent different components of a system. In this diagram, every component represents an individual module that encompasses all its attributes and operations. The user component can access all the resources. The user component consists of the resources, health A–Z, news and experts as it can access those directly. The database subsystem consists of all the artefacts that are required for the system. The service provider is a service that takes care of the processes like financing, placing order to buy those drugs that are out of stock. The drug supplier component supplies the drugs to the service providers for which the payment is done (Figures 2.11 and 2.12).

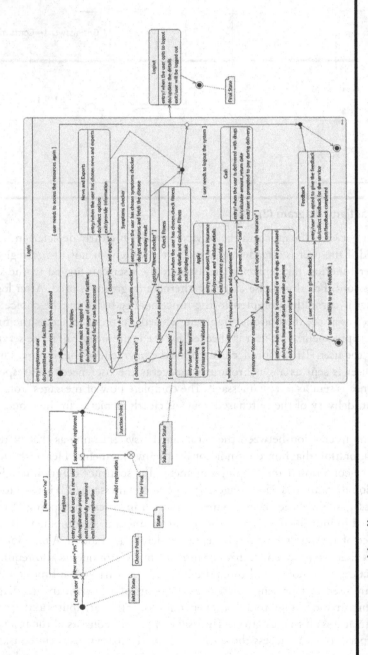

Figure 2.8 UML state machine diagram.

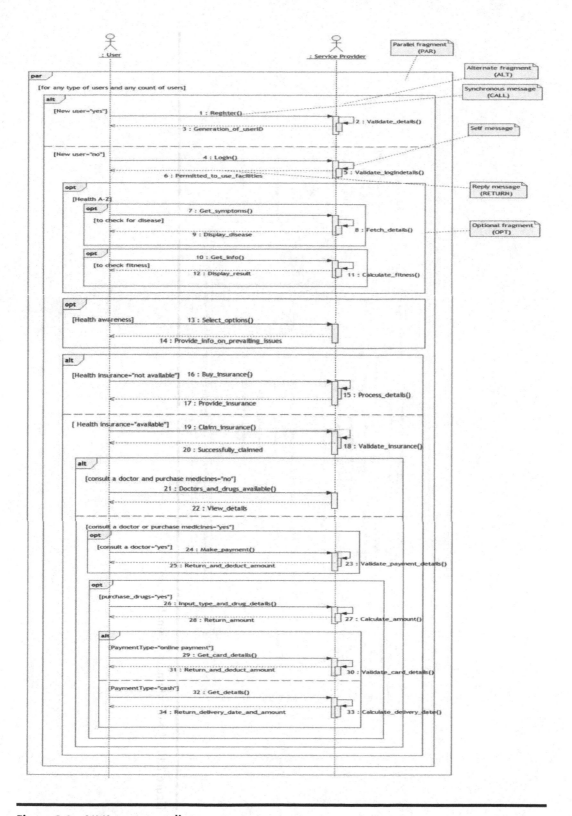

Figure 2.9   UML sequence diagram.

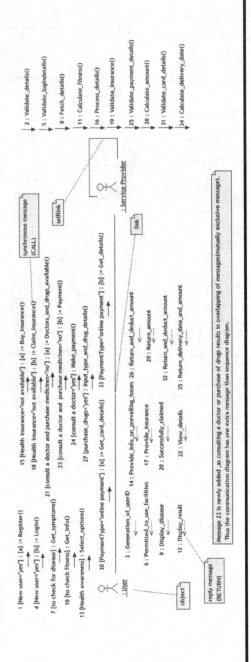

Figure 2.10   UML communication diagram.

The nodes and the Execution Environment Node are used to represent the OS, database and the web browser. The attributes and the operations are represented using parts as that of the component diagram. The database is maintained in the service provider as it needs to search for the details of the patient in the event of register, login, finding a doctor and payment. The drug supplier node is used to illustrate the attributes and operations involved in representing the ordering and purchasing of the drugs. The protocol that is used between the user and the service provider is Secure and Auditable Agent-based Communication Protocol (SAACP). SAACP is often used by most of the hospitals to maintain the details of the patients in a secure way. Each node has parts that denote the attributes and operations that it can involve.

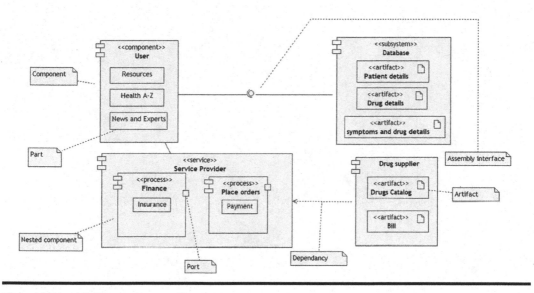

Figure 2.11   UML component diagram.

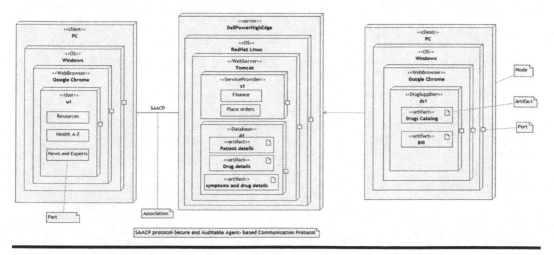

Figure 2.12   UML deployment diagram.

Chapter 3

Design of UML Diagrams for Inventory Management System

3.1 Problem Statement

This chapter aims to create an inventory management system for the efficient management of goods. The performance will be guided by clear and concise strategic practices for each functional unit by an ongoing quest for perfection. The current systems use a manual method to keep track of the records at stores, but the current system is difficult to maintain due to the difficulty in searching and retrieving products, cost of material, human errors, less data integrity, and feasible loss of records and retrieving files. Therefore, by developing such a system, we propose to increase sales by creating the complete inventory records of stock, receipt, details of purchasers and sellers at the store and also to facilitate the salespersons and inventory managers. The ever-growing population creates a high demand. Thus, the responsibility of delivering goods on time lies in the hands of an effective inventory management system. The inventory management system will be installed in both the warehouse and at the billing counter thereby enabling the salespersons and the inventory managers to get instantaneous information and use it on demand. The customer billing process will happen at the main counter and the inventory management will happen in the background in the warehouse.

3.2 Software Requirements Specification

The current inventory system is difficult to maintain due to the difficulty in searching and retrieving products, cost of material, human errors, less data integrity, and feasible loss of records and retrieving files. So there is a need to create robust inventory management software that ensures a reduction in customer's complaints as well as the reduction in inventory cost. The demand for goods accrues from the growing population. To meet these demands, the inventory managers and salespersons require an application with on-demand information retrieval and update. The system will feature a secure login for salespersons and inventory managers. At the warehouse, the inventory application will manage the available goods and resources. At the billing counter, the application will have the ability to create bills along with proper discount and tax evaluations.

DOI: 10.1201/9781003287124-3

3.3 Functional Requirements

Authentication – Login: This will allow inventory managers and salespersons to log in to the system.
Change Password: This will allow inventory managers and salespersons to change the password.
Add Goods: This will allow adding goods and their corresponding details to the current inventory.
Remove Goods: This will allow removing goods from the current inventory.
Place Order: This will allow placing a wholesale order to the supplier.
Invoice Generation: This will allow generating an invoice for the order request to the supplier.
Search Item: This will allow searching the item details in the current inventory.
Receipt Generation: This will generate a bill for the customer selected items from the inventory.
Discount and Tax Generation: This will calculate the discount and tax based on the quantity selected by the customer.
Replace Item: This will replace the item in the current inventory.
Cancel Receipt: This will cancel the currently generated receipt.
Price Updating: This will update the price details of the corresponding item.
Customer Request: This will log an item request from the customer.
View Summary Report: This will generate the summary report for all the transactions that have taken place.
Expired Goods: This will notify about the removal of goods from the current inventory.

3.4 Design and Design Constraints

The constraints are that a lot of information should not be displayed on the screen while placing the order or using the interface. By reducing it to a minimalistic interface, we are able to deliver an elevated user experience (Figures 3.1–3.11).

INVENTREE
an inventory management system

username

password

login

Figure 3.1 Login functionality (home dashboard).

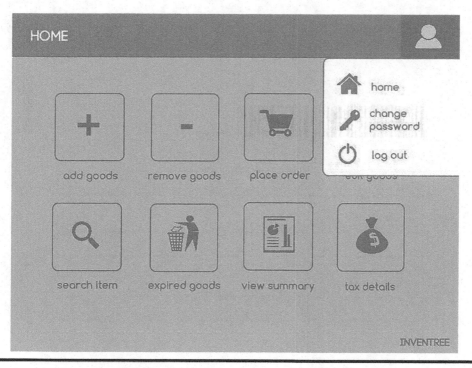

Figure 3.2   Dashboard popup.

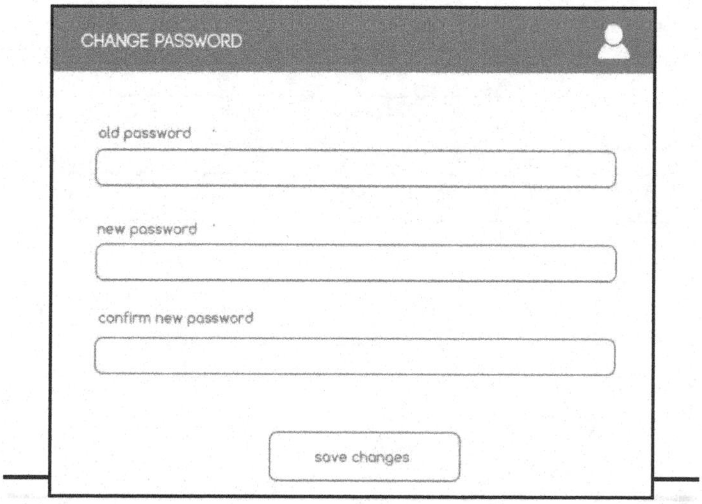

Figure 3.3   Change password.

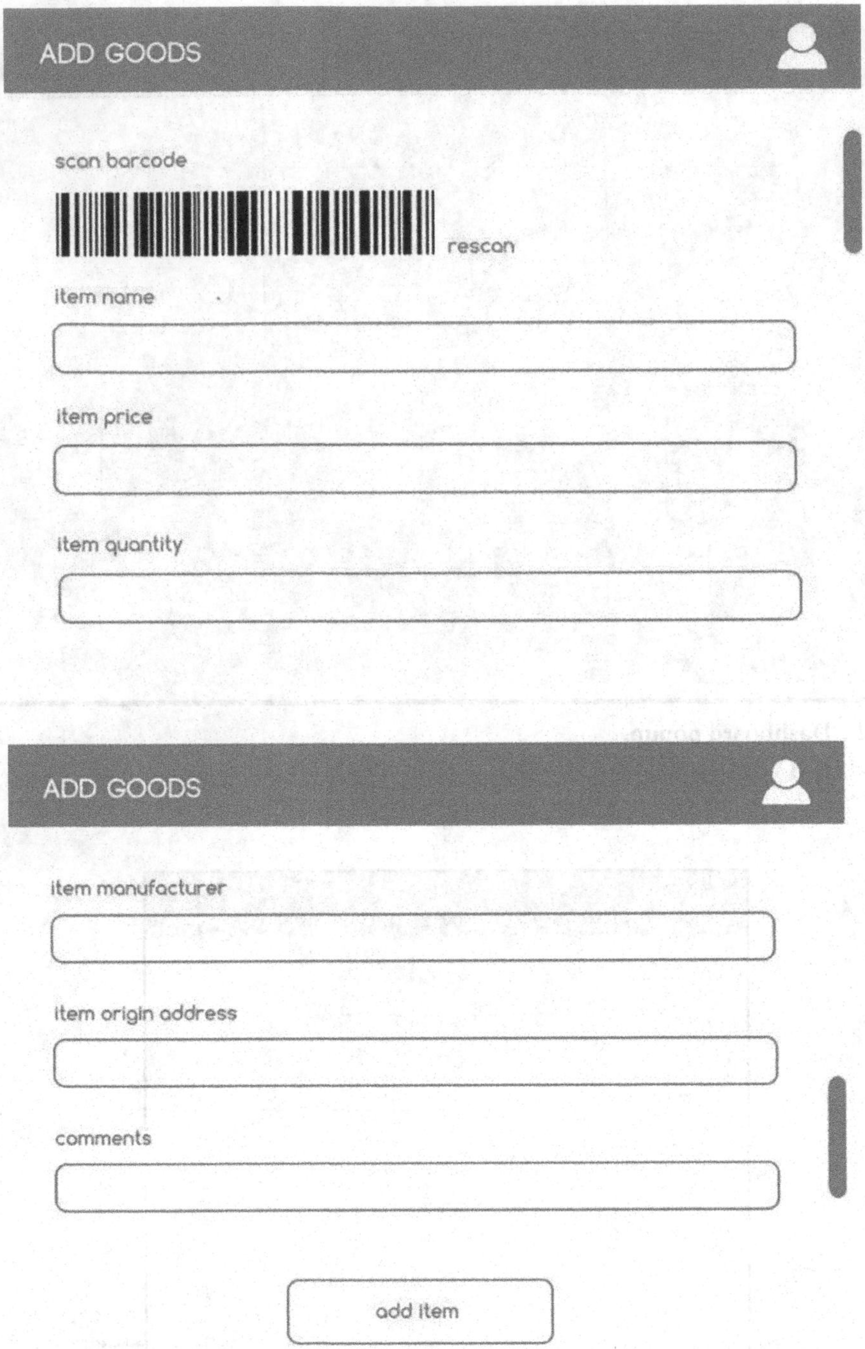

Figure 3.4 Add goods.

REMOVE GOODS

scan barcode

rescan

item id

item quantity

remove item

Figure 3.5   Remove goods.

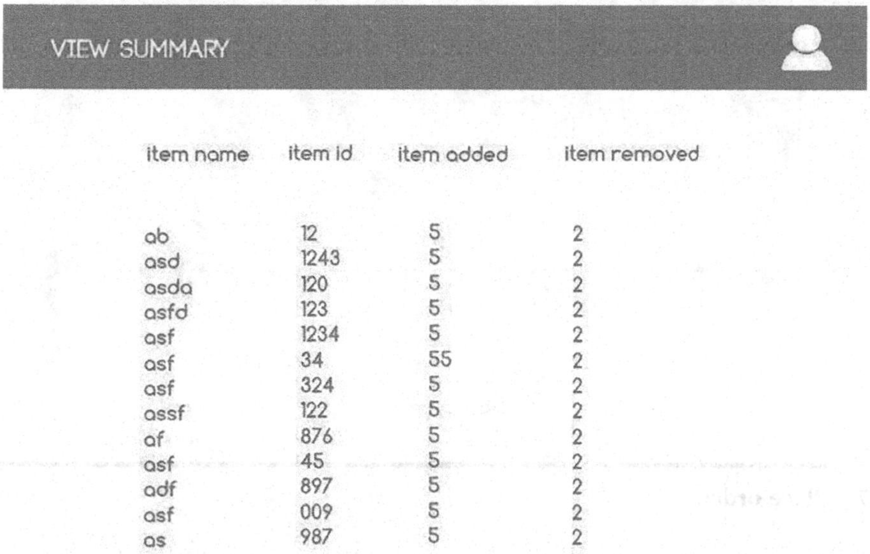

VIEW SUMMARY

item name	item id	item added	item removed
ab	12	5	2
asd	1243	5	2
asda	120	5	2
asfd	123	5	2
asf	1234	5	2
asf	34	55	2
asf	324	5	2
assf	122	5	2
af	876	5	2
asf	45	5	2
adf	897	5	2
asf	009	5	2
as	987	5	2

Figure 3.6   View summary.

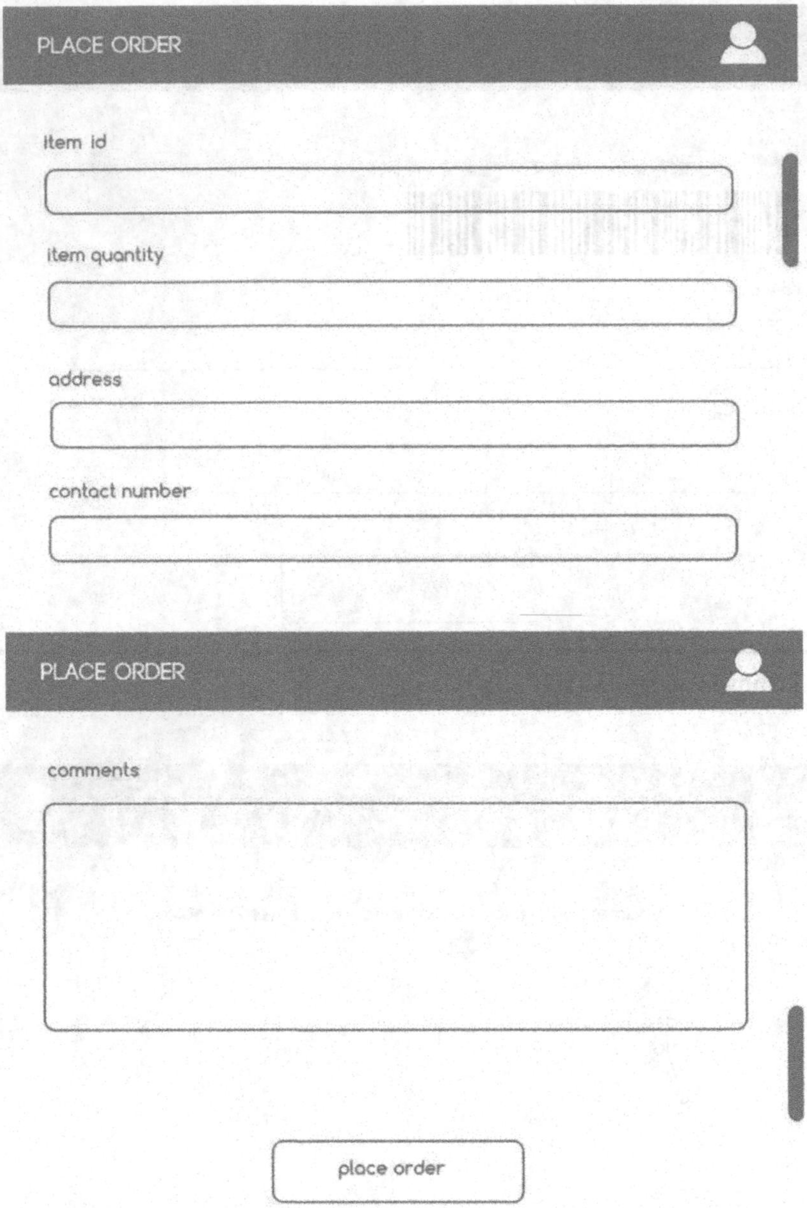

Figure 3.7 Place order.

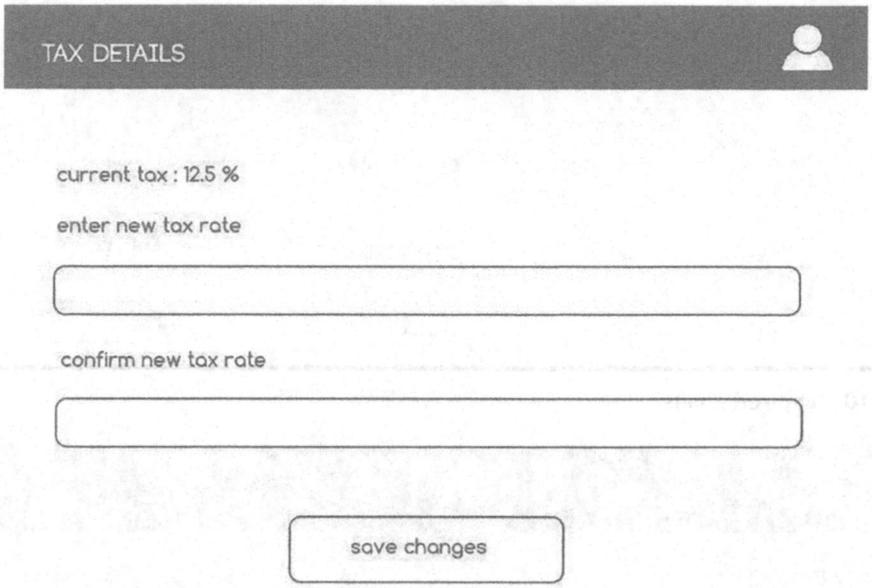

Figure 3.8   Tax details.

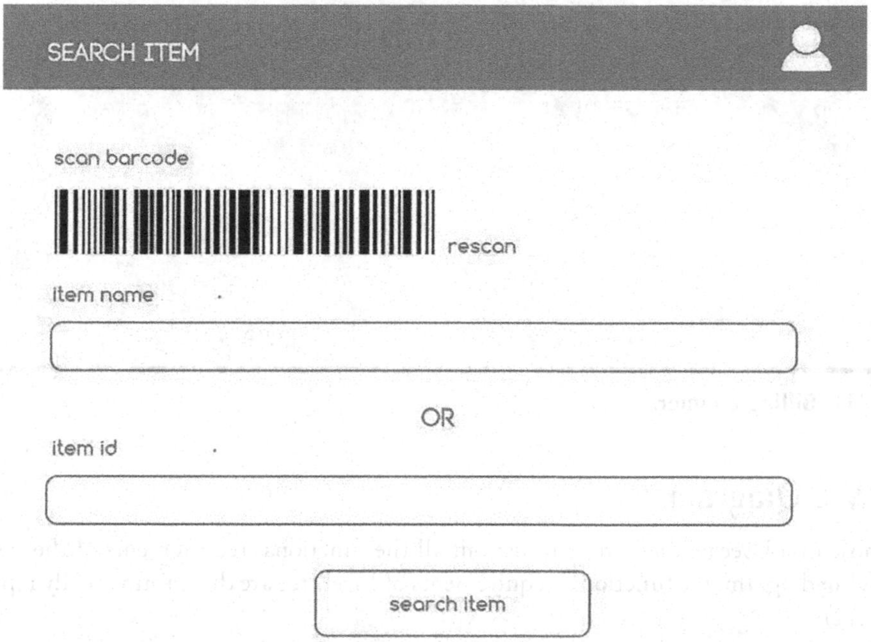

Figure 3.9   Search item.

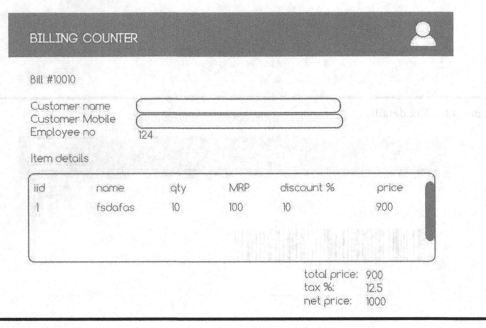

Figure 3.10   Expired goods.

Figure 3.11   Billing counter.

3.5 UML Diagrams

The purpose of a Usecase diagram is to list out all the functional requirements of the system. In the following diagram, the functional requirements of Inventree are diagrammatically represented (Figure 3.12)

Actor Specification

1. **Administrator** – The functionality of this actor is to authenticate users who have registered to the system. More importantly, if a change has occurred in an inventory such as price updation, removing expired goods, these changes are made subsequently by the administrator.
2. **Inventory manager** – This actor takes care of the inventory, its associated goods and the transactions that occur within the inventory.

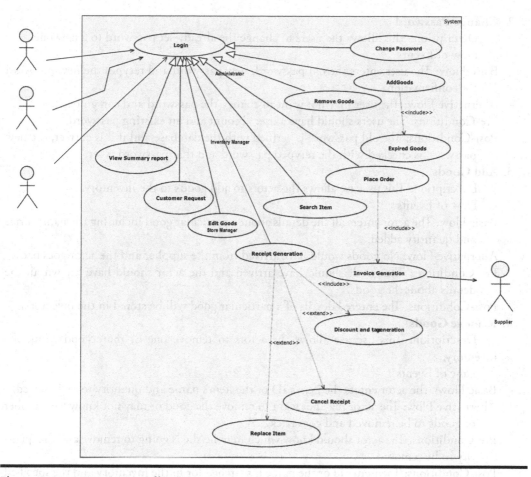

Figure 3.12   UML usecase diagram.

3. **Store manager** – The store manager would effectively manage the stored goods that are obtained from the supplier and dispatch, when requested.
4. **Supplier** – The work of this actor is to supply the goods that are requested by the store, subsequently responding to requests made at regular instants of time.

Usecase Specification

1. **Login**

    Description: This usecase allows the actors to login to the system with the credentials.
    Flow of Events

    Basic Flow: The actor enters the username and password and clicks on login button.

    Alternative Flow: The actor may have forgotten the password and clicks on Forgot password button.

    Pre-Conditions: The actors should have already registered and should have their credentials ready.

    Post-Conditions: The entered credentials will be checked and if the entries are correct, the actor is let in.

2. **Change Password**

   Description: This allows the users to change the already set password to a new one.
   Flow of Events

   Basic Flow: The user enters the old password, new password and retypes the new password for confirmation.

   Alternative Flow: The user may not want to change the password and can go back.

   Pre-Conditions: The users should have a user account and an existing password.

   Post-Conditions: The old password is verified with the database and if it is correct, the new password is checked with the retyped password and that password is set.

3. **Add Goods**

   Description: This usecase allows the actors to add goods to the inventory.
   Flow of Events

   Basic Flow: The actor enters all the details about a particular good including the name, price and quantity added.

   Alternative Flow: No goods would have arrived from the supplier and the actor goes back.

   Pre-Conditions: The goods should have arrived and the actor should have known all the details about the goods.

   Post-Conditions: The entered details of a particular good will be stored in the inventory.

4. **Remove Goods**

   Description: This usecase allows the actors to remove one or more goods from the inventory.
   Flow of Events

   Basic Flow: The actor enters the item's ID or the item's name and quantity to be removed.

   Alternative Flow: The actor may not want to remove the good or may not know the number of goods to be removed and goes back.

   Pre-Conditions: The actor should know which item he/she is going to remove and the quantity to be removed.

   Post-Conditions: The item's id or the name is searched for in the inventory and the specified number of that item is removed.

5. **Expired Goods**

   Description: This usecase allows the actors to view all the expired goods and allow them to remove those goods from the inventory.
   Flow of Events

   Basic Flow: The expired goods are displayed and the actor clicks on the remove button to remove that item.

   Alternative Flow: The expired goods are displayed but the actor decides to have them on the inventory and goes back.

   Pre-Conditions: There should be atleast one expired good for this usecase to function.

   Post-Conditions: The expired good is removed from the inventory.

6. **Place Order**

   Description: This usecase allows the actors to place an order from the inventory.
   Flow of Events

   Basic Flow: The actor chooses the item he/she wants to buy, specifies the quantity, gives the address and contact details and clicks on place order.

   Alternative Flow: The actor may decide not to buy anything at that instant and goes back.

   Pre-Conditions: The actor is allowed to choose only between the items that are available in the inventory.

Post-Conditions: The requested item and the quantity is recorded and the item is delivered to the specified address.

7. **Invoice Generation**

Description: This usecase generates the invoice for the items that are bought from the supplier.

Flow of Events

Basic Flow: The item's name, price and quantity are taken and the total amount is calculated.

Alternative Flow: The required details may not be present and thus invoice is not generated.

Pre-Conditions: The requested item by the inventory manager should be available with the supplier.

Post-Conditions: The invoice is generated and the item is received.

8. **Search Item**

Description: The usecase allows the actors to search for an item that is present in the inventory.

Flow of Events

Basic Flow: The actor enters the item's id or the item's name and clicks on the search button.

Alternative Flow: The actor may not know which item he/she wants to search and goes back.

Pre-Conditions: The item that is to be searched must be present in the inventory.

Post-Conditions: The entered item is searched and displayed.

9. **Edit Goods**

Description: This usecase allows the actors to edit the details regarding the goods that have been entered already.

Flow of Events

Basic Flow: The required item is searched, old details are deleted and the new details are entered.

Alternative Flow: The item that is searched for may not be present in the inventory.

Pre-Conditions: The searched item should be present in the inventory.

Post-Conditions: The details that are changed are updated and stored.

10. **Customer Request**

Description: This usecase allows the customers (actors) to place a request for the item they need.

Flow of Events

Basic Flow: The actor enters the item and the quantity he/she needs.

Alternative Flow: The actor may not know what he/she needs clearly and can go back.

Pre-Conditions: The requested item should not exist in the inventory.

Post-Conditions: The requested item is stored and it is placed as an order to the supplier.

11. **Receipt Generation**

Description: This usecase generates the receipt for the items that the customers buy.

Flow of Events

Basic Flow: The item, quantity the customer buys is entered and the bill amount is calculated.

Alternative Flow: The customer may not buy any item.

Pre-Conditions: The items should be present in the inventory.

Post-Conditions: The bill amount is generated and the customer is notified.

12. **Discount and Tax Generation**
Description: This usecase calculates the discount and tax for the total bill amount.
Flow of Events
Basic Flow: The net total amount is taken and the corresponding discount and the tax is calculated and added to the net total to get the grand total.
Alternative Flow: There may not be any discounts.
Pre-Conditions: The net total should be calculated for the items bought.
Post-Conditions: The grand total is calculated and the customer is notified.

13. **Cancel Receipt**
Description: This allows the actors to cancel a generated receipt.
Flow of Events
Basic Flow: The actor enters the bill number and clicks on the Cancel button.
Alternative Flow: The receipt may not be cancelled and it is correct.
Pre-Conditions: The searched receipt that needs to be cancelled should be generated previously.
Post-Conditions: The selected receipt is cancelled and the respective items are added back to the inventory.

14. **Replace Item**
Description: This usecase allows the actors to replace an item from the inventory.
Flow of Events
Basic Flow: The actor enters the item to be replaced.
Alternative Flow: The actor does not want to replace and goes back.
Pre-Conditions: The item to be replaced must be bought beforehand.
Post-Conditions: The specified item is replaced with another item from the inventory.

15. **View Summary Report**
Description: This usecase allows the actors to view the summary report of all transactions.
Flow of Events
Basic Flow: The actor views the summary report that is generated.
Alternative Flow: The actor goes back without viewing.
Pre-Conditions: There must be some transactions that should have taken place.
Post-Conditions: The summary report is generated and is viewed by the actors.

UML Class Diagram: It focuses on the relationship among various attributes along with the operations associated with each of them, with respect to classes (Figure 3.13).

UML Activity Diagram: The purpose of the activity diagram is to have a visual depiction of the flow of activities in the system (Figure 3.14).

UML State Machine Diagram: The purpose of the state machine diagram is to design and understand time-critical systems. It helps in understanding the behaviour of the system and it expresses the behaviour in terms of a series of steps, triggering events and the actions that may occur (Figure 3.15).

UML Sequence Diagram: The purpose of this diagram is to order the events identified earlier using usecase, class and activity diagram. It is also used to trace the execution of the problem domain (Figure 3.16).

UML Communication Diagram: The diagram focuses on how strongly objects communicate with each other with the help of messages (Figure 3.17).

UML Component Diagram: It focuses on how every component collaborates with every other component using available interfaces to provide the major functionalities of the system (Figure 3.18).

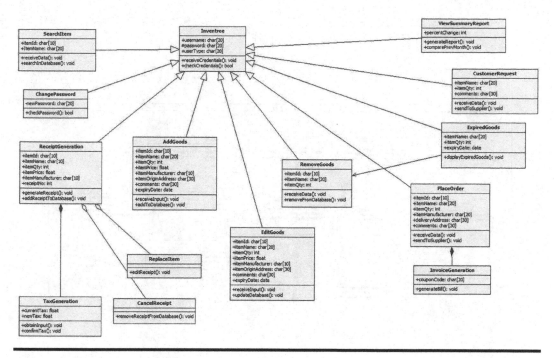

Figure 3.13   UML class diagram.

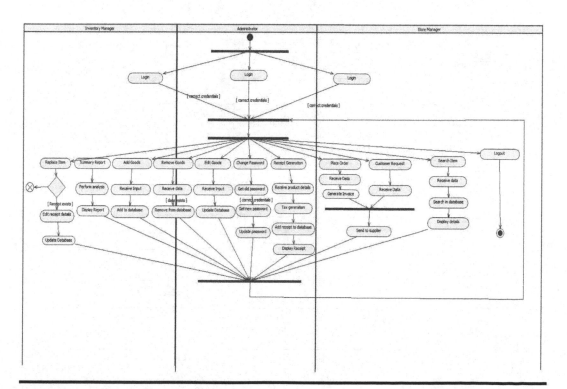

Figure 3.14   UML activity diagram.

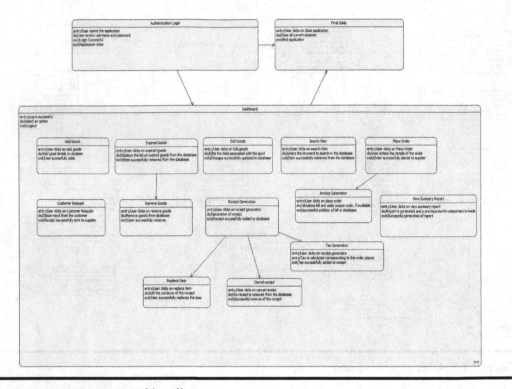

Figure 3.15   UML state machine diagram.

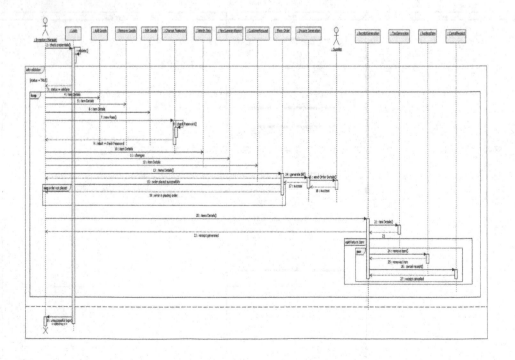

Figure 3.16   UML sequence diagram.

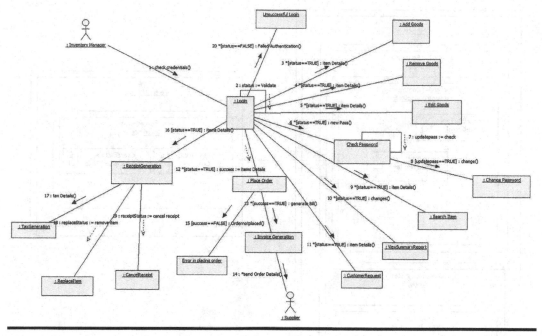

Figure 3.17   UML communication diagram.

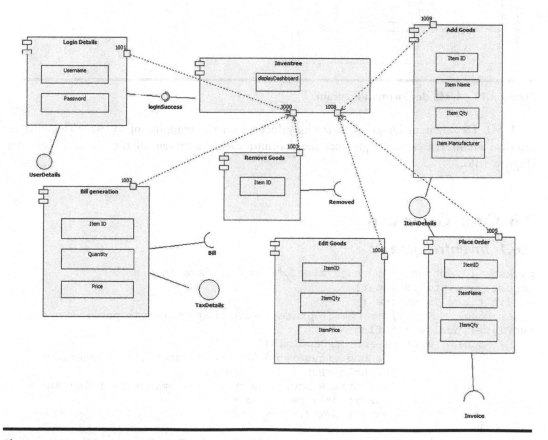

Figure 3.18   UML component diagram.

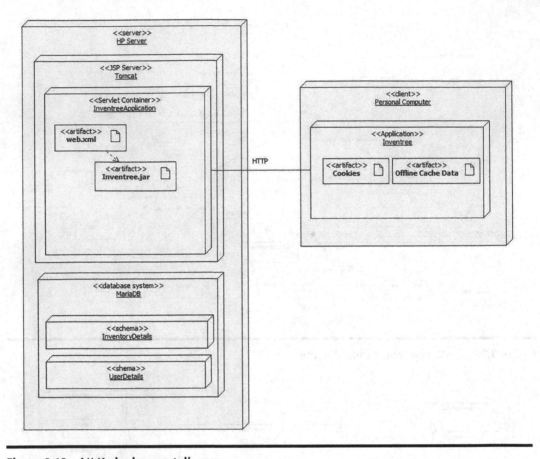

Figure 3.19 UML deployment diagram.

UML Deployment Diagram: It strongly focuses on the mapping of software elements to physical architectures and represents the communication between all the physical elements (Figure 3.19).

3.6 Code Generated

3.6.1 Inventree.java

```
package Inventree; import java.sql.*; import java.io.*;
import java.util.Scanner;
public class Inventree {
        public String username; protected String password; public String
userType; public int flag;
        public void receiveCredentials() {
                    Scanner scuser=new Scanner(System.in); System.out.
                    println("Enter username");
                    username = scuser.next(); System.out.println("Enter
                    password"); password =
                    scuser.next();
        }
```

```
    public boolean checkCredentials() {
        //System.out.println("Comes here"); receiveCredentials();
        if(username.equals("admin")&&password.equals("admin"))
        return true;
        else
                                            } }
    return false;
```

3.6.2 AddGoods.java

```
import java.sql.*; import java.io.*;
import java.util.Scanner; import Inventree.Inventree; import java.
util.*;
public class AddGoods extends Inventree { public String itemId;
        public String itemName; public int itemQty; public double
        itemPrice;
        public String itemManufacturer; public String
        itemOriginAddress; public String comments;
        public Date expiryDate;
        public void receiveInput() { if(checkCredentials()){
                Scanner sc = new Scanner(System.in);
                System.out.print(String.format("%40s","Add Goods\n"));
                System.out.println("\n\n");
                System.out.println("Enter the item Id"); itemId =
                sc.next();
                System.out.println("Enter the item Name"); itemName =
                sc.next();
                System.out.println("Enter the item Qty"); itemQty =
                sc.nextInt();
                System.out.println("Enter the item Price"); itemPrice
                = sc.nextDouble();
                System.out.println("Enter the item Manufacturer");
                itemManufacturer =
                sc.next(); System.out.println("Enter the item Origin
                Address");
                itemOriginAddress = sc.next();
                System.out.println("Enter the item comments");
                comments = sc.next();
        }
    }
    public void addToDatabase() {
    }
    public static void main(String[] argv){ int choice;
        Scanner sc=new Scanner(System.in); AddGoods obj=new
        AddGoods();
        do{     System.out.println("\n\n"); System.out.print(String.
        format("%40s","Inventree\n")); System.out.print(String.
        format("%50s","Inventory Management

System.out.println("Choose an option"); System.out.print(String.forma
t("%15s%40s","1","Login\n")); System.out.print(String.
format("%15s%40s","2" ,"About\n"));
System.out.print(String.format("%15s%40s","3", "EXIT\n")); choice =
sc.nextInt();
```

```
switch(choice){
        case 1:  obj.receiveInput(); break;
        case 2: System.out.println("Developed by TEAM 5"); break;
        case 3: break;
        default: System.out.println("Enter a correct option"); break;
            }
            }
        while(choice!=3);
    } }
```

3.6.3 Screenshots of the Project

See Figures 3.20–3.22

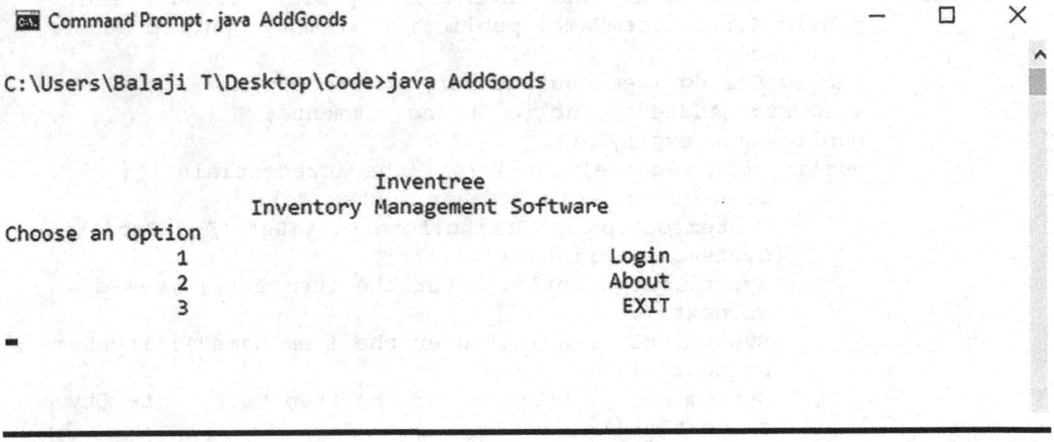

Figure 3.20　Case 1.

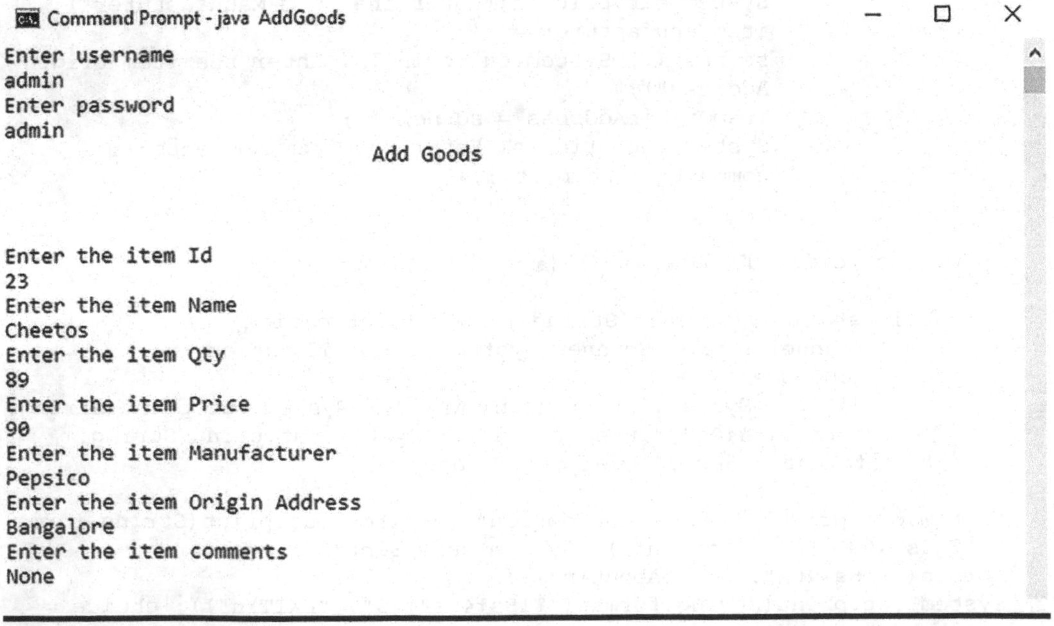

Figure 3.21　Case 2.

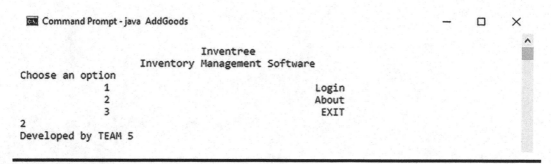

Figure 3.22 Case 3.

Chapter 4

Design of UML Diagrams for Business Process Outsourcing (BPO) Management System

4.1 Problem Statement

The proposed software will be user-friendly, so that all interactions between a BPO (Business process outsourcing) organization and clients can be done through the software. The required source documents can be easily uploaded and sent to the BPO organization and vice versa. One of the problems is the communication between the client and the BPO organization being limited to face-to-face interaction for assurance, which is costly and time-consuming. There are costs due to printing and the security of documents, which can be prevented as document are stored in digital form with high security. The system should mainly focus on providing login for the separate users (client and BPO organization), and a facility to search the other party to initiate any project agreements. Source documents can be easily uploaded, and the service provided by the BPO organization can also be uploaded for quality testing. The core motive of the software is to provide communication between the users, with the least cost. The BPO management system proves to be essential because of the over growth of the BPO segment in the present economy. This system will be crucial when organizations wish to outsource their work. It will affect the BPO organizations and the clients who wish to seek their service. If this software gets implemented, conveying information will be easier as it is through the internet.

4.2 Functional Requirements

Login – provides a personalized profile for each user, to ensure security. Profile changes – each user can personalize their account, and change their password. Post project request – clients post their request with requirements for BPO organizations to choose from. Search project requests – BPO organizations can search and respond to the requests. Upload source documents – the documents required by the BPO organization can be transferred through the system, and the receiver can

DOI: 10.1201/9781003287124-4

download them. Check progress – clients should be constantly updated with the progress of the work. Quality check and testing – the clients can check their product and quote any modifications. Upload product/service – BPO organization should upload their product/service for the further procedure (payment, shipment, etc.). Payment – clients should pay the BPO organization at the end of their agreement. Shipment – the product/service should be delivered to the clients. Rating – the clients can rate the service provided by the BPO organization (Figures 4.1–4.19).

4.3 Design and Design Constraints

Usecase Specification

1. **Accept Request**
    Description: It allows BPO organization to accept the request.
    Flow of Events
  Basic Flow: BPO organization accepts the request and thereby initiates the deal.

Figure 4.1   Login page.

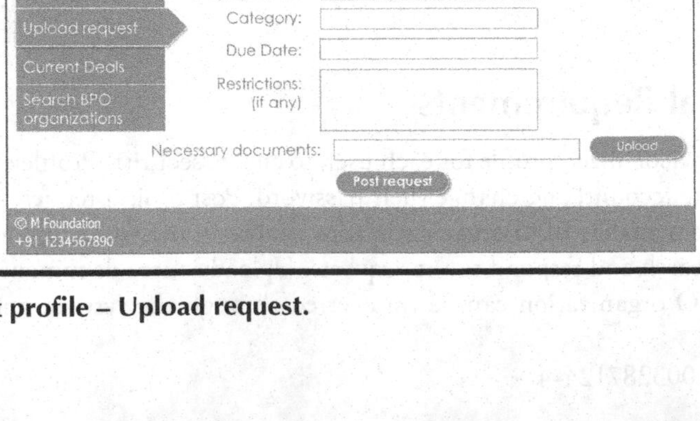

Figure 4.2   Client profile – Upload request.

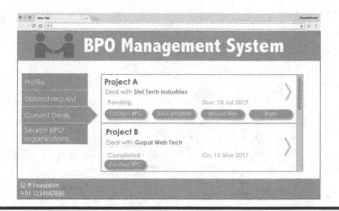

Figure 4.3   Client profile – Current deals.

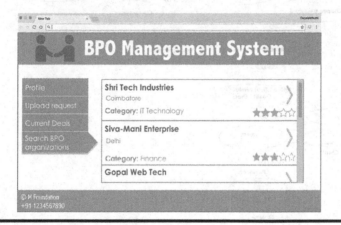

Figure 4.4   Client profile – Search BPO Organization.

Alternative Flow: BPO organization can search for other clients.
Pre-Conditions: The client should post a request.
Post-Conditions: It should be added into the current deals.

2. **Card**

Description: It is sub-usecase of payment, where this method can be chosen in case the client wishes to pay by card.

Flow of Events

Basic Flow: The final amount of money will be displayed, and once paid; the BPO organization can verify the status of the agreement to 'paid'.

Alternative Flow: The BPO can sue the client using the evidence of their agreement from the database.

Pre-Conditions: Previous procedures, such as upload the final product and quality check must be completed.

Post-Conditions: The status of the agreement should be updated in the database as 'paid' or 'completed'.

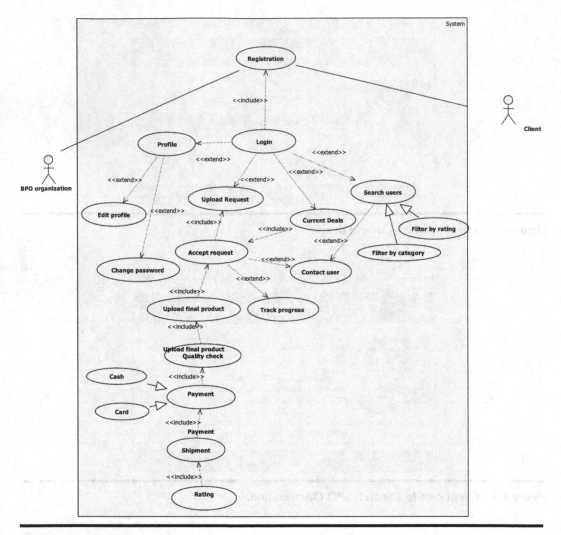

Figure 4.5   UML usecase diagram.

3. **Cash**

  Description: It is sub-usecase of payment, where this method can be chosen in case the client wishes to pay by cash.

  Flow of Events

Basic Flow: The final amount of money will be displayed, and once paid, the status of the agreement will be updated.

Alternative Flow: The BPO can sue the client using the evidence of their agreement from the database.

Pre-Conditions: Previous procedures, such as upload the final product and quality check must be completed.

Post-Conditions: The status of the agreement should be updated in the database as 'paid' or 'completed'.

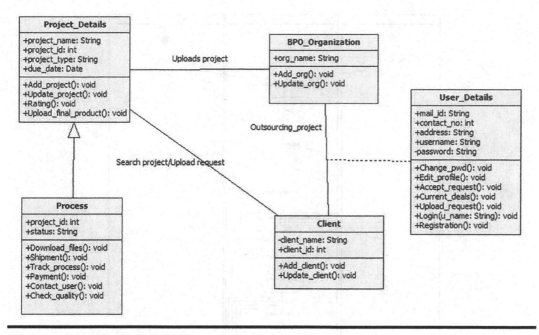

Figure 4.6 UML class diagram.

4. **Change Password**
    Description: This allows you to change your password.
    Flow of Events
   Basic Flow: The user can change their password for security purposes.
   Alternative Flow: They can stick with their old password itself.
   Pre-Conditions: They should enter into their profile page.
   Post-Conditions: Changes should be updated in the database successfully.

5. **Contact User**
    Description: This provides a communication between users.
    Flow of Events
   Basic Flow: The users are allowed to communicate with each other.
   Alternative Flow: Try alternate methods of contacting.
   Pre-Conditions: Contact details should be available for users.
   Post-Conditions: None.

6. **Current Deals**
    Description: The users are allowed to view all of their deals.
    Flow of Events
   Basic Flow: The users can view their pending and completed deals.
   Alternative Flow: They can contact the other user involved in the deal.
   Pre-Conditions: The user should have at least one deal to view.
   Post-Conditions: They can track the progress of the pending deals.

7. **Edit Profile**
    Description: The users are allowed to edit their profiles.
    Flow of Events
   Basic Flow: The user can edit their profile and save the changes.

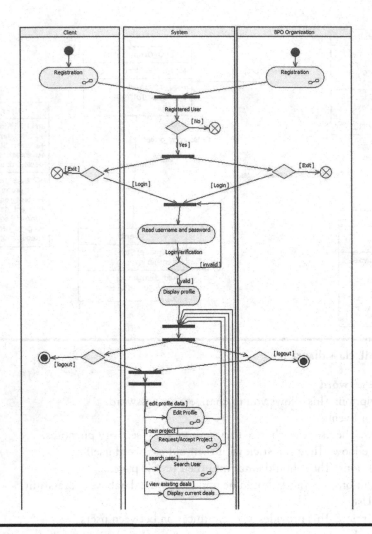

Figure 4.7 UML activity diagram (part 1).

Alternative Flow: They can just view the profile.

Pre-Conditions: They should enter into the profile page.

Post-Conditions: Changes should be updated to the database successfully.

8. **Filter by Category**

Description: This is a sub-usecase of searching users, where the users can be filtered by category (finance, etc.).

Flow of Events

Basic Flow: The category type should be specified by the user and that category will be compared with the database to retrieve the required users.

Alternative Flow: The user can filter by rating or can view all users without any filters.

Pre-Conditions: The user should have an authenticated profile by registering in the system to search other profiles.

Post-Conditions: The user can contact any other user.

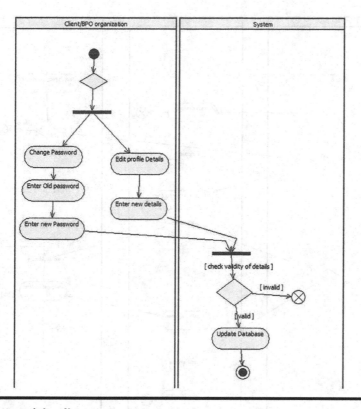

Figure 4.8   UML activity diagram (part 2).

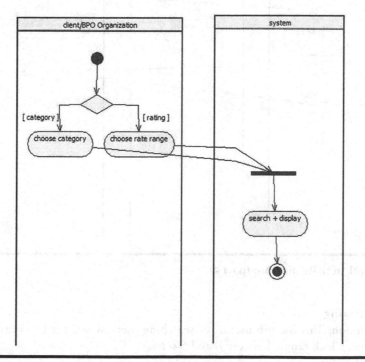

Figure 4.9   UML activity diagram (part 3).

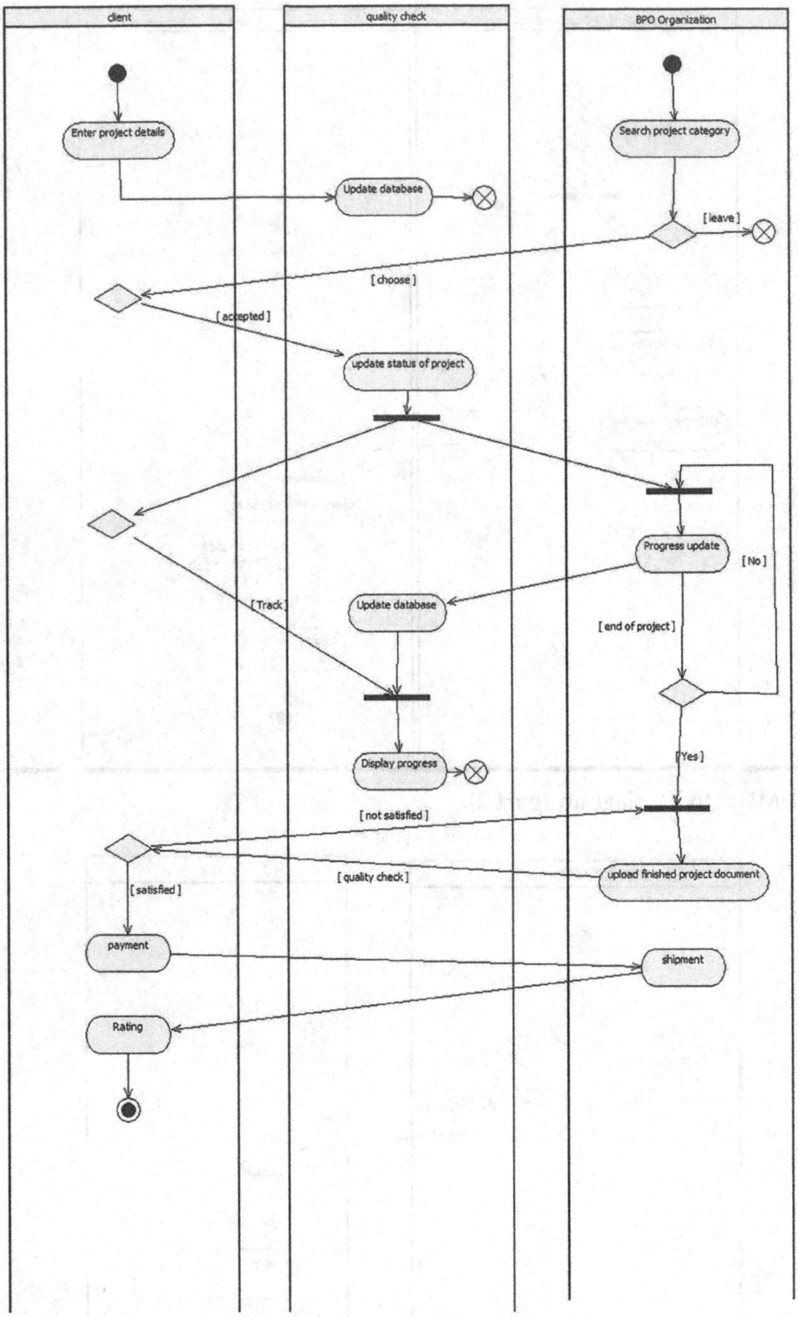

Figure 4.10 UML activity diagram (part 4).

9. **Filter by Rating**

Description: This is a sub-usecase of searching users, where the users can be filtered by rating value, which ranges between 0 and 5 stars.

Flow of Events

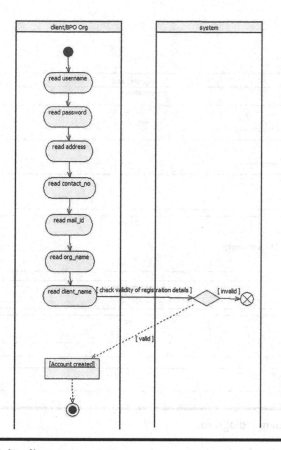

Figure 4.11   UML activity diagram (part 5).

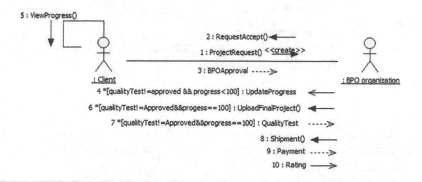

Figure 4.12   UML collaboration diagram.

Basic Flow: The range of rating should be specified by the user and that rating range will be compared with the database to retrieve the required users.

Alternative Flow: User can filter by category or can view all users without any filters.

Pre-Conditions: User should have an authenticated profile by registering in the system to search other profiles.

Post-Conditions: The user can contact any other user.

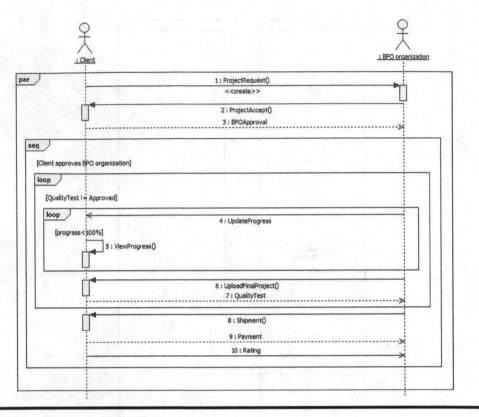

Figure 4.13 UML sequence diagram.

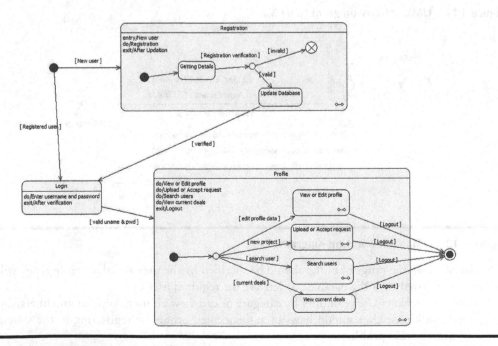

Figure 4.14 UML state machine diagram (part 1).

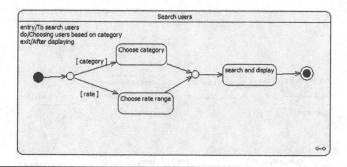

Figure 4.15 UML state machine diagram (part 2).

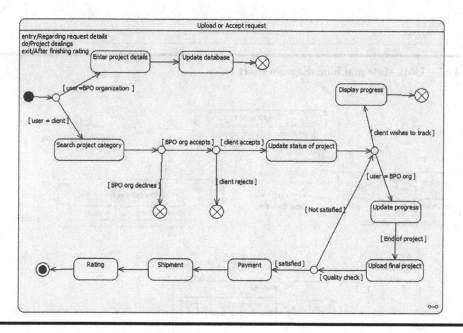

Figure 4.16 UML state machine diagram (part 3).

10. **Login**

    Description: The users are allowed to login.

    Flow of Events

    Basic Flow: The user can login to the system with a valid username and password.

    Alternative Flow: They can register as a fresh user.

    Pre-Conditions: They should be an authenticated user to login.

    Post-Conditions: Basic details of the user will be retrieved to be displayed on all the other sections using username.

11. **Payment**

    Description: At the end of the deal, the client should pay the BPO organization for their service, which will be provided by this functionality.

    Flow of Events

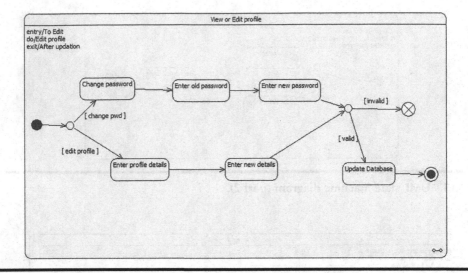

Figure 4.17   UML state machine diagram (part 4).

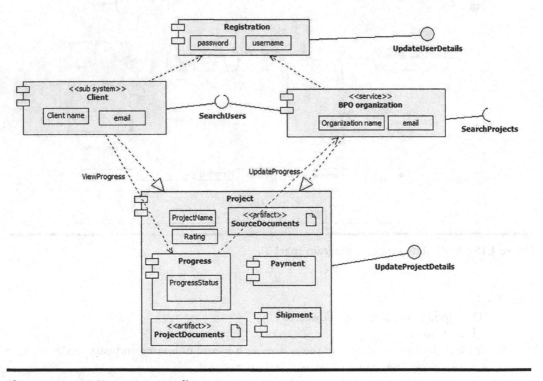

Figure 4.18   UML component diagram.

Basic Flow: The client will choose the method of payment, provide the necessary details to complete the transaction.

Alternative Flow: The BPO can sue the client using the evidence of their agreement from the database.

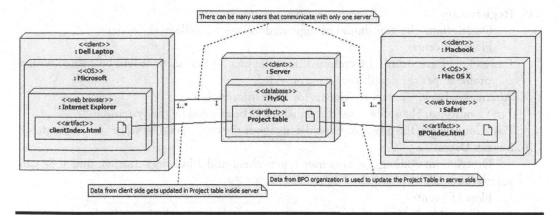

Figure 4.19   UML deployment diagram.

Pre-Conditions: Previous procedures, such as upload the final product and quality check must be completed.

Post-Conditions: The status of the agreement should be updated in the database as 'paid'.

12. **Profile**

Description: The user can view their basic provided details in the profile view

Flow of Events

Basic Flow: The username from login will be used to compare in the database to retrieve the basic details and display them in the profile.

Alternative Flow: They can choose to do other functionalities like change password, search users, etc.

Pre-Conditions: User should have an authenticated profile by registering in the system.

Post-Conditions: No changes will be made as it is only displayed functionality.

13. **Quality Check**

Description: The client should be able to check the quality of the product before proceeding to payment.

Flow of Events

Basic Flow: The uploaded final product from the BPO organization can be retrieved and reviewed for quality and testing.

Alternative Flow: Quality and testing can be skipped to the payment procedure at the end.

Pre-Conditions: BPO organization should upload documents of the final product.

Post-Conditions: Comments from the client should be sent to the BPO organization.

14. **Rating**

Description: One user can rate the other user's service based on their previous dealings.

Flow of Events

Basic Flow: At the end of the deal, the two users involved in the agreement should rate the other on a rating of 5 based on their service.

Alternative Flow: The user can choose to rate later or ignore.

Pre-Conditions: The status of agreement should be closed – payment and shipment stages should be completed

Post-Conditions: The rating given should be averaged with previous ratings and stored in database for data retrieval when displaying.

15. **Registration**

    Description: The user should be registered to have a profile in the system

    Flow of Events

    Basic Flow: Basic details are collected from the user and an account will be created with a profile as per the details they have provided.

    Alternative Flow: Contact developers for more information.

    Pre-Conditions: Should be a valid user, who will be affected by the system.

    Post-Conditions: The provided basic details about the user should be stored in the database.

16. **Search Users**

    Description: Among the two user types, client and BPO organization, and they can search the other.

    Flow of Events

    Basic Flow: All the users of the other user type should be searched and displayed from the database.

    Pre-Conditions: User should have an authenticated profile by registering in the system to search other profiles.

    Post-Conditions: The user can contact the other user.

17. **Shipment**

    Description: The product after payment can be shipped from the BPO organization to the client as per the client's wish.

    Flow of Events

    Basic Flow: The status of payment should be verified, then the product is collected from the BPO organization and delivered to the client.

    Alternative Flow: The client and BPO organization can have their methods of shipment and skip this procedure.

    Pre-Conditions: Payment procedure should be done (verified either by cash or card).

    Post-Conditions: The status of the agreement should be updated in the database as 'completed'.

18. **Track Progress**

    Description: The client can track the progress of their product or service that has been service.

    Flow of Events

    Basic Flow: BPO organization should constantly update the status of their progress so that the client can view them.

    Alternative Flow: Previous updates of progress should be displayed in case the BPO organization fails to give a recent update.

    Pre-Conditions: BPO organization and the client should agree with the request.

    Post-Conditions: The current status of BPO organization with respect to the service should be updated in database.

19. **Upload Request**

    Description: This allows the client to post a request

    Flow of Events

    Basic Flow: The clients will have to enter the category, due date and description of their request along with an uploaded document.

    Alternative Flow: Contact BPO organization and deal directly.

    Pre-Conditions: Client should be a registered user.

    Post-Conditions: Request information and ID should be stored in the database.

20. **Upload Final Product**

Description: It will allow the BPO organization to upload their end product/service for further procedures (quality check, payment, shipment).

Flow of Events

Basic Flow: BPO organization can upload necessary documents.

Alternative Flow: Contact client and extend due date to upload final product

Pre-Conditions: BPO organization and the client should be in agreement with the request.

Post-Conditions: The document will be stored in database.

Chapter 5

Design of UML Diagrams for E-Ticketing for Buses

5.1 Problem Statement

In this case study, a software package to automate the manual procedures of reserving a bus ticket is made through Software Maintenance and Development Center (SMDC) Travels. Specifically, the objectives of this case study consist of providing a web-based bus ticket reservation function where a customer can buy a bus ticket through the online system without a need to queue up at the counter to purchase a bus ticket, enabling customers to check the availability and types of buses online. Customer can check the time departure for every Indian Tourist Centre (ITC) bus through the system, easing bus ticket payment by obtaining a bank pin after payments is made to the various designated banks, the ability of customers to cancel their reservation, admin user privileges in updating and cancelling payment, route and vehicle records (Figures 5.1–5.11).

DOI: 10.1201/9781003287124-5

5.2 UML Diagrams

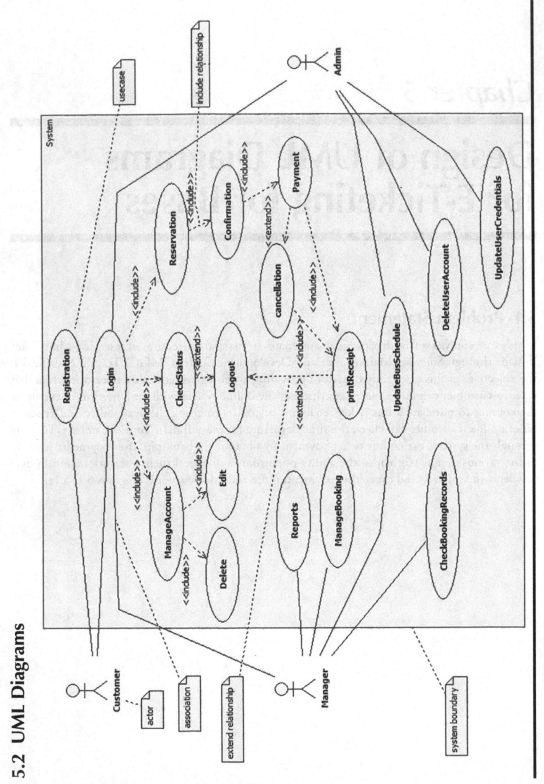

Figure 5.1 UML usecase diagram.

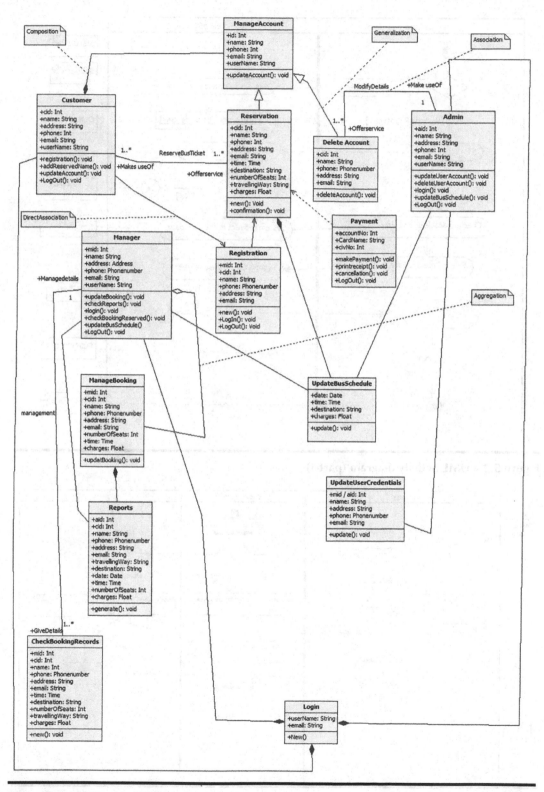

Figure 5.2   UML class diagram.

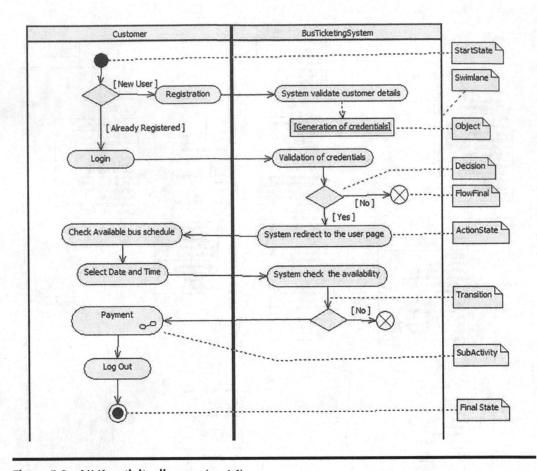

Figure 5.3 UML activity diagram (part-1).

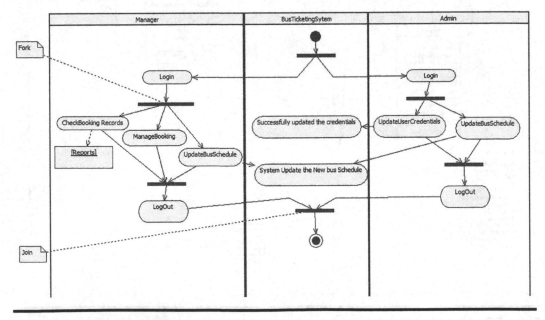

Figure 5.4 UML activity diagram (part-2).

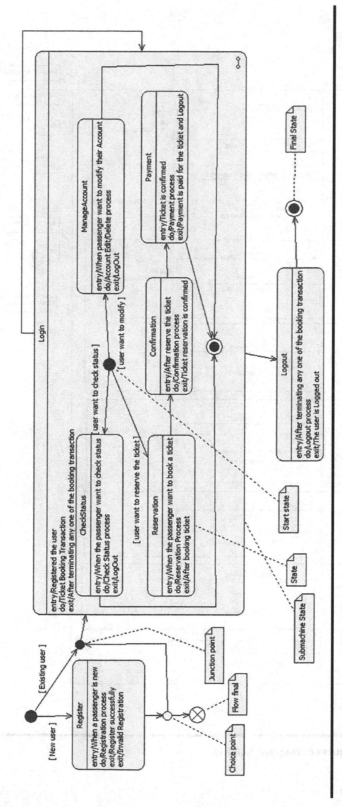

Figure 5.5   UML state machine diagram.

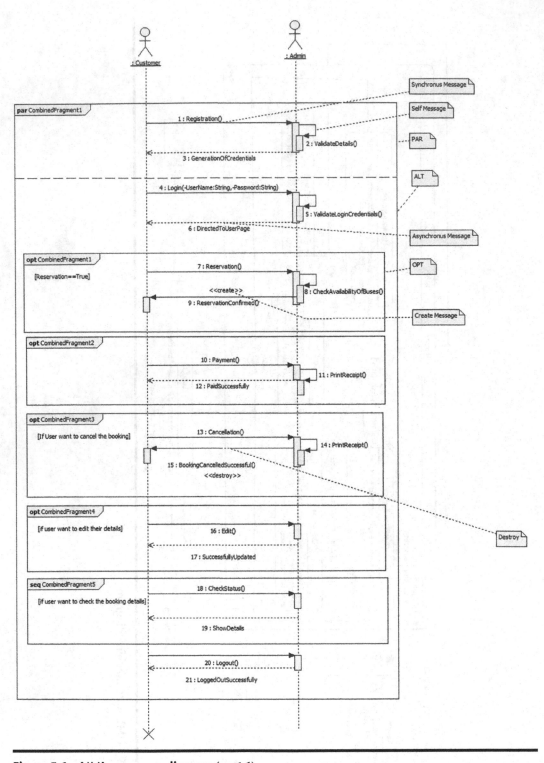

Figure 5.6   UML sequence diagram (part-1).

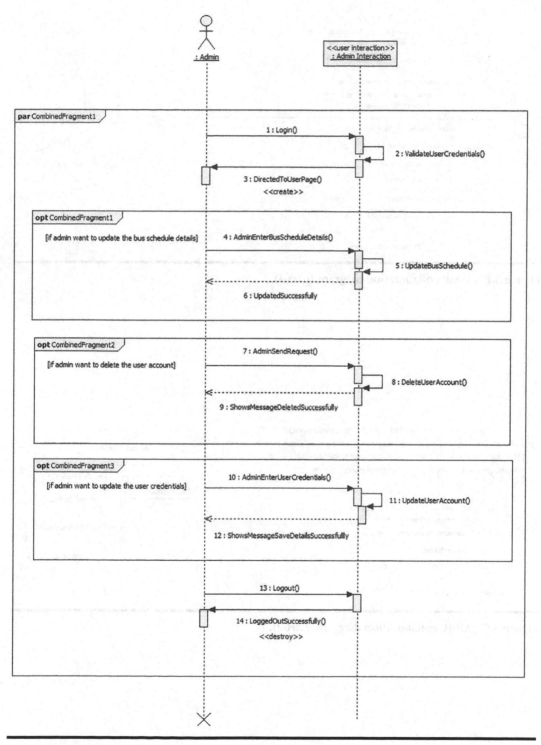

Figure 5.7   UML sequence diagram (part-2).

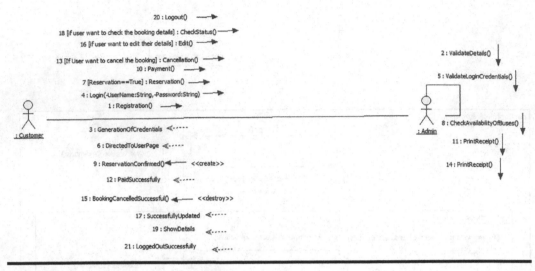

Figure 5.8   UML collaboration diagram (part-1).

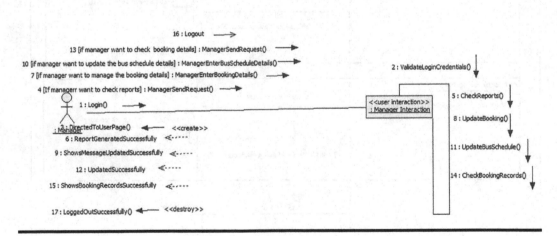

Figure 5.9   UML collaboration diagram (part-2).

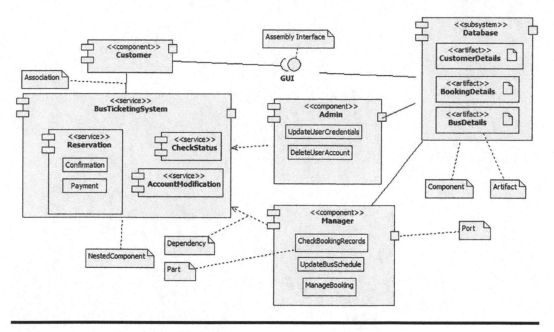

Figure 5.10   UML component diagram.

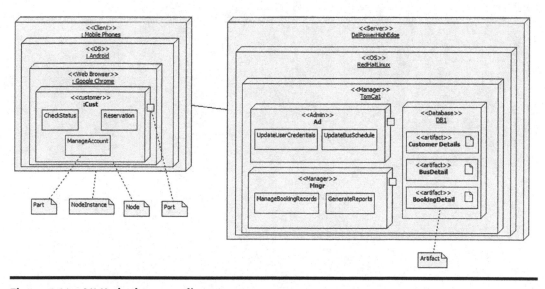

Figure 5.11   UML deployment diagram.

Chapter 6

Design of UML Diagrams for Weather Monitoring System

6.1 Problem Statement

This Weather Monitoring Case study allows people to directly check the weather status online. The functionalities are Weather Status, Live Updating, Alert, Graphical Representation, Future Prediction and Weekly. Weather Status – With this function, temperature, humidity, rainfall, pressure and dew point are measured using sensors. Live Updating – Data are live updated to be viewed by the user. Alert – This functionality provides tips and alerts to the user on certain weather conditions. Graphical Representation – Plotting of graphs based on variations in temperature for easier analysis. Future Prediction – This functionality helps in predicting the weather for the next few days. Weekly Analysis – Displaying the average, the highest and lowest temperature of the week. The final goal is to provide detailed weather conditions for the user based on his/her location (Figures 6.1 and 6.2).

6.2 Data Flow Diagrams

Functionalities:

1. Weather Status: With this function temperature, humidity, rainfall, pressure and dew point are measured using sensors.
2. Live Updation: Data are live updated to be viewed by the user.
3. Alert: This functionality provides tips and alerts to the user on certain weather conditions.
4. Graphical Representation: Plotting of graphs based on variations in temperature for easier analysis.

Figure 6.1 Level 0 DFD.

DOI: 10.1201/9781003287124-6

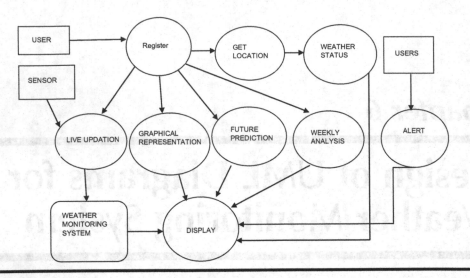

Figure 6.2   Level 1 DFD.

4. Future Prediction: This functionality helps in predicting the weather for the next few days.
5. Weekly Analysis: Displaying the average, the highest and lowest temperature of the week.

Finally, this case study aims to provide detailed weather conditions for the user based on his/her location (Figures 6.3–6.10).

6.3 UML Diagrams

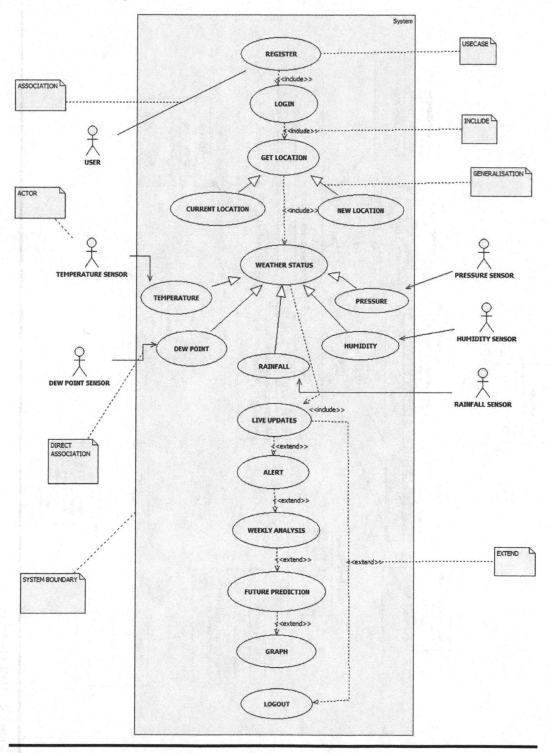

Figure 6.3   UML usecase diagram.

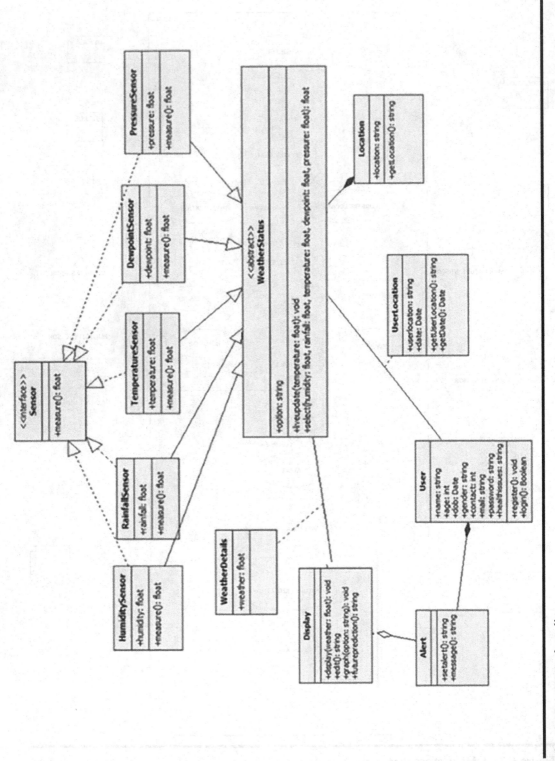

Figure 6.4 UML class diagram.

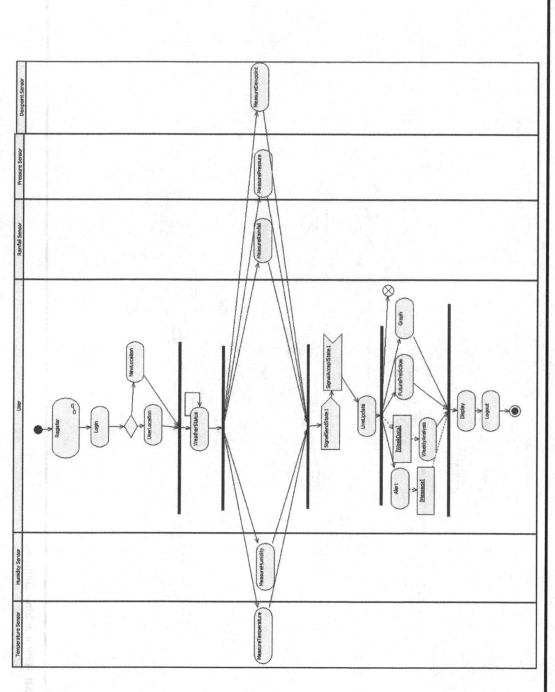

Figure 6.5 UML activity diagram.

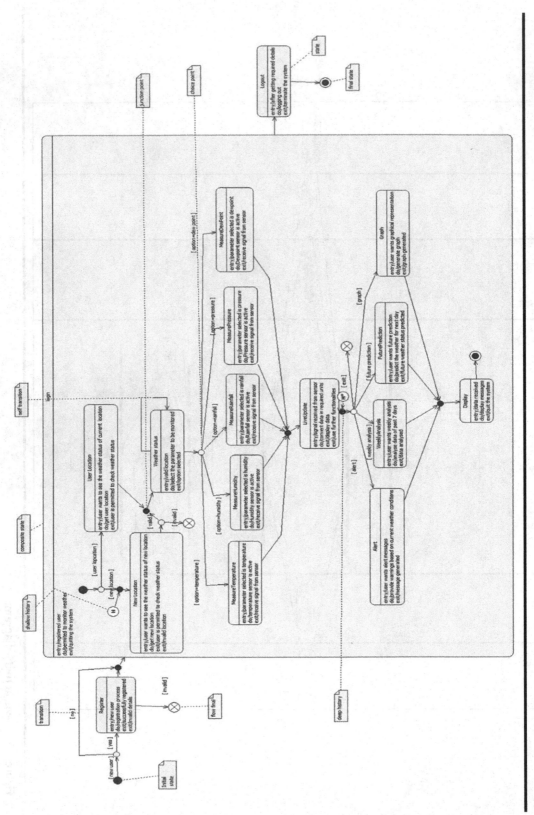

Figure 6.6 UML state machine diagram.

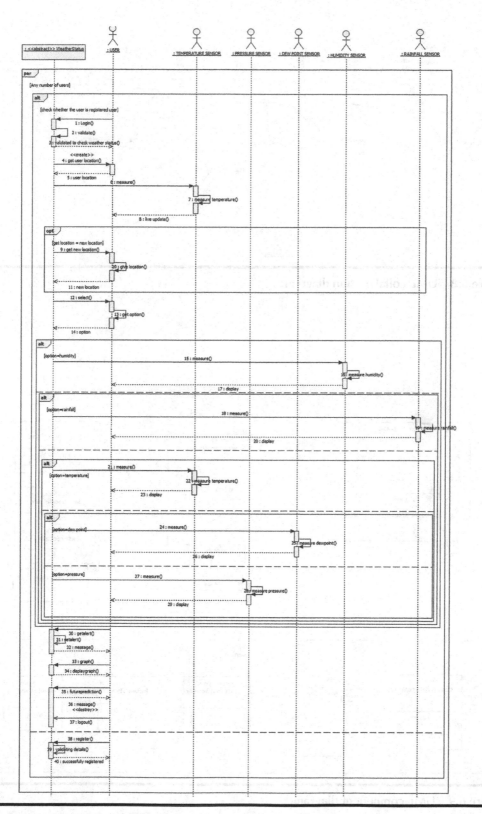

Figure 6.7   UML Sequence Diagram.

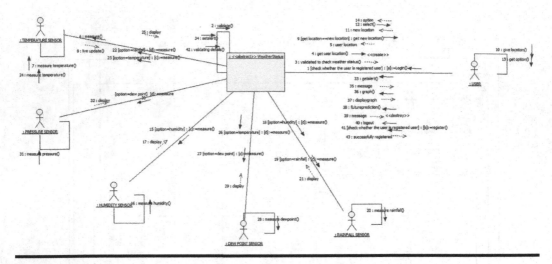

Figure 6.8 UML collaboration diagram.

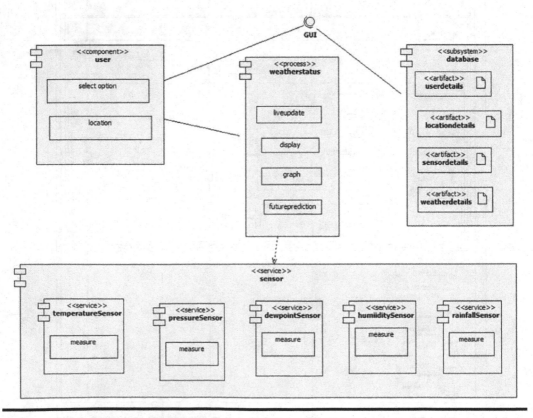

Figure 6.9 UML component diagram.

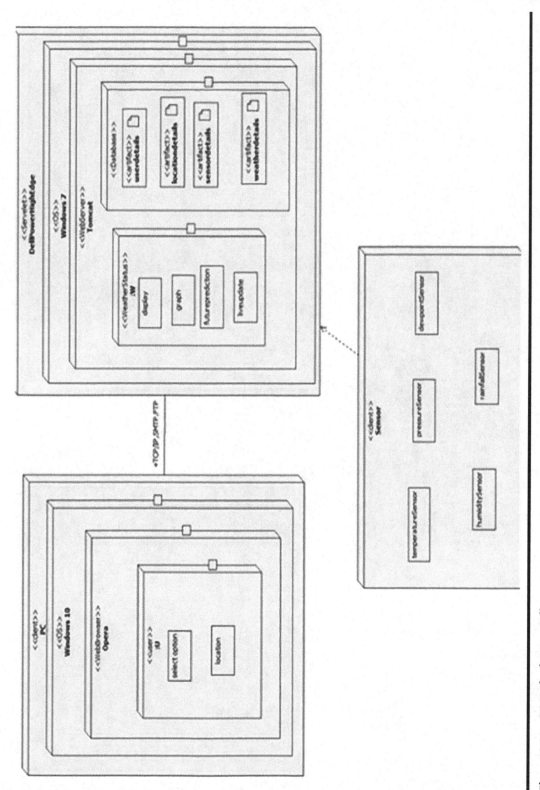

Figure 6.10 UML deployment diagram.

Chapter 7

Design of UML Diagrams for E-Province

7.1 Problem Statement

Citizens in every district face the difficulty with the of government certificates like birth/death certificates, income and caste certificates, old age and widow pensions, etc. This can be done with e-Province. This case study demonstrates how make the government services available to the citizens in a convenient, efficient and transparent manner, by enabling it simple by reliable access over the Internet. The main objective is to bring the public services closer to the citizens. To fulfil the vision of providing an easy and convenient service to the citizens through remote access primarily through Common Service Centre (CSCs), e-Province project is created. This case study aims to develop a State Portal (SP) to provide all the citizens of the respective province to access the services under a single interface mechanism in the form of the Portal. The various modules in the e-Province project are an Admin module that creates, updates, deactivates the users and performs various other tasks. A Login module that allows the users to login with their unique Application number with approved status. A User module that allows the approved users to register for the respective certificates. A User Profile module that creates the pre-requisite information of the user that needs to be stored in the database. The Certificate module contains the required forms that are to be filled with the information of the users (Figures 7.1–7.8).

DOI: 10.1201/9781003287124-7

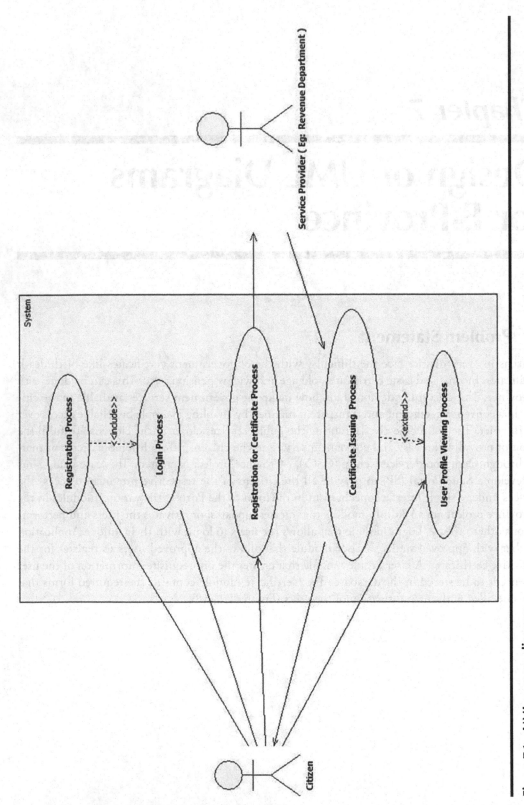

Figure 7.1 UML usecase diagram.

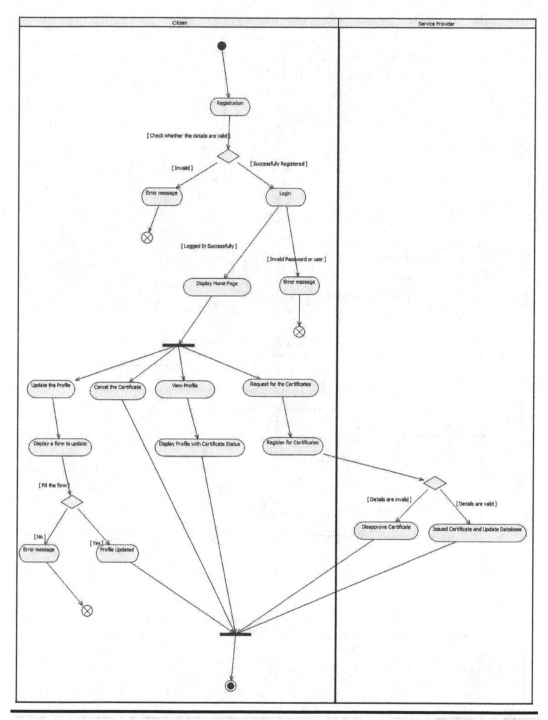

Figure 7.2   UML activity diagram.

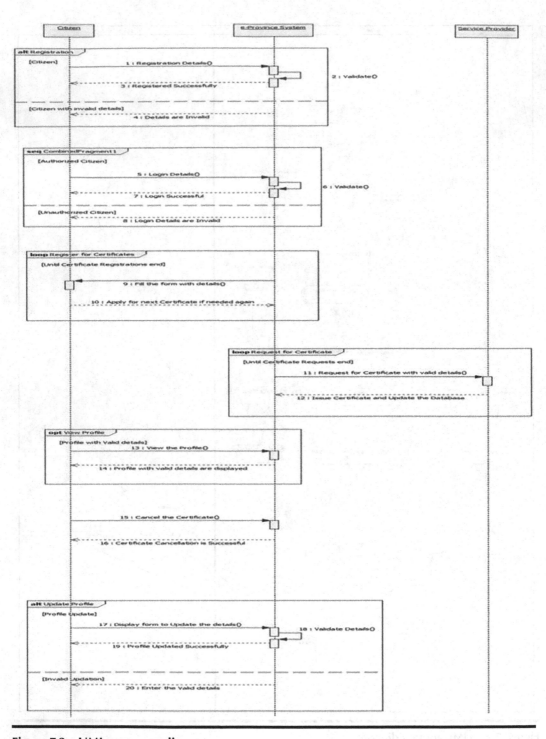

Figure 7.3 UML sequence diagram.

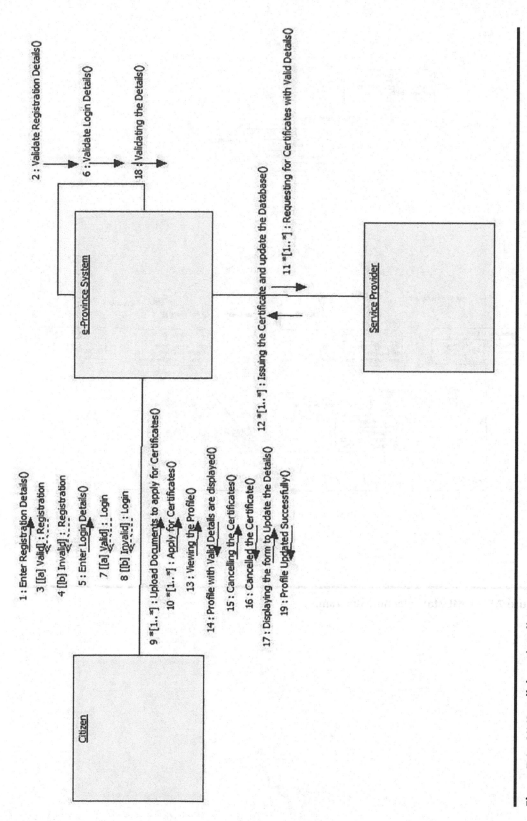

Figure 7.4   UML collaboration diagram.

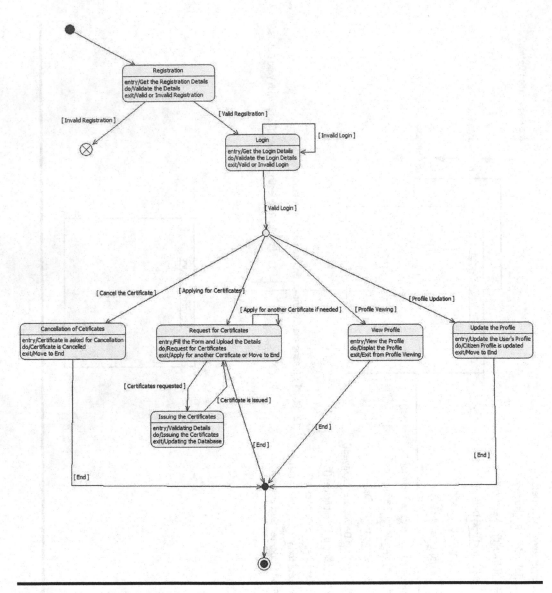

Figure 7.5   UML state machine diagram.

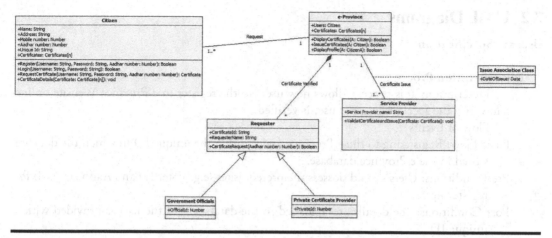

Figure 7.6   UML class diagram.

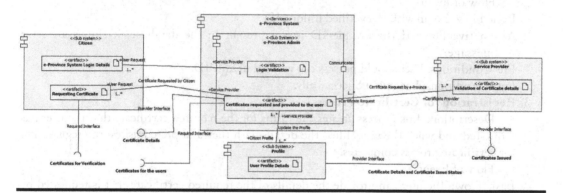

Figure 7.7   UML component diagram.

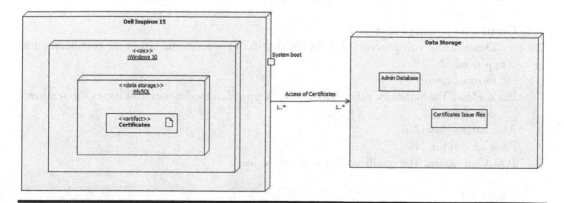

Figure 7.8   UML deployment diagram.

7.2 UML Diagrams

Usecase Specification

1. **Registration Process**

    Description: This process allows new users to the register to e-Province Website online and verify the account once the user is verified.

    Flow of Events

    Basic Flow: Registering to the e-Province and creating the unique ID in which the data are stored in the e-Province database.

    Pre-Conditions: Users should possess the prerequisites (e.g. Voter ID and Aadhaar card) for registering.

    Post-Conditions: The details are uploaded to the database and the user is provided with a unique ID.

2. **Login Process**

    Description: This process allows the authorized users to login to the website using their unique ID.

    Flow of Events

    Basic Flow: Login with the verified unique ID.

    Alternative Flow: If the unique ID is not present in the database, it shows an error message.

    Pre-Conditions: User should possess the verified unique ID.

    Post-Conditions: Logged in Successfully.

3. **Registration for Certificate Process**

    Description: This process creates the forms for the required certificate that the user has requested and when the users filled the details with the valid prerequisites, the registration for certificate process completes.

    Flow of Events

    Basic Flow: The user can provide the details of the required certificate that is requested by him, and the data are stored in e-Province database for further process.

    Alternative Flow: If the details are not provided correctly it displays an error message.

    Pre-Conditions: User should possess the details that are requested by the form to be filled (e.g. Aadhaar card, Voter ID).

    Post-Conditions: Form is filled with the required details and he requests the certificate from the issuer.

4. **Certificate Issuing Process**

    Description: This process validates the details of the form and issues the certificates if it is approved.

    Flow of Events

    Basic Flow: The authority validates the details provided by the user and issues the required certificate.

    Alternative Flow: Nil.

    Pre-Conditions: Nil.

    Post-Conditions: The certificate is issued to the user.

5. **User Profile Viewing Process**

   Description: This process allows the user whenever he needs to view his profile and even he is updated when the certificate is approved.

   Flow of Events

   Basic Flow: User can view his profile whenever needed and he is intimated by the portal if he received the certificate.

   Alternative Flow: Nil.

   Pre-Conditions: Document is uploaded by the user to update the profile.

   Post-Conditions: The complete user profile is displayed in the portal.

Chapter 8

Design of UML Diagrams for DigiDocLocker

8.1 Problem Statement

Maintaining the authentic documents physically in a single location is considered to be a challenging task. Thus, digitizing documents enables centralized storage of all the physical documents enabling easy retrieval from anywhere at anytime. It also prevents the troubles caused by missing any of those physical certificates. This can be achieved through the DigiDocLocker which is a platform for issuance and verification of documents and certificates in a digital format, thereby eliminating the use of physical documents. DigiDocLocker aims at benefitting all the citizens of the country by providing to access authentic documents/certificates such as driving licence, vehicle registration and academic mark sheet in digital format from the original issuers of these certificates. DigiDocLocker has the following functionalities:

   i. A Registration module allows the users to register and a Login module that allows the authorized users.
   ii. An Upload Document module allows the users to upload documents such as driving licence, vehicle registration, academic mark sheet and other relevant documents in various file formats.
   iii. A Profile module displays the complete profile of the user as available in the database.
   iv. An Issuer module displays the certificate issuers' names and the number of documents issued to the user by the issuer. For example, the Income Tax Department, Government of India has provided PAN Verification Records to Indian citizens via DigiLocker.
   v. A Requester module displays the requesters' names and the number of documents requested from the user by the requesters. For example, Citizen applying through Union Public Service Commission (UPSC)'s Online Recruitment Application (ORA) can upload documents through DigiDocLocker as well (Figures 8.1–8.8).

DOI: 10.1201/9781003287124-8

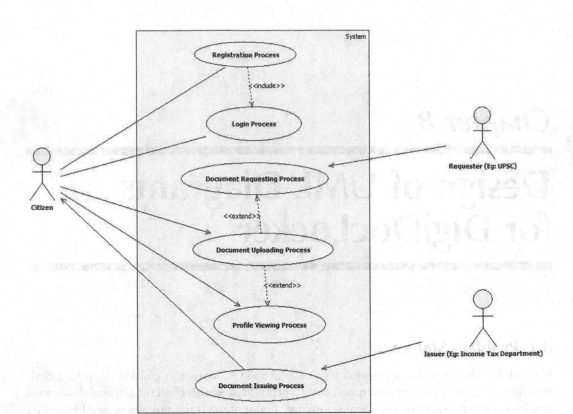

Figure 8.1   UML usecase diagram.

8.2 UML Diagrams

Usecase Specification

1. **Registration Process**

    Description: This process enables the new users to register with the DigiDocLocker System.
    Flow of Events

    Basic Flow: Register with the DigiDocLocker System successfully.

    Alternative Flow: Display an error message if the registration details provided by the user are not valid or Nil.

    Pre-Conditions: The user must possess a valid national identity card (Aadhaar).

    Post-Conditions: The user is registered with the DigiDocLocker System successfully and this is reflected in the registered users' database.

2. **Login Process**

    Description: This process enables the authorized users to login into the DigiDocLocker System.

    Flow of Events

    Basic Flow: Login into the DigiDocLocker System.

    Alternative Flow: Display an error message if the credentials are not valid or Nil.

    Pre-Conditions: The user should be registered with the system prior to the login process.

    Post-Conditions: The user is successfully logged in to the DigiDocLocker System.

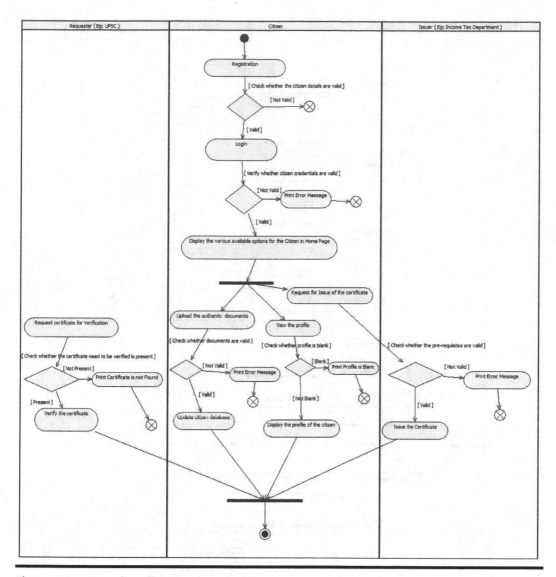

Figure 8.2   UML class diagram.

3. **Document Requesting Process**

Description: This process enables the Requesters (e.g. UPSC) to request for various authentic documents/certificates of the citizens that are to be verified online.

Flow of Events

Basic Flow: Display the requested certificate.

Alternative Flow: Request for another certificate or Nil.

Pre-Conditions: The certificate requested by the Requester must have been uploaded by the user prior.

Post-Conditions: The requested certificate is displayed to the Requester for verification.

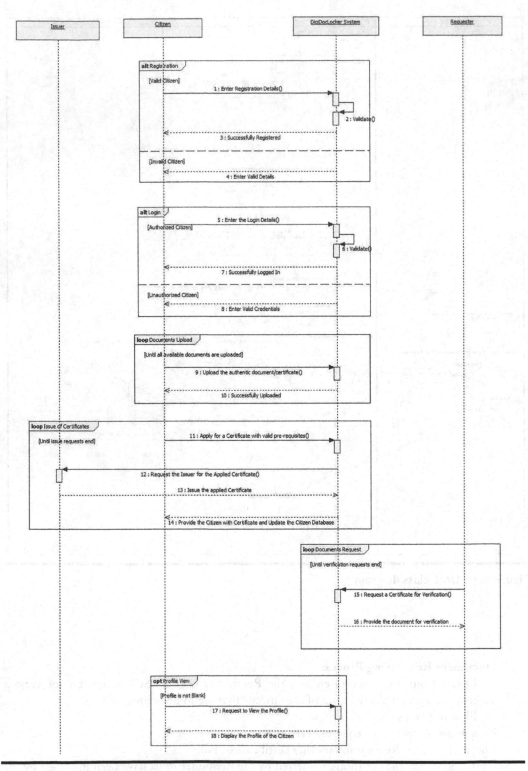

Figure 8.3 UML sequence diagram.

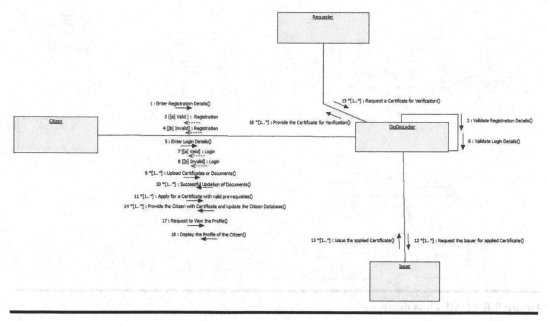

Figure 8.4 UML collaboration diagram.

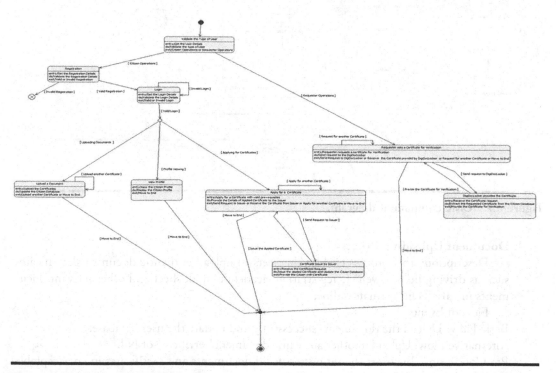

Figure 8.5 UML state machine diagram.

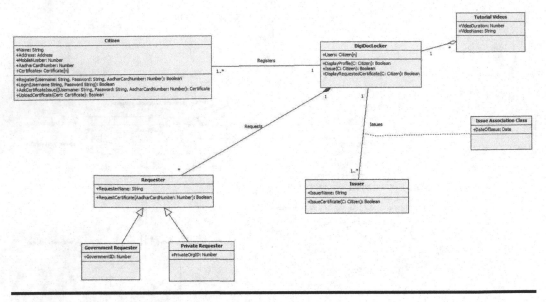

Figure 8.6   UML class diagram.

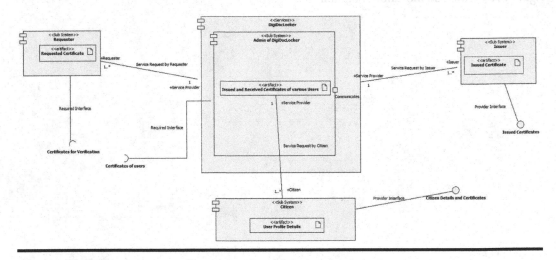

Figure 8.7   UML component diagram.

4. Document Uploading Process

Description: This process enables the users to upload authentic documents/certificates such as driving licence, vehicle registration, academic mark sheet and other relevant documents in various file formats online.

Flow of Events

Basic Flow: Upload the documents successfully and update the user database.

Alternative Flow: Upload another authentic document/certificate or Nil.

Pre-Conditions: The users should possess valid documents and certificates in an acceptable file format.

Post-Conditions: The document gets uploaded into the user database.

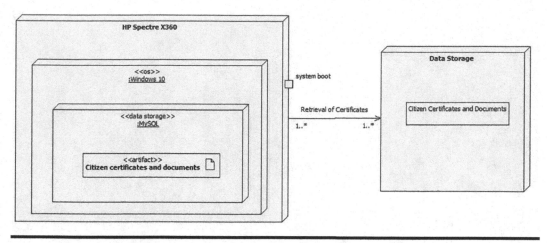

Figure 8.8   UML deployment diagram.

5. **Profile Viewing Process**

Description: This process enables the users to view their complete profile as available in the database.

Flow of Events

Basic Flow: Display the complete profile of the user.

Alternative Flow: Display an error message if no documents are available for the user in his profile or Nil.

Pre-Conditions: The documents should be uploaded by the user prior.

Post-Conditions: The complete profile of the user is displayed.

6. **Document Issuing Process**

Description: This process enables the citizens to apply for various authentic documents/certificates online which will be provided by the Issuers (e.g. Income Tax Department).

Flow of Events

Basic Flow: Apply for a certificate to the corresponding authority.

Alternative Flow: Apply for another certificate or Nil.

Pre-Conditions: The user must possess the pre-requisite documents (e.g. Aadhaar card) in order to apply for a specific certificate.

Post-Conditions: The certificate application process is successfully completed.

Chapter 9

Design of UML Diagrams for Online Marketplace

9.1 Problem Statement

Various new small scale and medium scale sellers face difficulties to reach out to the customers and sell their products along with other competing products in the market. This increases their overall cost, thus reducing their profit or even causing loss. E-Retail is an online marketplace application case study where small and medium scale sellers can list, showcase, advertise and sell their products directly to the customers without any physical store. E-Retail aims in providing a dynamic platform for all small and medium scale sellers to reach out and sell their products directly to all range of customers at a competing price without the need of any physical store. This enables the sellers to eliminate the cost of rent or maintenance of a physical store and to minimize other related costs. It also aims in promoting direct communication between the seller and customer, hence providing a trusted relationship between them. New sellers can easily authenticate and signup to the portal and sell their products in the portal. The application offers separate login for sellers and customers, where the sellers and customers can sign in and start using the application. Customers can view all the products available from various sellers and buy those products. It also facilitates online payments for purchasing the products. Customers can rate or give a review for the product and seller. Customers can also report a seller for any violations in delivery or if the product does not meet the specified requirement. Customers can also view the contact information and the rating of the seller before buying the product (Figures 9.1–9.9).

DOI: 10.1201/9781003287124-9

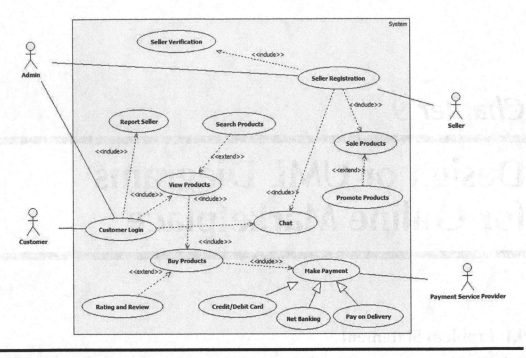

Figure 9.1 UML usecase diagram.

9.2 UML Diagrams

Actor Specification

1. **Admin** – Admin authenticates the new customers logging in to the system and verifies the new seller that registers to the system. Admin also verifies the reports issued by the customers against the sellers.
2. **Customers** – Customers are the users who logins into the system, to view and buy products sold by different sellers in the application.
3. **Payment Service Provider** – Payment service providers act as a mediator between merchants, customers, card brand networks and other financial institutions to process the electronic payment transactions in the application.
4. **Sellers** – Sellers are small or medium scale businesses, who can sell their products directly to potential customers using the applications.

Usecase Specification

1. **Customer Login**
   Description: Each customer has to login to the system using a username and password for using the application.
   Flow of Events
   Basic Flow: Authenticates the user and grants access to the system.
   Alternative Flow: Invalid username and password, try correct username and password.
   Pre-Conditions: Valid username and password.
   Post-Conditions: Nil.

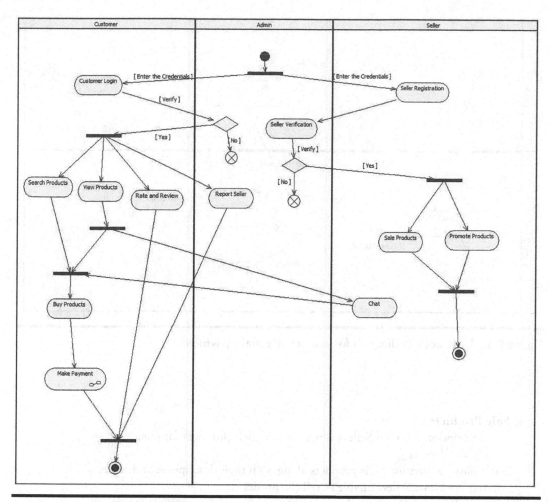

Figure 9.2   UML activity diagram (part 1).

2. **Seller Registration**

   Description: Each Seller has to register themselves in the system to sell their products.
   Flow of Events

   Basic Flow: Sellers register with valid credentials.

   Alternative Flow: Invalid credentials and retry.

   Pre-Conditions: Valid credentials.

   Post-Conditions: The registered seller is authenticated and they are verified.

3. **Seller Verification**

   Description: After registration, each seller is verified before being able to sell.
   Flow of Events

   Basic Flow: The registered seller is verified and they can sell their products.

   Alternative Flow: Verification of the seller is failed and they cannot sell their products.

   Pre-Conditions: Each seller must be registered.

   Post-Conditions: Nil.

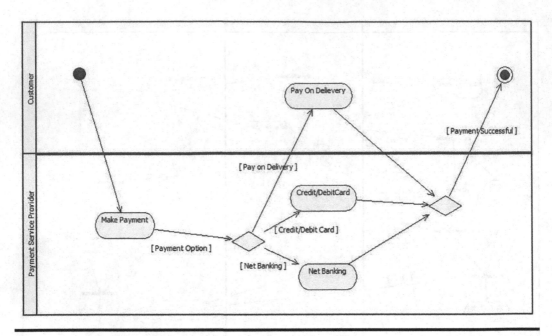

Figure 9.3 UML activity diagram for sub-activity make payment.

4. **Sale Products**

   Description: Verified Sellers can showcase their products for sale.

   Flow of Events

   Basic Flow: Sellers list their products along with their description and price.

   Alternative Flow: Sellers unable to sell the products.

   Pre-Conditions: Sellers must be verified before listing the products for sale.

   Post-Conditions: Nil.

5. **Promote Products**

   Description: Sellers can promote their products listed for sale.

   Flow of Events

   Basic Flow: Sellers promoting their products

   Alternative Flow: Sellers unable to promote their products

   Pre-Conditions: The Seller must be verified and should list their product for sale before promoting it.

   Post-Conditions: Promoted products are displayed on the home page.

6. **View Products**

   Description: Customers can view all the products listed for sale from various sellers.

   Flow of Events

   Basic Flow: Customers viewing the products available.

   Alternative Flow: Products unavailable to view.

   Pre-Conditions: Customer must be logged in.

   Post-Conditions: Customers can select a product to buy that product.

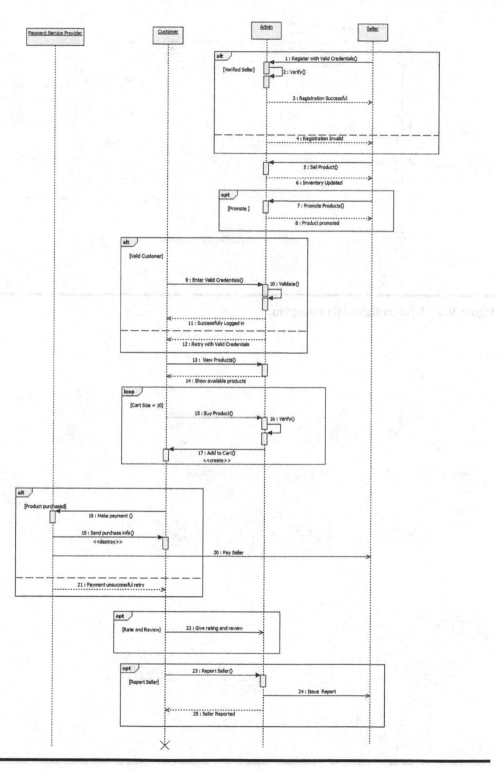

Figure 9.4 UML sequence diagram.

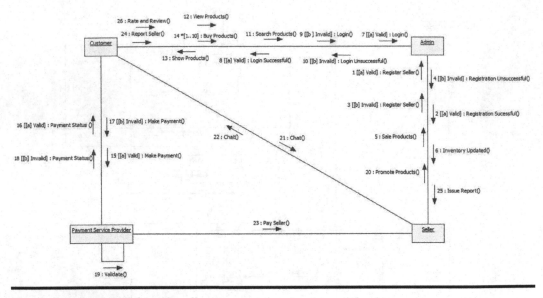

Figure 9.5   UML collaboration diagram.

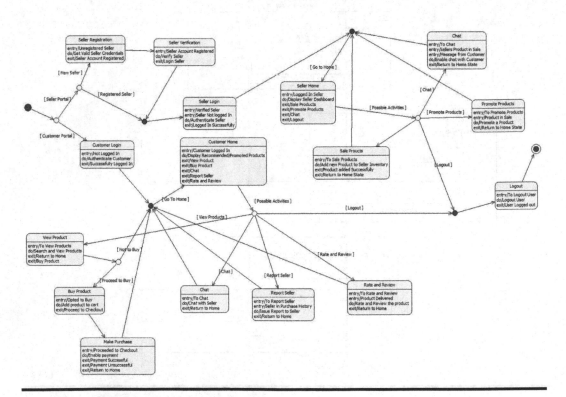

Figure 9.6   UML state machine diagram.

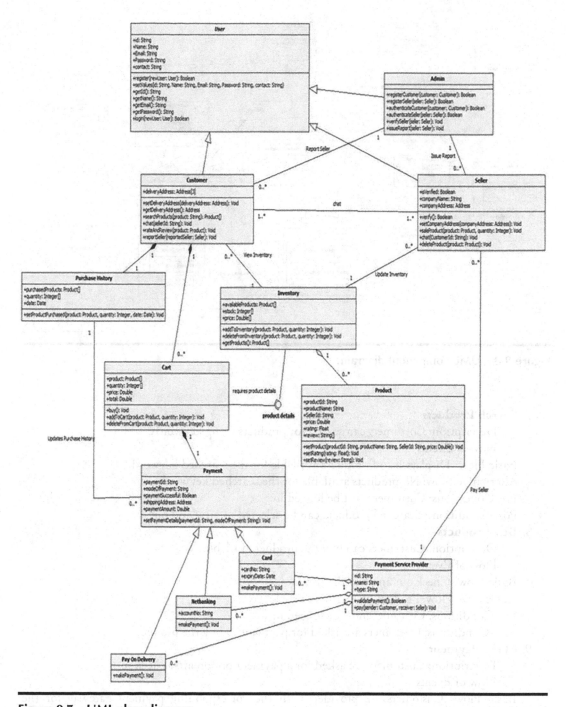

Figure 9.7   UML class diagram.

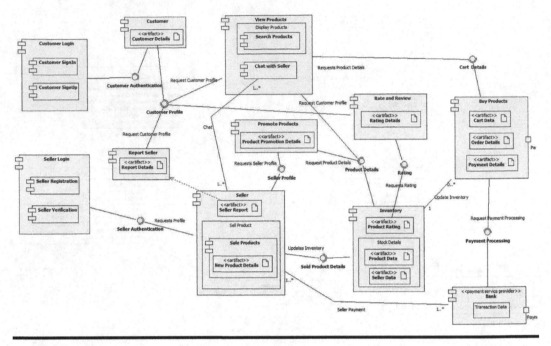

Figure 9.8 UML component diagram.

7. **Search Products**
   Description: Customers can search for products using keywords.
   Flow of Events
   Basic Flow: Displays list of products available for the searched keyword.
   Alternative Flow: No products available for the searched keyword.
   Pre-Conditions: Customer must be logged in.
   Post-Conditions: Searched products can be selected to view and buy.

8. **Buy Products**
   Description: Customers can buy the product available.
   Flow of Events
   Basic Flow: Check out and buy the product.
   Alternative Flow: Product unavailable for sale.
   Pre-Conditions: Customer must be logged in.
   Post-Conditions: Customers are asked for payment to buy the product.

9. **Make Payment**
   Description: Customers are asked for a payment option after checkout
   Flow of Events
   Basic Flow: Customers are provided with the corresponding payment gateway for the selected payment option in case of digital payment. Customers are asked for the delivery address in case of Pay on Delivery.
   Alternative Flow: Selected Payment option is unavailable.
   Pre-Conditions: Customer must choose to buy the product.
   Post-Conditions: Product purchase is updated and the order details are sent to the customer.

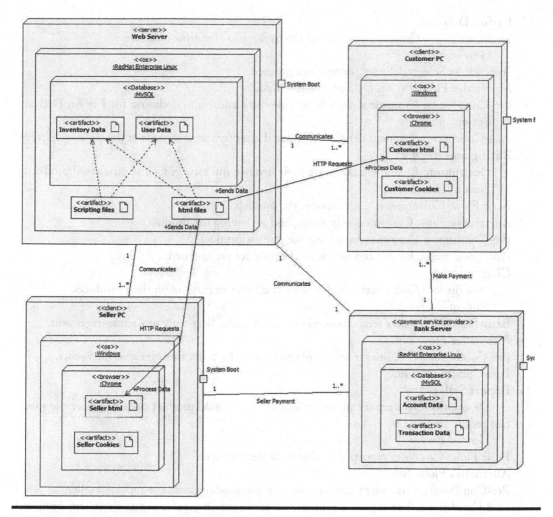

Figure 9.9 UML deployment diagram.

10. **Credit/Debit Card**
    Description: Products can be purchased using Credit/Debit card for payment.
    Flow of Events
  Basic Flow: Credit/Debit card payment is successful.
  Alternative Flow: Credit/Debit card payment is unsuccessful.
  Pre-Conditions: Customers must choose to make payments through Credit/Debit card.
  Post-Conditions: Payment details are updated.
11. **Net Banking**
    Description: Products can be purchased by using net banking for payment.
    Flow of Events
  Basic Flow: Net Banking payment is successful
  Alternative Flow: Net Banking payment is unsuccessful
  Pre-Conditions: Customers must choose to make payment through net banking.
  Post-Conditions: Payment details are updated.

12. **Pay on Delivery**
    Description: Customers can make the payment at the time of delivery.
    Flow of Events
Basic Flow: Selects delivery address and proceed.
Alternative Flow: Pay on Delivery is unavailable.
Pre-Conditions: Customers must have a delivery address and choose for Pay on Delivery option.
Post-Conditions: Payment details are updated after payment is made at the time of delivery.

13. **Rating and Review**
    Description: Customers can share their reviews and ratings for the purchased product.
    Flow of Events
Basic Flow: Customers rate and review the product.
Alternative Flow: Customers skip rating and reviewing the product.
Pre-Conditions: Customer must have bought the product.
Post-Conditions: Rating and review of the product are updated.

14. **Chat**
    Description: Customers can chat with the Seller to enquire on their products.
    Flow of Events
Basic Flow: Customers sends messages to sellers and sellers reply to the messages sent.
Alternative Flow: Nil.
Pre-Conditions: Customer must be logged in and the Seller must be a verified seller.
Post-Conditions: Nil.

15. **Report Seller**
    Description: Customer can report a seller if their sold product does not meet the specified requirement.
    Flow of Events
Basic Flow: Customer reports the seller with description.
Alternative Flow: Nil.
Pre-Conditions: Customer must have bought the product from the reported seller.
Post-Conditions: The report is sent to the corresponding seller for explanation. Frequent reports against specific sellers can remove the seller from the portal.

Chapter 10

Design of UML Diagrams for Product Recommendation System

10.1 Problem Statement

This case study focuses on using web scrapping for product comparison across websites to reduce the amount of time and effort involved in finding and comparing the products. To assist and enable online shopaholics to buy products with ease (Figures 10.1–10.8).

10.2 UML Diagrams

Usecase Specification

1. **Register**
   Description: Allows the user to register/login to use the system.
   Flow of Events
   Basic Flow: Allows into the system.
   Alternative Flow: Retry to login.
   Pre-Conditions: Nil.
   Post-Conditions: Control goes to the search product page.
2. **Search Product**
   Description: Allows the user to search for the product of their choices such as medicines, clothes and machinery.
   Flow of Events
   Basic Flow: Displays the search result for the product.
   Alternative Flow: Nil.
   Pre-Conditions: Users must have logged in.
   Post-Conditions: Nil.

DOI: 10.1201/9781003287124-10

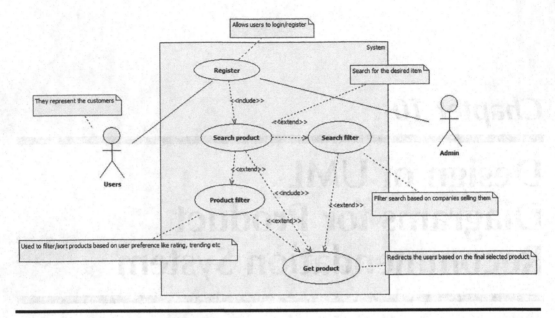

Figure 10.1   UML usecase diagram.

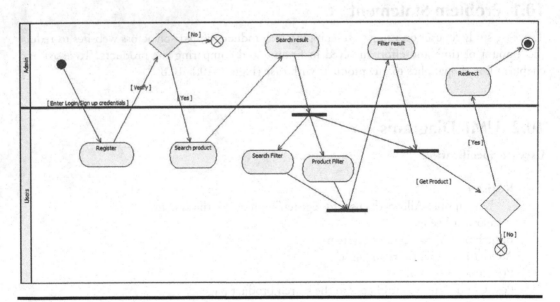

Figure 10.2   UML activity diagram.

3. **Search Filter**

Description: This allows the user to specify the website on which their product has to be searched. Example: Search in Amazon.

Flow of Events

Basic Flow: Shows more desired and user-specific results.

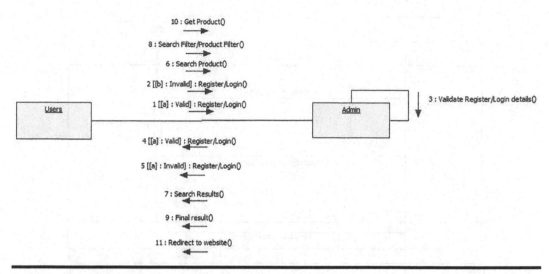

Figure 10.3   UML collaboration diagram.

Alternative Flow: Nil.
Pre-Conditions: Search product.
Post-Conditions: Nil.

4. **Product Filter**

Description: Filter the product results based on user's choice like rating, reviews, and number of purchases.

Flow of Events

Basic Flow: Shows more desired and user-specific results.
Alternative Flow: Nil.
Pre-Conditions: Search product.
Post-Conditions: Nil.

5. **Get Product**

Description: Redirects the user to the user-selected product's website. Then, the user can purchase the product.

Flow of Events

Basic Flow: Enables the user to purchase the product.
Alternative Flow: Nil.
Pre-Conditions: Search product.
Post-Conditions: Nil.

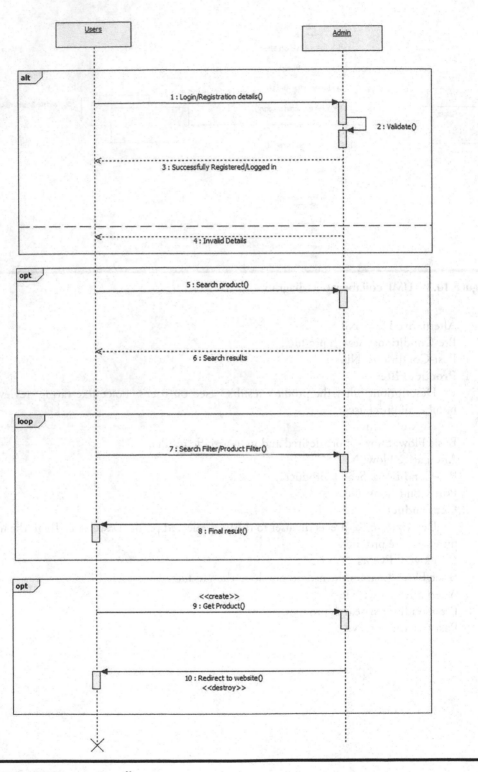

Figure 10.4 UML sequence diagram.

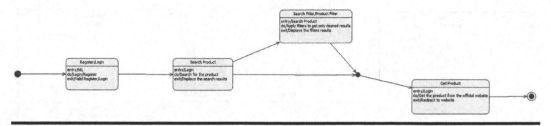

Figure 10.5   UML state machine diagram.

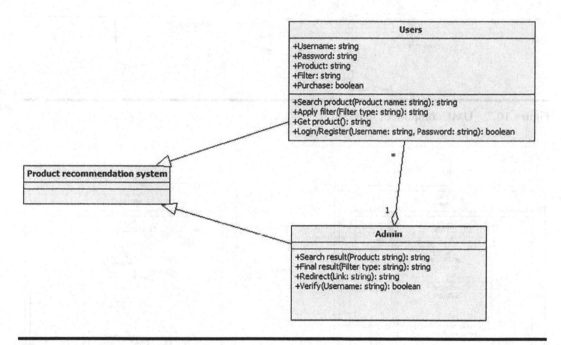

Figure 10.6   UML class diagram.

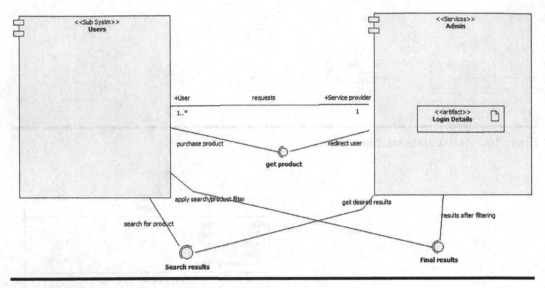

Figure 10.7   UML component diagram.

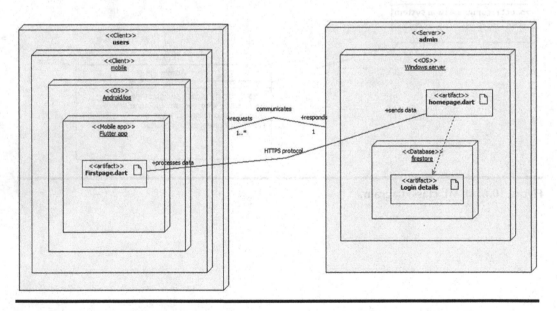

Figure 10.8   UML deployment diagram.

Chapter 11

Design of UML Diagrams for Advocate Diary

11.1 Problem Statement

The need for law and enforcement in a country with a high population like India is salient. Lawyers play a major role in maintaining most of their data as hard copies. This project is mainly designed for lawyers to make their work more easy and efficient. It is a responsive web application that would provide lawyers with various services that would help them to maintain their documents. The services include a logbook that has details about the cases along with a calendar. The lawyers can also upload and save documents related to their case. It contains formats of model forms and links to online filing. It also provides quick references of common cases and detailed information about laws through e-books. Information about the judicial exams for lawyers is also made available. Furthermore, the web application contains news updates for lawyers, blogs and feedback. This case study will serve as a small hand tool for lawyers to maintain the soft copies of their data (Figures 11.1–11.8).

11.2 UML Diagrams

Usecase Specification

1. **Register**
   Description: Register allows a new lawyer to create an account.
   Flow of Events
   Basic Flow: User enters proper credentials.
   Alternative Flow: If improper credentials are entered.
   Pre-Conditions: Nil.
   Post-Conditions: The data entered are saved in the database. The user is allowed to login.
2. **Login**
   Description: It allows a valid user to login to the page.
   Flow of Events
   Basic Flow: Enters user id and password.

DOI: 10.1201/9781003287124-11

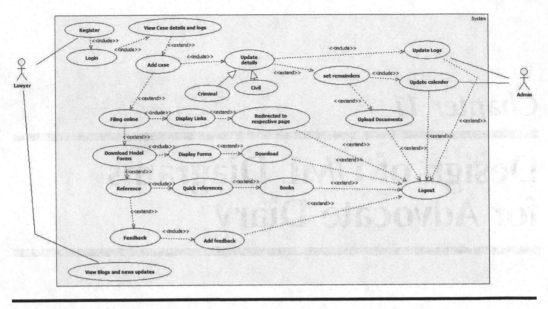

Figure 11.1   UML usecase diagram.

Alternative Flow: Invalid ID or password leads to improper login.
Pre-Conditions: The user should have registered.
Post-Conditions: Nil.

3. **View Case Details and Logs**
Description: Displays details about both existing and completed cases along with the calendar.
Flow of Events
Basic Flow: Allows user to view and edit details.
Alternative Flow: Nil.
Pre-Conditions: Nil.
Post-Conditions: If edited, the remainders will be reflected in the calendar.

4. **Add Case**
Description: Allows user to add new case.
Flow of Events
Basic Flow: User can add details about new cases.
Alternative Flow: User may not add details.
Pre-Conditions: Nil.
Post-Conditions: Nil.

5. **Update Details**
Description: This allows the user to enter specific details about the case.
Flow of Events
Basic Flow: User enters the proper details.
Alternative Flow: User may enter wrong details.
Pre-Conditions: User must have details about the cases.
Post-Conditions: The details are reflected in the View table.

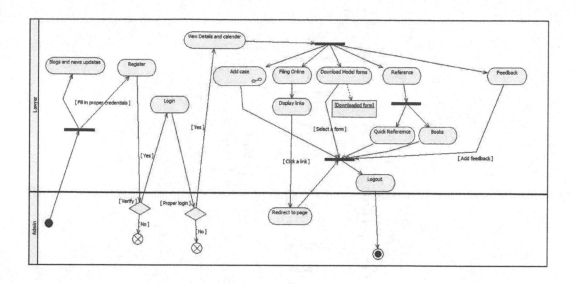

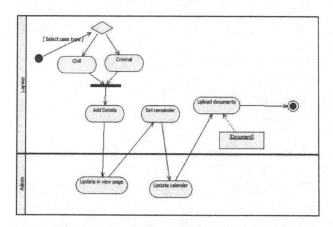

Figure 11.2   UML activity diagrams.

6. **Criminal**
    Description: It specifies whether the case is a criminal case.
    Flow of Events
  Basic Flow: The user selects if it is a criminal case.
  Alternative Flow: The user doesn't select it if it's not a criminal case.
  Pre-Conditions: Nil.
  Post-Conditions: The information is reflected in the view table.
7. **Civil**
    Description: It specifies whether the case is a civil case.
    Flow of Events
  Basic Flow: The user selects if it is a civil case.
  Alternative Flow: The user doesn't select it if it's not a civil case.

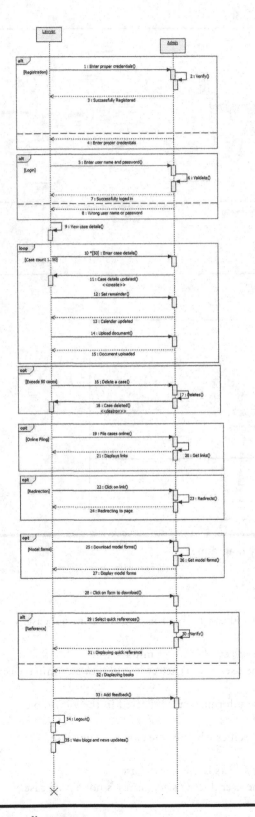

Figure 11.3   UML sequence diagram.

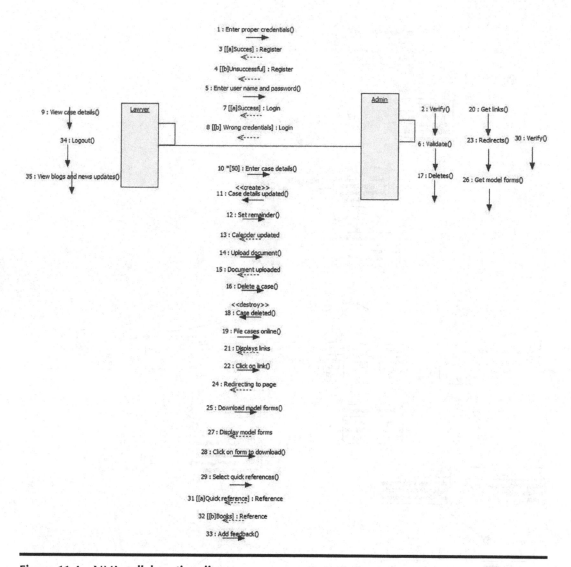

Figure 11.4   UML collaboration diagram.

Pre-Conditions: Nil.
Post-Conditions: The information is reflected in the view table.
8. **Update Logs**
Description: This updates the view table with the data provided.
Flow of Events
Basic Flow: The data given is added to the view table.
Alternative Flow: Nil.
Pre-Conditions: The details should be entered by the user.
Post-Conditions: Nil.
9. **Set Remainders**
Description: It allows users to add date and time details for the case.
Flow of Events

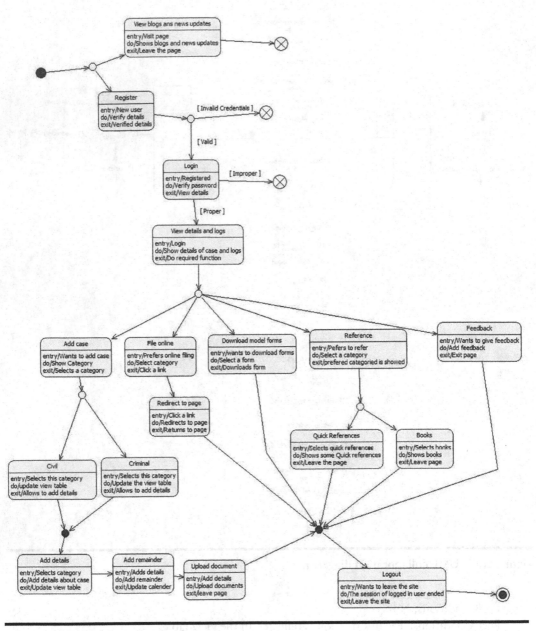

Figure 11.5 UML state machine diagram.

Basic Flow: The user enters the date and time the case will be held.

Alternative Flow: The user may not enter the date and time.

Pre-Conditions: The user should have entered details of the case.

Post-Conditions: The remainder is reflected in the view and calendar table.

10. **Update Calendar**

Description: This function updates the calendar with the remainder.

Flow of Events

Basic Flow: The calendar is updated with the remainders.

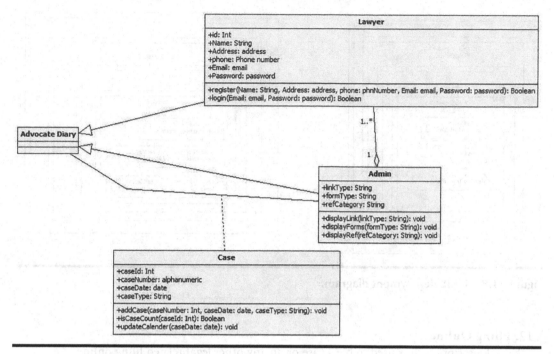

Figure 11.6   UML class diagram.

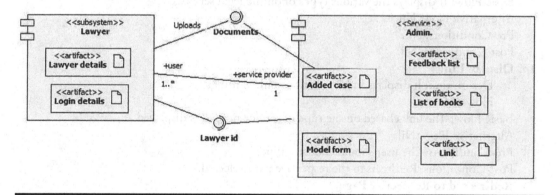

Figure 11.7   UML component diagram.

Alternative Flow: Nil.

Pre-Conditions: The user should have set remainders.

Post-Conditions: Nil.

11. **Upload Document**

Description: A user can upload the documents related to the case.

Flow of Events

Basic Flow: The user uploads the document.

Alternative Flow: The user may not upload the document.

Pre-Conditions: The details of the case must be entered.

Post-Conditions: The documents are saved in the drives.

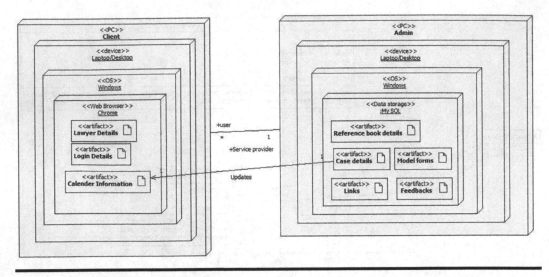

Figure 11.8   UML deployment diagram.

12. **Filing Online**

   Description: It is used to file a case or do any other legal related filing online.

   Flow of Events

   Basic Flow: It displays the various types of online legal services.

   Alternative Flow: Nil.

   Pre-Conditions: Nil.

   Post-Conditions: Nil.

13. **Display Links**

   Description: It displays links to various online filings.

   Flow of Events

   Basic Flow: The links based on the type of service needed is displayed.

   Alternative Flow: Nil.

   Pre-Conditions: The user should choose a type.

   Post-Conditions: Redirects to the respective page selected.

14. **Redirected to Respective Page**

   Description: This redirects to the link selected.

   Flow of Events

   Basic Flow: The page of the link selected for online filing is displayed.

   Alternative Flow: Nil.

   Pre-Conditions: A link should be clicked.

   Post-Conditions: Nil.

15. **Download Model Forms**

   Description: This allows users to download model forms.

   Flow of Events

   Basic Flow: This displays different categories of cases.

   Alternative Flow: Nil.

   Pre-Conditions: Nil.

   Post-Conditions: Nil.

16. **Display Forms**
   Description: It displays various forms on the category selected.
   Flow of Events
Basic Flow: The user can select any form to be downloaded.
Alternative Flow: Nil.
Pre-Conditions: The category must be selected.
Post-Conditions: Nil.

17. **Download**
   Description: This allows the user to download a model form.
   Flow of Events
Basic Flow: It displays the option to view and download the form.
Alternative Flow: Nil.
Pre-Conditions: The form to be downloaded must be selected.
Post-Conditions: The downloaded document will be saved in the system.

18. **Reference**
   Description: It displays quick references and books for the user to choose.
   Flow of Events
Basic Flow: The user selects for quick reference or books.
Alternative Flow: Nil.
Pre-Conditions: Nil.
Post-Conditions: Nil.

19. **Quick Reference**
   Description: It displays various information about the most common cases.
   Flow of Events
Basic Flow: The important information for the most common cases are listed.
Alternative Flow: Nil.
Pre-Conditions: Nil.
Post-Conditions: Nil.

20. **Books**
   Description: Helps the user to get information via law e-books.
   Flow of Events
Basic Flow: It displays the title of the book.
Alternative Flow: Nil.
Pre-Conditions: Nil.
Post-Conditions: The book selected will be displayed.

21. **Feedback**
   Description: This allows users to add feedbacks.
   Flow of Events
Basic Flow: The user is allowed to add feedbacks.
Alternative Flow: Nil.
Pre-Conditions: Nil.
Post-Conditions: Nil.

22. **Add Feedback**
   Description: This allows the user to type in and send feedbacks.
   Flow of Events
Basic Flow: The user sends the feedback.
Alternative Flow: Nil.

Pre-Conditions: Nil.
Post-Conditions: If any problem, it'll be rectified by the developer.

23. **View Blogs and Updates**

Description: It allows users to view blogs and news updates.

Flow of Events

Basic Flow: Both registered and unregistered users can see blogs and news updates regarding legal activities.

Alternative Flow: Nil.

Pre-Conditions: Nil.

Post-Conditions: Nil.

Chapter 12

Design of UML Diagrams for My Helper

12.1 Problem Statement

This case study is helpful to people who forget their mobile phones at home as a part of their busy daily routines. Keeping tick of essentials in this fast-paced life sometimes turns out to be quite demanding. People sometimes forget their phones at home. What if we need to make an important call and we don't remember the contact number? Sometimes our phones just get disappeared and the scariest part is when the phone is put on silent mode. We sometimes want to lock our phones when they aren't around us. Need to know the exact location of your phone? Therein comes the use of 'My Helper'. The solutions to all the problems stated above can be solved easily and very quickly if u have the application 'My Helper' pre-installed on your phone and u have completed configuring the app. All you need to do is just send an SMS to your mobile number from any phone that you have access to...and there goes your problem solved. The scope of this system is increasing every day across the entire world where everything is happening at the speed of a Formula 1 Car on a race track. The objective of this system is to provide help to people facing these types of problems instantly with the help of advanced technology. The alluring features of this system are Remote Access without the Internet, Track your phone through an SMS, Hassle-Free as no OTP and ID PASSWORD is required and an SMS can help you change the sound profile of your phone (silent to normal) without Internet. The system is user friendly and the application will be available to even basic smartphones (Figures 12.1–12.8).

DOI: 10.1201/9781003287124-12

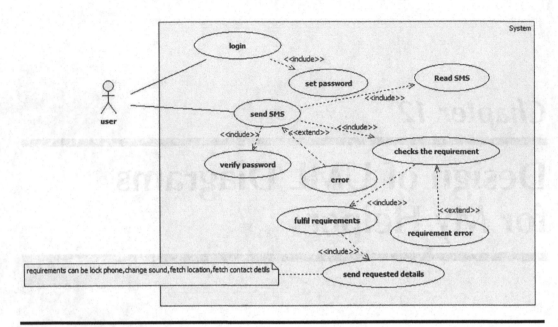

Figure 12.1   UML usecase diagram.

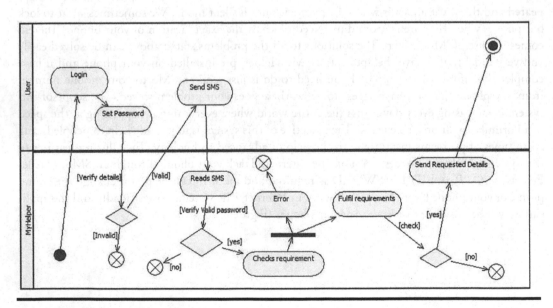

Figure 12.2   UML activity diagram.

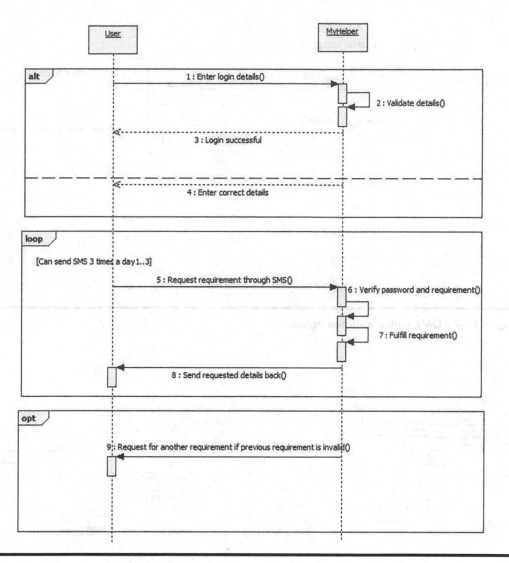

Figure 12.3   UML sequence diagram.

12.2 UML Diagrams

Usecase Specification

1. **Login**
   Description: This usecase allows the user to get started with the system.
   Flow of Events
   Basic Flow: Entering valid details to get started with the system.
   Alternative Flow: If invalid details are entered, the user is redirected to fill out correctly.
   Pre-Conditions: Nil.
   Post-Conditions: User gets registered, data of the user gets stored into the database.

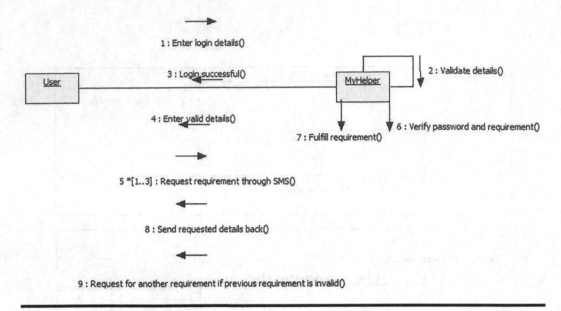

Figure 12.4 UML collaboration diagram.

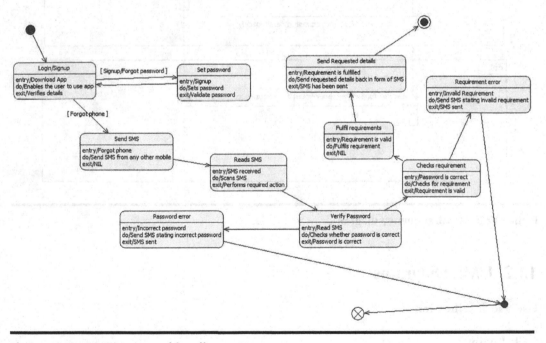

Figure 12.5 UML state machine diagram.

2. **Set Password**

Description: Allows user to set a strong password to use it later.

Flow of Events

Basic Flow: Setting a strong password (e.g. Using numbers, Special characters, Lowercase and uppercase letters).

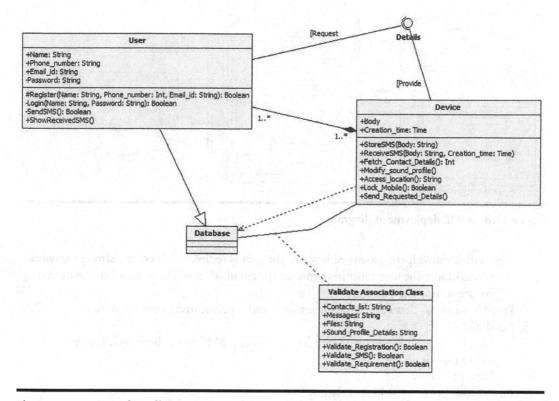

Figure 12.6 UML class diagram.

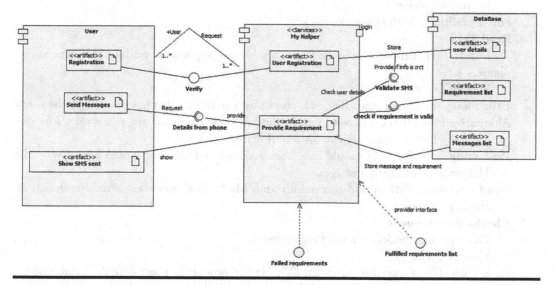

Figure 12.7 UML component diagram.

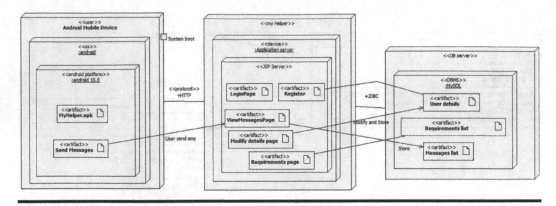

Figure 12.8 UML deployment diagram.

Alternative Flow: If the password is weak, the user is redirected to enter a strong password.

Pre-Conditions: The user must have entered the email address, phone number and username before setting the password.

Post-Conditions: Password is set successfully and it gets stored in the database.

3. **Send SMS**

Description: This usecase allows the user to send SMS to his/her's mobile number from any other mobile phone.

Flow of Events

Basic Flow: Sending SMS successfully.

Alternative Flow: If SMS sending is failed due to any issue, the user should resend the SMS.

Pre-Conditions: The user must have completed configuring the 'MY HELPER' system on his mobile phone.

Post-Conditions: SMS is successfully sent.

4. **Read SMS**

Description: This usecase is about the 'My Helper' application reading SMS sent to the phone.

Flow of Events

Basic Flow: The system reads the SMS, checks for a password that has been set by the user.

Alternative Flow: If the password sent in the SMS doesn't match the password set by the user, My Helper sends back an SMS stating invalid details.

Pre-Conditions: The SMS should have been received and the user should have given 'My Helper' access to read messages.

Post-Conditions: SMS is read successfully and 'My Helper' now starts checking details of the requirement.

5. **Checks Requirement**

Description: Checks for a valid requirement.

Flow of Events

Basic Flow: If it is a valid requirement, 'My Helper' now starts processing the requirement.

Alternative Flow: If the requirement is not valid, My Helper sends back an SMS stating invalid details.

Pre-Conditions: SMS should have been received and successfully read.

Post-Conditions: The requirement fulfilment process gets started.

6. **Error**

   Description: If SMS sending fails, it results in an error.
   Flow of Events

   Basic Flow: Error in sending.

   Alternative Flow: Send another SMS or Nil.

   Pre-Conditions: Nil.

   Post-Conditions: Send SMS again (or) Don't send an SMS.

7. **Fulfil Requirement**

   Description: Performs operations and satisfies user requirements.
   Flow of Events

   Basic Flow: After scanning the requirement, start processing the requirement.

   Alternative Flow: Requirement processing is failed, request another requirement.

   Pre-Conditions: Requirement should be read and valid.

   Post-Conditions: After fetching the requirement, send the requested details back to the user.

8. **Requirement Error**

   Description: If the requirement cannot be satisfied by 'My helper', it results in an error.
   Flow of Events

   Basic Flow: Requirement has been read, and it resulted in an error.

   Alternative Flow: Request another requirement or satisfy the requirement if it is valid.

   Pre-Conditions: Nil.

   Post-Conditions: Send another requirement or Nil.

9. **Send Requested Details**

   Description: Fetch user requirements and send them to the user in the form of SMS.
   Flow of Events

   Basic Flow: Requirement details have been fetched completely and send it to the user.

   Alternative Flow: Requested detail fetching has been failed or Nil.

   Pre-Conditions: Requirement details should have been fetched.

   Post-Conditions: Nil.

10. **Verify Password**

    Description: Verifying if the password sent in SMS matches the user-set-password
    Flow of Events

    Basic Flow: Verify password.

    Alternative Flow: Wrong password.

    Pre-Conditions: Should have received SMS.

    Post-Conditions: Password is successfully verified.

Chapter 13

Design of UML Diagrams for COVID-19 Management System

13.1 Problem Statement

The all in one COVID-19 management system simplifies the entire process of decreasing the virus load in the community by digitalization. It includes tracking and treating COVID-19 patients and monitoring the spread of the virus. It aims to assist healthcare organizations and governments to assess patient risk profiles and provide awareness to common people by connecting them with virtual care capabilities. With the current epidemiological situation of COVID-19, there is a high demand to reduce contact between persons and digitize the whole process. This will effectively reduce the infection rate, help the common people and empower medical professionals across the world to help more patients through telemedicine and virtual care.

Functionalities:

1. Medical Professionals (Doctors/Nurses): Can monitor the oxygen level, blood pressure level, temperature, symptoms, medicine intake and diet of the registered patient. All the information of the patients from screening to discharge can be viewed. Medicines can also be prescribed to a specific patient.
2. COVID-19 Patients: View the data shared by the doctor, home quarantined patients can update data and checklist of medical shops in their locality.
3. Common People: Check the number of people infected (symptomatic and asymptomatic) and death in their locality ranging from current street, 500 m, 1 km, 5 km, 10 km and view a blog where recovered persons share their experience.
4. COVID-19 Essentials Seller: Can stock up essentials like masks and gloves according to infection in an area. Medical shops nearby the area will be listed.

DOI: 10.1201/9781003287124-13

5. Corporation Worker Head: Workers will be assigned to disinfect Covid-affected areas regularly based on infection data and updates status.
6. Admin: Updates current number of infected persons in a locality (Figure 13.1–13.9).

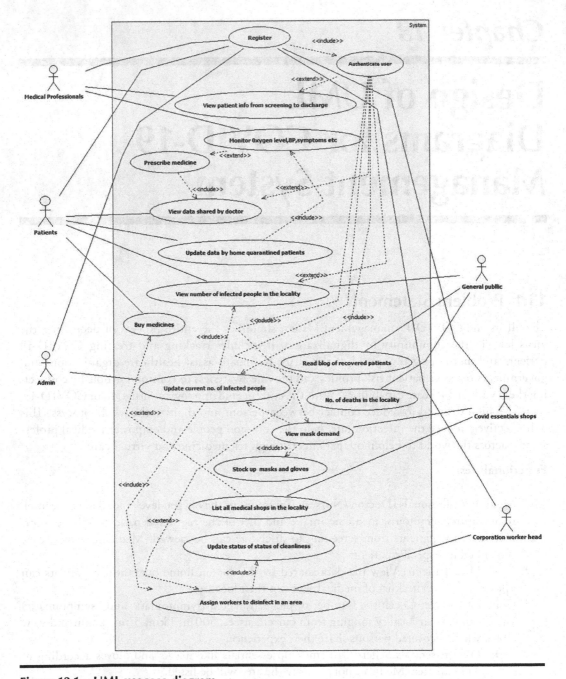

Figure 13.1   UML usecase diagram.

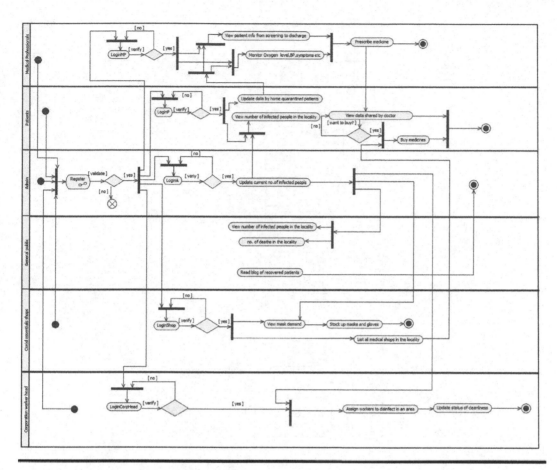

Figure 13.2   UML activity diagram (part 1).

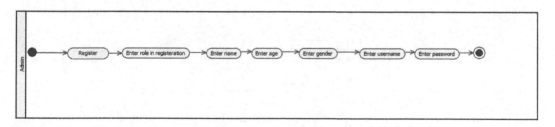

Figure 13.3   UML activity diagram (part 2).

13.2 UML Diagrams

Usecase Specification

1. **Monitor Oxygen Levels, BP, Symptoms, etc.**
   Description: To monitor the oxygen level, blood pressure level, temperature, symptoms, medicine intake and diet of the registered patient.
   Flow of Events

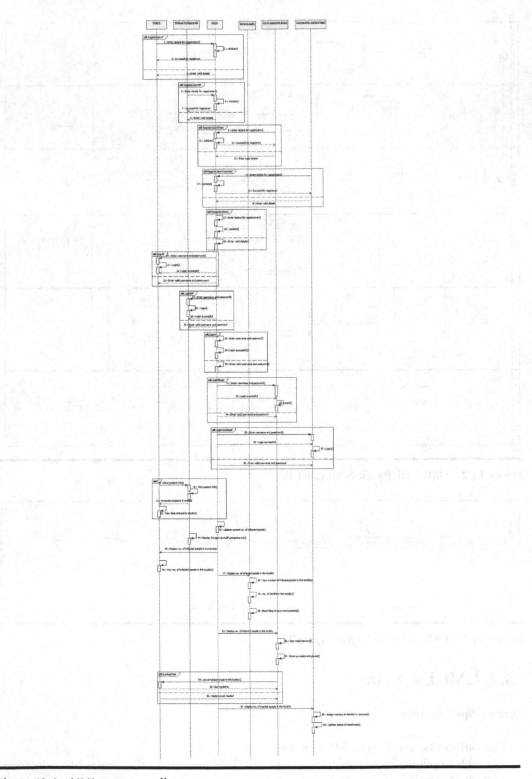

Figure 13.4   UML sequence diagram.

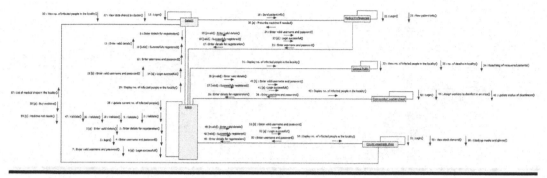

Figure 13.5   UML collaboration diagram.

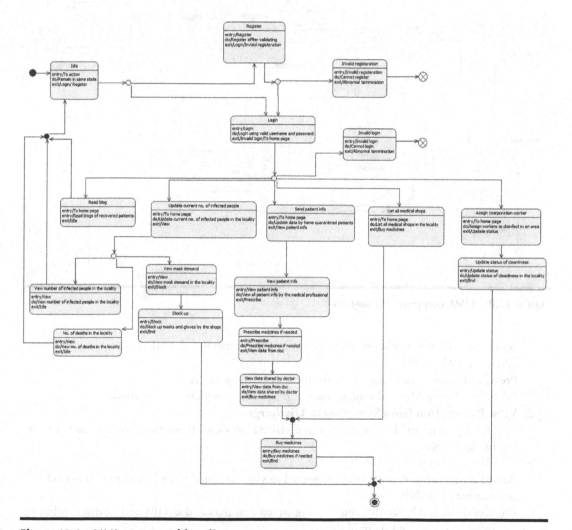

Figure 13.6   UML state machine diagram.

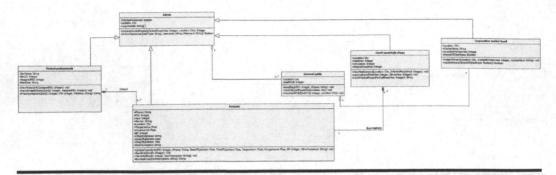

Figure 13.7 UML class diagram.

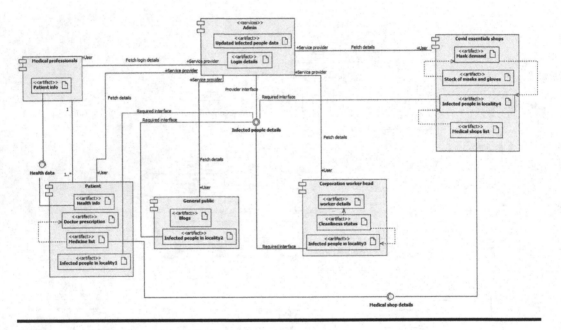

Figure 13.8 UML component diagram.

Basic Flow: Correctly choose a patient to view the respective details.

Alternative Flow: Nil.

Pre-Conditions: Patient has to record the set of details precisely.

Post-Conditions: Medical professionals can prescribe medicines if required.

2. **View Patient Info from Screening to Discharge**

Description: Enables the medical professional to view all patients' records from screening to discharge.

Flow of Events

Basic Flow: Date and time must be entered to view patients' records within that period.

Alternative Flow: Nil.

Pre-Conditions: All patients must be registered and personal details and health conditions must be entered with credibility.

Post-Conditions: Nil.

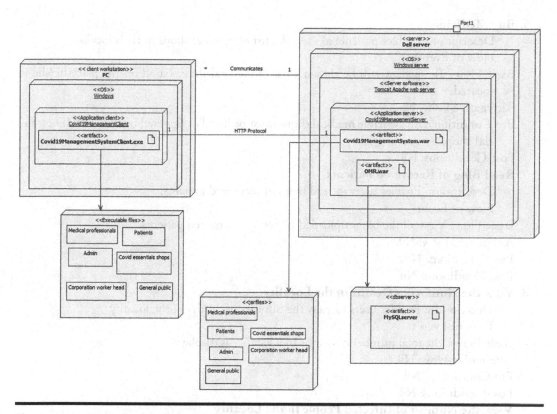

Figure 13.9   UML deployment diagram.

3. **Prescribe Medicines**
   Description: Enables doctors to prescribe medicines to specific patients.
   Flow of Events
   Basic Flow: Enter the appropriate medicine with dosage for the patient.
   Alternative Flow: Nil.
   Pre-Conditions: Doctors must have viewed the patient's health conditions.
   Post-Conditions: Nil.
4. **Update Data by Home Quarantined Patients**
   Description: Enable home quarantined patients to update their health conditions.
   Flow of Events
   Basic Flow: Enter temperature, oxygen level and other symptoms.
   Alternative Flow: Nil.
   Pre-Conditions: Patients must be registered with credible credentials.
   Post-Conditions: Nil.
5. **View Data Shared by Doctor**
   Description: Enables patient to view prescription and other remarks of the doctor.
   Flow of Events
   Basic Flow: View the data shared by the doctor when notified.
   Alternative Flow: Nil.
   Pre-Conditions: Nil.
   Post-Conditions: Nil.

6. **Buy Medicine**

Description: Enables patients to view the list of medical shops in their locality.

Flow of Events

Basic Flow: The patient will be shown a list of medical shops based on the place he/she is located.

Alternative Flow: Nil.

Pre-Conditions: All available medical shops must be listed or updated by the COVID essential shop.

Post-Conditions: Nil.

7. **Read Blog of Recovered Patients**

Description: Enables users to read blogs of recovered patients.

Flow of Events

Basic Flow: View all the blogs uploaded by several recovered patients.

Alternative Flow: Nil.

Pre-Conditions: Nil.

Post-Conditions: Nil.

8. **View the Number of Deaths in the Locality**

Description: Enables users to view the number of deaths in the locality.

Flow of Events

Basic Flow: The total number of deaths in a locality is displayed.

Alternative Flow: Nil.

Pre-Conditions: Nil.

Post-Conditions: Nil.

9. **View the Number of Infected People in the Locality**

Description: Enables users to view the exact number of infected people in their locality.

Flow of Events

Basic Flow: The exact number of infected people in a particular locality is displayed.

Alternative Flow: Nil.

Pre-Conditions: Nil.

Post-Conditions: Nil.

10. **List all Medical Shops in the Locality**

Description: Enables the COVID essentials shops to list all the medical shops in the locality.

Flow of Events

Basic Flow: All available medical shops in the locality is entered and listed.

Alternative Flow: Nil.

Pre-Conditions: COVID essential shops should be registered.

Post-Conditions: Can be viewed by patients who want to buy medicines.

11. **Update Status of Cleanliness**

Description: Enables corporation worker head to update the status of cleanliness after a particular area has been disinfected.

Flow of Events

Basic Flow: Updating the status of cleanliness like cleaned/not cleaned/in progress.

Alternative Flow: Nil.

Pre-Conditions: Checking of the number of infected people in the locality.

Post-Conditions: Assign workers to disinfect the particular area.

12. **Assign Workers to Disinfect in an Area**

Description: Workers are assigned according to the infection rate in the locality.

Flow of Events

Basic Flow: After assigning workers, status is changed by the corporation worker head to 'assigned workers'.

Alternative Flow: Nil.

Pre-Conditions: The head has to view the number of infected people in the locality from time to time.

Post-Conditions: Update status of cleanliness.

13. **Register**

Description: All users except the general public must register to ensure their access control and make use of their distinct functions in the COVID-19 management system.

Flow of Events

Basic Flow: All the details must be filled correctly before submitting.

Alternative Flow: Invalid credentials leads to improper registration.

Pre-Conditions: Nil.

Post-Conditions: Authentication is performed to ensure the proper functioning of access control list.

14. **Authenticate User**

Description: To check the access control of the user in this system.

Flow of Events

Basic Flow: The profile of the user is checked and given distinct functions respectively.

Alternative Flow: In case of failed authentication, the user won't be able to use the system.

Pre-Conditions: Registration.

Post-Conditions: Nil.

15. **Update the Current Number of Infected People**

Description: Enables the admin to update the exact number of infected people belonging to a place frequently.

Flow of Events

Basic Flow: Enter the number of people infected and their place.

Alternative Flow: Nil.

Pre-Conditions: Admin must be registered to have administrative rights over updating the number of people infected.

Post-Conditions: Nil.

16. **Stock Up Masks and Gloves**

Description: Enables the Covid essentials shops to show their updated stock of the essentials like masks, gloves, hand sanitizers and other disinfectants.

Flow of Events

Basic Flow: Update/increase stock of essential products.

Alternative Flow: Nil.

Pre-Conditions: View mask demand.

Post-Conditions: Nil.

17. **View Mask Demand**

Description: Enables the COVID essential shops to view the demand for masks as the number of infected people in locality increases.

Flow of Events

Basic Flow: Analyze mask demand by viewing number of infected people in a locality.

Alternative Flow: Nil.

Pre-Conditions: Nil.

Post-Conditions: Stock up all essentials.

Chapter 14

Design of UML Diagrams for Car Care

14.1 Problem Statement

Most of the car owners do not know whether their car is at risk and needs to be serviced. This considerably increases the risk of malfunctioning of major parts of a car such as the braking system and engine which lead to accidents.

Car Care is a multi-brand car service and maintenance application that maintains the date at which the specific part of a car is installed and notifies the expiry date of the parts of the car for both the driver and authorized service centre, so that the car can be serviced.

This application enables car owners and service centres to separately login and enter their cars information. After issuing the car, the service centre employee enters the estimated expiry dates of parts of the car in this app.

This application notifies the car owners and service centres when the expiry date for parts of the car is reached. Then the service centre employee contacts the owner of a car about service, once the owner accepts service request, the service centre employee picks up the car from home, this saves the time for owner of car.

And then service centre employee examines the entire car and prepares the list of the damaged parts of the car and send it to the owner of the car through this app, once the owner selects the damaged parts to be serviced, the employee services the owner selected parts and updates the information about changed parts in the app so that the car can be service again on the expiry date of changed parts. Thus, this application helps in exchanging information between car owners and service centres. This application also enables the online payment for the services (Figures 14.1–14.8).

DOI: 10.1201/9781003287124-14

14.2 UML Diagrams

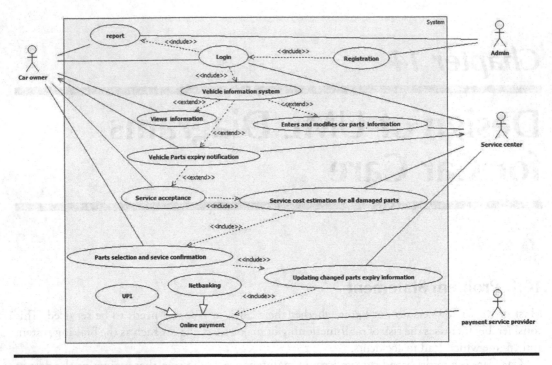

Figure 14.1 UML usecase diagram.

Usecase Specification

1. **Registration**
   Description: Registration of car owner and service centre is required to use the system.
   Flow of Events
   Basic Flow: Profile for a car owner and service centre is created.
   Alternative Flow: If the car owner and service centre are already registered, they can go with login and get access to the system.
   Pre-Conditions: Nil.
   Post-Conditions: Allows the car owner and service centre to login into system.
2. **Login**
   Description: Login is required to get access to the system.
   Flow of Events
   Basic Flow: If the password is correct, then the car owner and service centre can get access to the system.
   Alternative Flow: If the password is incorrect, try with the correct password and forgot password facility is available.
   Pre-Conditions: Registration is required.

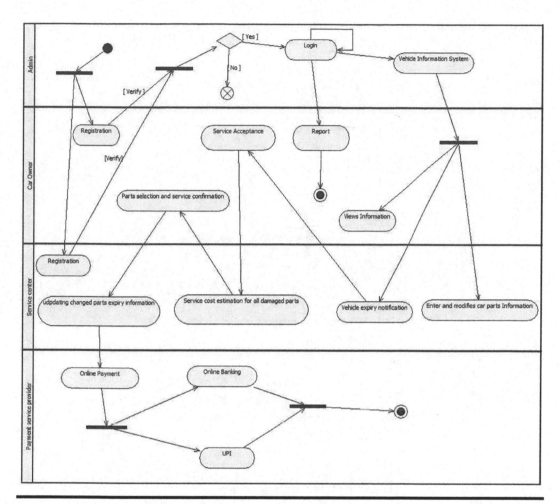

Figure 14.2   UML activity diagram.

Post-Conditions: This allows the car owner and service centre to access the Vehicle Information System.

3. **Vehicle Information System**

Description: Vehicle Information System maintains the information of the vehicle and when the expiry date of parts of car is reached, it notifies both the owner and service centre, so that car can be serviced.

Flow of Events

Basic Flow: Maintains the information of the vehicle and sends a notification when the expiry date of parts of the car is reached.

Alternative Flow: Nil.

Pre-Conditions: Login is required.

Post-Conditions: The car owner and service centre can view the information of car.

4. **Views Information**

Description: This allows the car owner and service centre to know the conditions of parts of the car and other information.

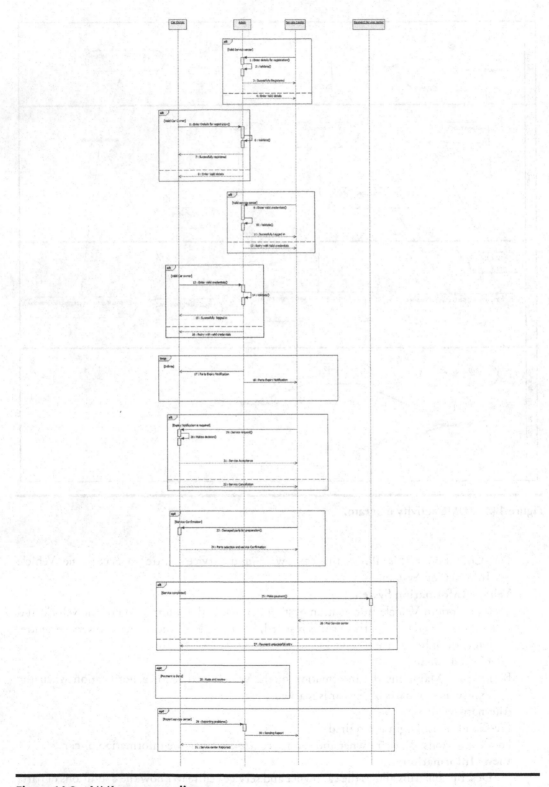

Figure 14.3   UML sequence diagram.

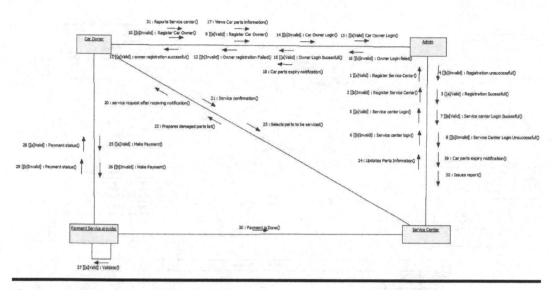

Figure 14.4   UML collaboration diagram.

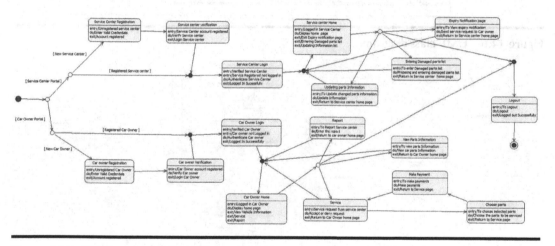

Figure 14.5   UML state machine diagram.

Flow of Events

Basic Flow: User gets to know the status of parts of the car.

Alternative Flow: Nil.

Pre-Conditions: Registration and login are required.

Post-Conditions: Nil.

5. **Enters and Modifies Car Parts Information**

Description: Service centre employee modifies the car parts information after every service.

Flow of Events

Basic Flow: Service centre employee updates the information in Vehicle Information System after every service which is helpful further services.

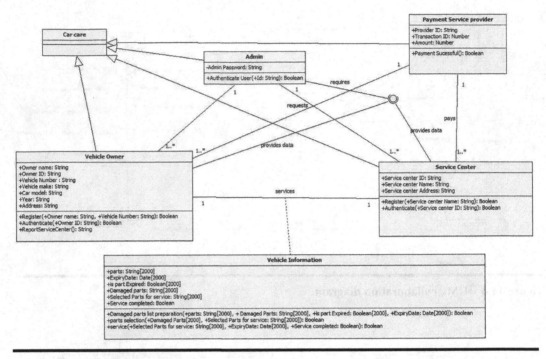

Figure 14.6   UML class diagram.

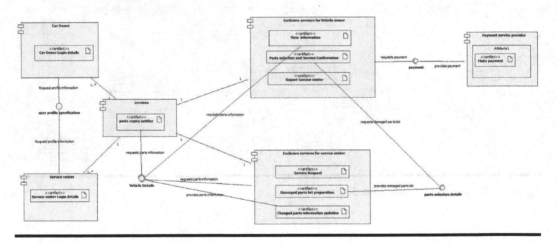

Figure 14.7   UML component diagram.

Alternative Flow: Nil.

Pre-Conditions: Registration and login of the service centre are required.

Post-Conditions: The information updated by the service centre employee is used for expiry notification of upcoming services.

6. **Vehicle Parts Expiry Notification**

Description: Expiry notification will be sent to the owner and service centre so that the car can be serviced.

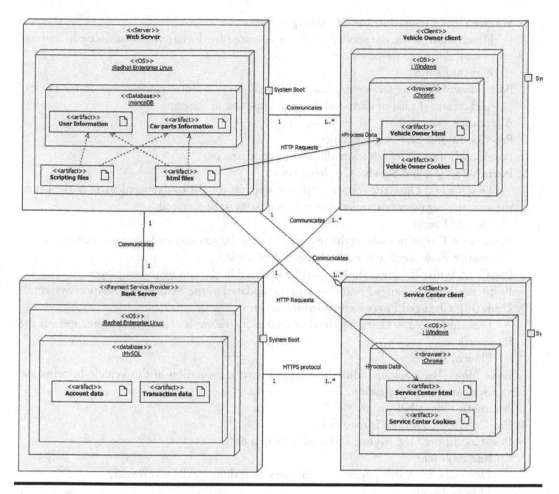

Figure 14.8 UML deployment diagram.

Flow of Events

Basic Flow: Once the expiry notification is received, service centre employee contacts car owner and asks for service.

Alternative Flow: Nil.

Pre-Conditions: Information of cars should be present in Vehicle Information System.

Post-Conditions: Service centre employee contacts car owner and asks for service.

7. **Service Acceptance**

Description: The Car owner may or may not accept the service request from service centre.

Flow of Events

Basic Flow: If the car owner accepts the service, further steps for service is carried out.

Alternative Flow: Car owner denies the service request.

Pre-Conditions: Service requests from the service centre is required.

Post-Conditions: Nil.

8. **Service Cost Estimation for all Damaged Parts**

    Description: Once the service request is accepted by the car owner, service cost estimation for all damaged parts will be carried out.

    Flow of Events

    Basic Flow: Once the service request is accepted, service centre employee examines the car and creates the list of damaged parts and updates in the app.

    Alternative Flow: Nil.

    Pre-Conditions: Service Acceptance.

    Post-Conditions: Parts selection and service confirmation.

9. **Parts Selection and Service Confirmation**

    Description: Once the service employee updates the list of damaged parts of the car in the app, the car owner can select the required parts to be serviced.

    Flow of Events

    Basic Flow: Car owner selects the required parts to be serviced and confirm the service.

    Alternative Flow: Service cancellation is also possible.

    Pre-Conditions: The selection list must be updated in the app by the employee.

    Post-Conditions: Changed parts list must be updated in the Vehicle Information System.

10. **Updating Changed Parts Expiry Information**

    Description: After changing the damaged parts the service centre employee, updates the information.

    Flow of Events

    Basic Flow: The employee edits the changed parts information in the Vehicle Information System of this application.

    Alternative Flow: Nil.

    Pre-Conditions: Service is required.

    Post-Conditions: The payment process is carried out.

11. **Online Payment**

    Description: Online payment for the service is done by the Car owner.

    Flow of Events

    Basic Flow: Payment Service provider provides an easy way to use interface for making payments.

    Alternative Flow: Nil.

    Pre-Conditions: All car service process should be completed.

    Post-Conditions: Car owner can report to admin.

12. **Net Banking**

    Description: Car owner can use net banking facility provided by the payment service provider.

    Flow of Events

    Basic Flow: Car owner can use net banking for making payments.

    Alternative Flow: Car owner can choose any other payment method.

    Pre-Conditions: All the car service processes should be completed.

    Post-Conditions: Car owner can report to admin.

13. **UPI**

    Description: Car owner can use UPI (Unified Payment Interface) facility provided by the payment service provider.

    Flow of Events

    Basic Flow: Car owner can use UPI for making payments.

Alternative Flow: Car owner can choose any other method for making payments.

Pre-Conditions: All the car service processes should be completed.

Post-Conditions: Car owner can report to admin.

14. **Report**

Description: Car owner reports to the admin about the service centre.

Flow of Events

Basic Flow: Car owner reports to admin so that necessary actions could be taken.

Alternative Flow: Car owner can give positive feedback as well.

Pre-Conditions: All service and payment process should be done.

Post-Conditions: Nil.

Chapter 15

Design of UML Diagrams for E-Ration Shop

15.1 Problem Statement

Public Distribution System (PDS) is an Indian food security system. It is established by the Government of India under the Ministry of Consumer Affairs, Food, and Public Distribution and managed jointly with state governments in India. The traditional PDS is used to distribute grocery items to India's poor who are valid ration cardholders. The validity and the allocation of the ration cards are monitored by the state governments. A ration cardholder should be given 35 kg of food grain as per the norms of PDS. However, there are concerns about the efficiency of the distribution process. In order to make it efficient and improve the current system of PDS, we are implementing e-Ration Shop. Here, we are going to make a website for shopping purposes. Using this website ration cardholder can order his/her grocery items from the PDS online. The main reason for using this website is to make this process computerized and to remove the drawbacks of the present way of issuing products based on the ration card. The main drawback in the current system is that the PDS has been criticized for its urban bias and its failure to serve the poorer sections of the population effectively. Also, many retail shopkeepers have a large number of bogus cards to sell food grains in the open market. Many PDS dealers resort to malpractice since they acquire less Salary so, by this project we are solving this problem too. Most of the time, users do not get their rightful entitlement in terms of quantity. What's meant for them or the farm produce procured by the PDS is diverted to the open market. So in order to avoid all these drawbacks, we are going to use the e-Ration Shop which will help us to avoid the corruption in PDS if not eradicate it. The various importance of the proposed case study is every shop's geo-location will be located on the map, all the information regarding shop and shopkeeper respective to the ration card and region, shop opening and closing details will be available, stock provided based on category, retailers can add, edit, delete and update their shop's other items also, retailers can advertise their shops, stock availability will be notified on regular basis, product delivery feature, complaint forum for complaints by users, easy payment system by PayTM, COD etc., admin and moderator features for government and shopkeepers and authentication system by Aadhaar number and One-Time Pin (OTP) (Figures 15.1–15.8).

DOI: 10.1201/9781003287124-15

15.2 UML Diagrams

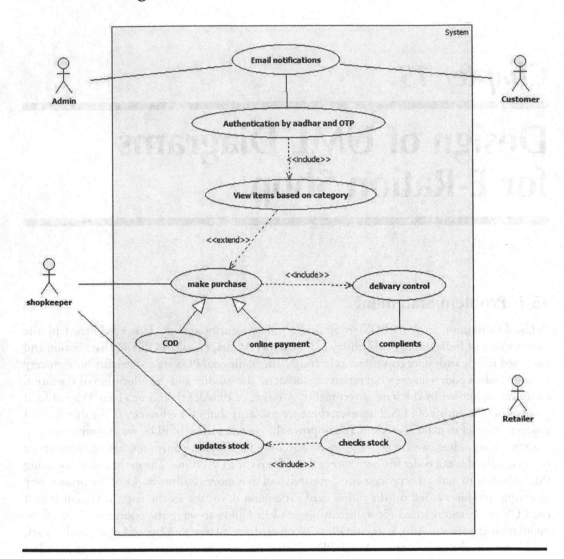

Figure 15.1   UML usecase diagram.

Usecase Specification

1. **Email notification**
   Description: Shop opening time closing time and other details about the shop will be mailed to the customer.
   Flow of Events
   Basic Flow: Sent the mail.
   Alternative Flow: Null.
   Pre-Conditions: Mail ids of users should be retrieved from the database.
   Post-Conditions: The users can buy from the link that we sent as an attachment to the mail.

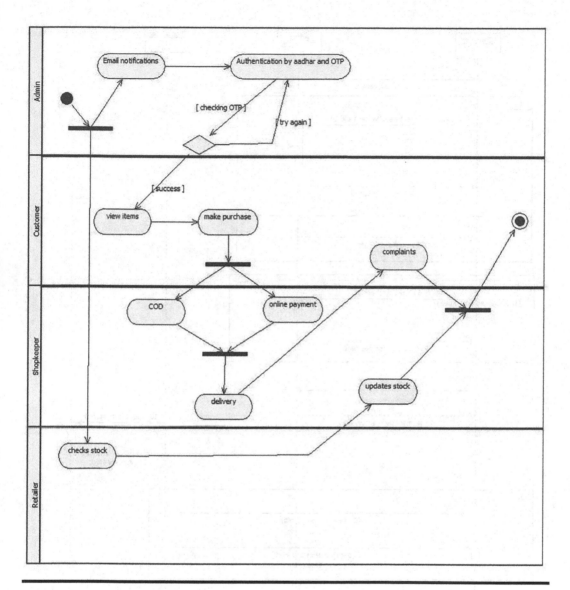

Figure 15.2   UML activity diagram.

2. **Authentication by Aadhaar and OTP**

    Description: One-time pin-based authentication: A OTP, with limited time validity, is sent to the mobile number and/ or e-mail address of the Aadhaar number holder registered with the Authority, or generated by other appropriate means. The Aadhaar number holder shall provide this OTP along with his Aadhaar number during authentication and the same shall be matched with the OTP generated by the Authority.

    Flow of Events

Basic Flow: View the website, request OTP through mobile.

Alternative Flow: Do not request for OTP can simply exit or users can be able to open the website, request OTP through mobile, invalid OTP, exit.

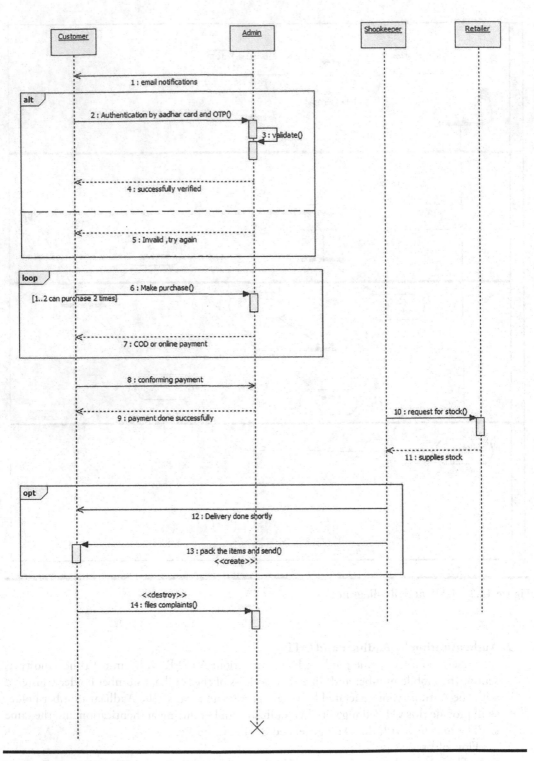

Figure 15.3   UML sequence diagram.

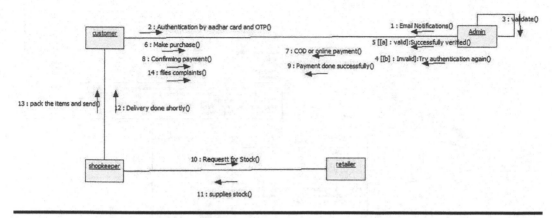

Figure 15.4   UML collaboration diagram.

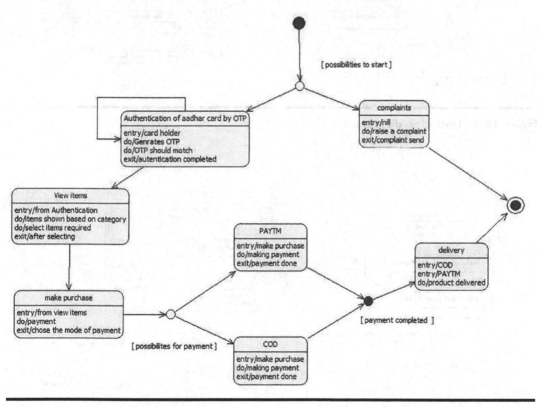

Figure 15.5   UML state machine diagram.

Pre-Conditions: Details Authority should generate OTP to the registered mobile number of the customer.

Post-Conditions: If the OTP matches to the generated one by the Authority then he can view the items.

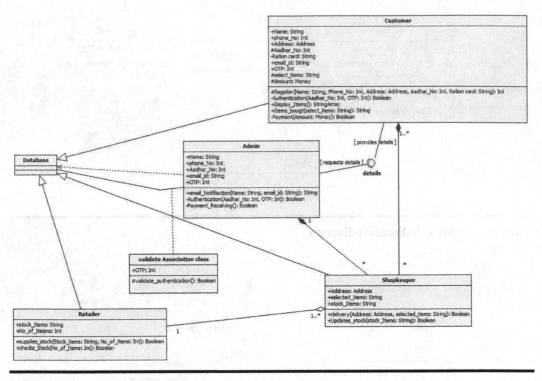

Figure 15.6   UML class diagram.

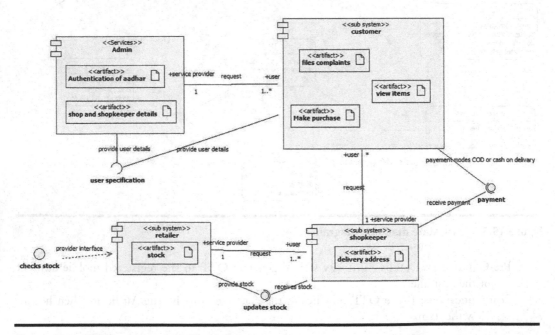

Figure 15.7   UML component diagram.

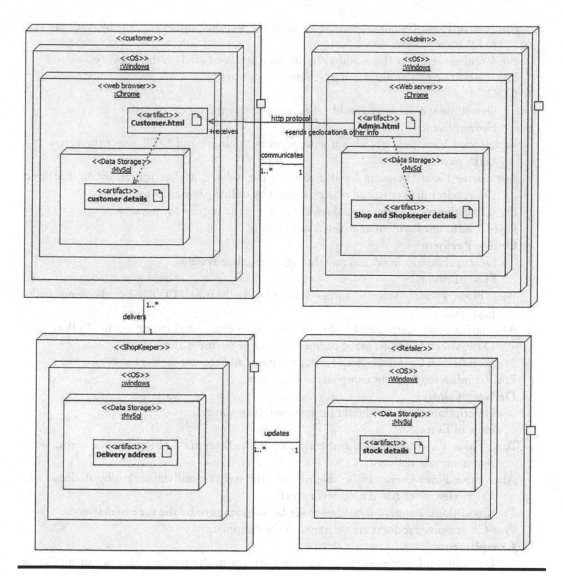

Figure 15.8   UML deployment diagram.

3. **View items based on category**
     Description: The customers can be able to view the product details based on the category.
     Flow of Events
 Basic Flow: View the website, authentication by Aadhaar and OTP, view the product details.
 Alternative Flow: Null.
 Pre-Conditions: View the product details.
 Post-Conditions: They can make the purchase if required.
4. **Make purchase**
     Description: Customers can select items needed and can purchase.
     Flow of Events
 Basic Flow: View the website, authentication by Aadhaar and OTP, select the items

Alternative Flow: Users can be able to open the website, authentication by Aadhaar and OTP, view product details, exit.

Pre-Conditions: Select the products in the list displayed based on the category

Post-Conditions: Customers can purchase by two ways.

5. **COD**

Description: customers should make payments by the means of cash.

Flow of Events

Basic Flow: View the website, authentication by Aadhaar and OTP, select the items, and make payment.

Alternative Flow: Users can be able to open the website, authentication by Aadhaar and OTP, select the items, and make payment by online payment also.

Pre-Conditions: Customer should select the items and request for payment

Post-Conditions: Payment completed successfully.

6. **Online Payment**

Description: customers can pay through the online systems.

Flow of Events

Basic Flow: View the website, authentication by Aadhaar and OTP, select the items, make payment.

Alternative Flow: Users can be able to open the website, authentication by Aadhaar and OTP, select the items, make payment by online payment also.

Pre-Conditions: Customer should select the items and request for payment.

Post-Conditions: Payment completed successfully.

7. **Delivery Control**

Description: Products should be delivered to customers.

Flow of Events

Basic Flow: View the website, authentication by Aadhaar and OTP, select the items, make payment, take delivery.

Alternative Flow: Users can be able to open the website, authentication by Aadhaar and OTP, view items based on category, exit.

Pre-Conditions: Payment should be made by any means or by the time of delivery.

Post-Conditions: Products are delivered to the customers.

8. **Compliments**

Description: Customers can raise a compliment in the product quantity or quality or any other issues.

Flow of Events

Basic Flow: View website, authentication by Aadhaar and OTP, raise compliment

Alternative Flow: View the website, authentication by Aadhaar and OTP, view product details, exit.

Pre-Conditions: None. They can raise compliments without buying a product.

Post-Conditions: Compliment is successfully given to the shopkeeper.

9. **Checks Stock**

Description: Stock should be checked on a regular based to display the items to the customers.

Flow of Events

Basic Flow: View the website, check stock.

Alternative Flow: Null.

Pre-Conditions: If the retailer can directly check the stock.

Post-Conditions: Go for update stock.

10. **Updates Stock**

 Description: The stock is updated by the retailer on regular basis.

 Flow of Events

Basic Flow: View the website, checks for stock, updates stock.

Alternative Flow: View the website, check for stock, exit.

Pre-Conditions: Check for stock.

Post-Conditions: New stock is updated successfully.

Chapter 16

Design of UML Diagrams for Textile Management System

16.1 Problem Statement

The 'Textile Management System' case study is designed to monitor all the processes in a textile manufacturing industry. There are various processes such as order receiving, purchase of raw materials, classification of raw materials, production of goods and selling the products. The main aim of this system is to ensure the reliability of data and to ease the process of manufacturing and transportation of garments and raw materials. This system ensures that the hardships prevailing in the manual systems are overridden by reducing the errors in data handling. The major functionalities are customer registration, sampling, stock checking, purchasing and processing of raw materials, production of garments, product checking and clearance, shipment, billing and report generation (Figures 16.1–16.8).

16.2 UML Diagrams

Usecase Specification

1. **Customer Registration**
   Description: Enables a user (customer) to register with the system.
   Flow of Events
   Basic Flow: Details to be correctly filled before completing the registration process.
   Alternative Flow: Nil.
   Pre-Conditions: Access to registration platform.
   Post-Conditions: Customers can place the order.
2. **Ordering Garments**
   Description: Allows registered customers to place the orders for the garments.
   Flow of Events
   Basic Flow: The particular order is placed and an order ID is generated.

DOI: 10.1201/9781003287124-16

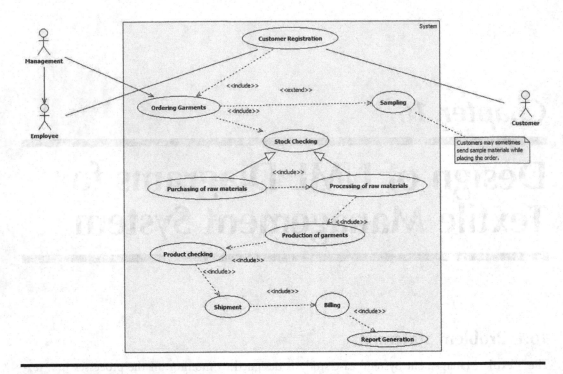

Figure 16.1   UML usecase diagram.

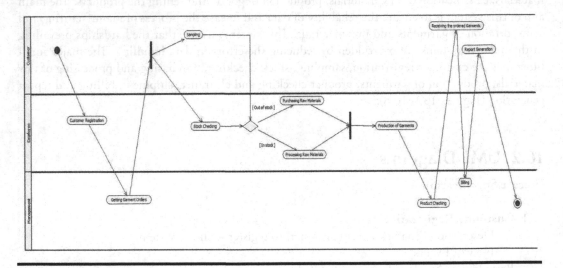

Figure 16.2   UML activity diagram.

> Alternative Flow: Nil.
> Pre-Conditions: Registration of customers.
> Post-Conditions: Customers may also send sample goods.

3. **Sampling**
> Description: This allows customers to send out sample materials.
> Flow of Events

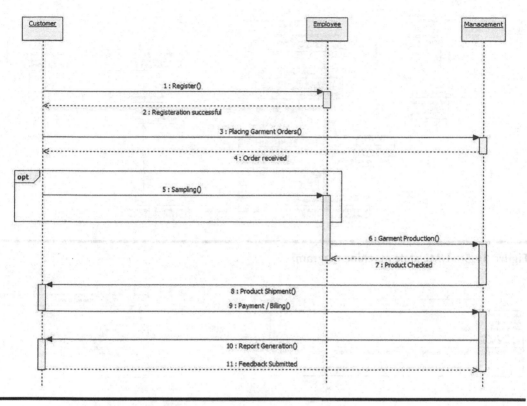

Figure 16.3   UML sequence diagram.

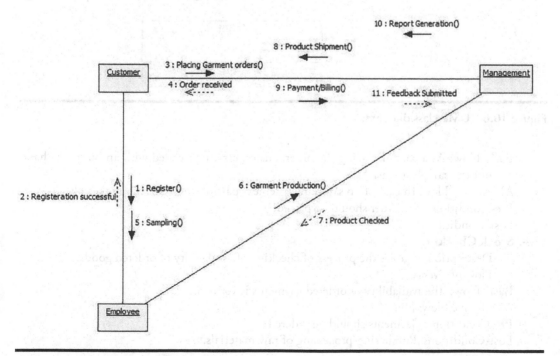

Figure 16.4   UML collaboration diagram.

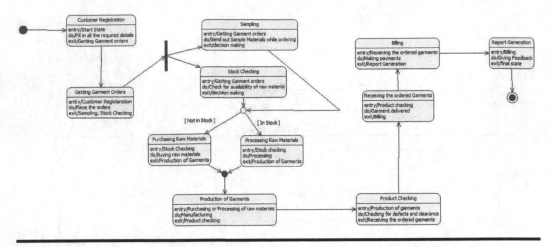

Figure 16.5   UML state machine diagram.

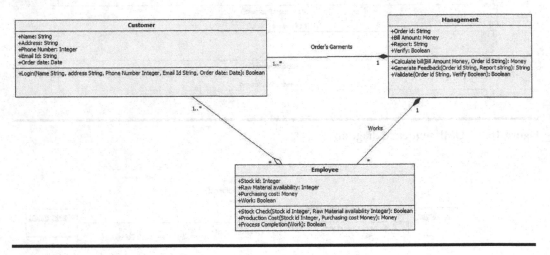

Figure 16.6   UML class diagram.

Basic Flow: As a part of placing the order, customers are provided with an option to hand
out the sample goods.

Alternative Flow: In case of no sampling, the next part of stock checking takes place.

Pre-Conditions: The order should be placed.

Post-Conditions: Nil.

4. **Stock Checking**

Description: Enables the process of checking of availability of ordered goods.

Flow of Events

Basic Flow: The availability of ordered garments is verified.

Alternative Flow: Nil.

Pre-Conditions: Garments should be ordered.

Post-Conditions: Purchasing/processing of raw materials.

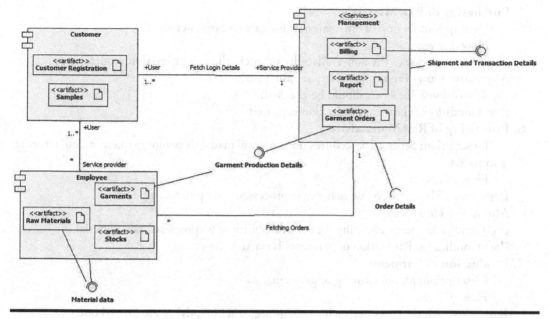

Figure 16.7   UML component diagram.

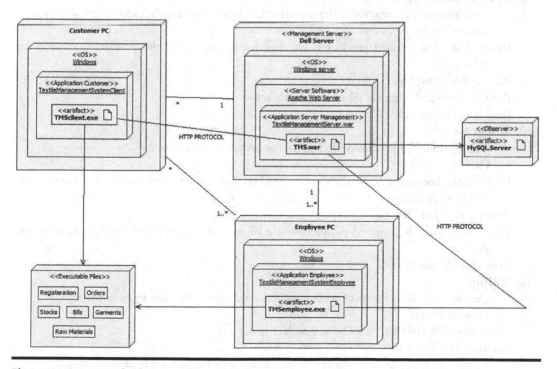

Figure 16.8   UML deployment diagram.

5. **Purchasing of Raw Materials**
   Description: Buying of raw materials for garment production.
   Flow of Events
   Basic Flow: In case of the non-availability of stock, the raw materials are purchased.
   Alternative Flow: The raw materials are processed.
   Pre-Conditions: The stock should be checked.
   Post-Conditions: Garment production is started.
6. **Processing of Raw Materials**
   Description: Series of procedures done on raw materials before garment manufacturing is initiated.
   Flow of Events
   Basic Flow: The required raw material is processed after purchasing.
   Alternative Flow: Nil.
   Pre-Conditions: Stock checking for the availability of preprocessed raw material.
   Post-Conditions: Production of garments is started.
7. **Production of Garments**
   Description: Manufacturing of garments.
   Flow of Events
   Basic Flow: All the processes such as designing, stitching, dying are carried out.
   Alternative Flow: Nil.
   Pre-Conditions: Raw materials should be processed.
   Post-Conditions: Product clearance.
8. **Product Checking**
   Description: The step where the manufactured garments are checked before shipment.
   Flow of Events
   Basic Flow: The finished product is checked for damages and the product is cleared for shipment.
   Alternative Flow: Nil.
   Pre-Conditions: Garments should be manufactured.
   Post-Conditions: Nil.
9. **Shipment**
   Description: The process of delivering the orders to the customers.
   Flow of Events
   Basic Flow: The ordered garments are dispatched and ready to be handed out to customers from the industry.
   Alternative Flow: Nil.
   Pre-Conditions: The finished product should be packed along with the order and payment details.
   Post-Conditions: Nil.
10. **Billing**
    Description: The process of preparing and sending out invoices to customers.
    Flow of Events
    Basic Flow: The bill for the ordered goods is generated.
    Alternative Flow: Nil.
    Pre-Conditions: The cost of all steps in the manufacturing process is necessary.
    Post-Conditions: Nil.

11. **Report Generation**
    Description: The queries and feedbacks related to the order are generated.
    Flow of Events
Basic Flow: The ratings, suggestions, feedback are maintained in this Final Step.
Alternative Flow: Nil.
Pre-Conditions: Product should be delivered and payment process should be completed.
Post-Conditions: Nil.

Chapter 17

Design of UML Diagrams for National Health ID 2020

17.1 Problem Statement

The Prime Minister of India has announced a new scheme of National Health ID on August 15, 2020. According to this proposal, every Indian will get a unique Health ID based on their mobile number or Aadhaar number. The National Health ID will be a repository of all health-related information of a person. According to the National Health Authority (NHA), every patient who wishes to have their health records available digitally must start by creating a Health ID. Each Health ID will be linked to a health data consent manager – such as the National Digital Health Mission (NDHM) which will be used to seek the patient's consent and allow for seamless flow of health information from the Personal Health Records module. This Health ID prevents various insurance frauds committed by several health agencies, hospitals including both doctors and patients. This will reduce the paper works and help patients easily maintain their health records. It can be used for further diagnosis. Children who are born after the implementation of the National Health ID will have all their medications recorded including the vaccines, etc. (Figures 17.1–17.8).

17.2 UML Diagrams

Usecase Specification

1. **Verification**
   Description: People are verified for Indian citizenship through their individual identities such as Aadhaar card or voter ID.
   Flow of Events
   Basic Flow: Collection of data.
   Pre-Conditions: To have an Aadhaar card or voter id.
   Post-Conditions: Those who don't have unique identities will be rejected.

DOI: 10.1201/9781003287124-17

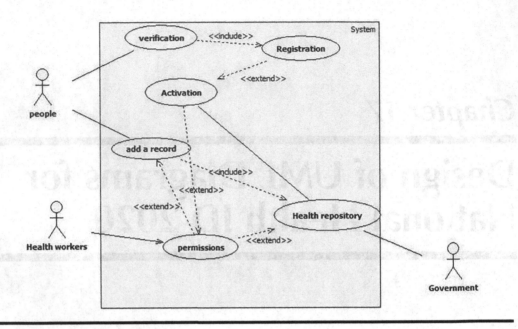

Figure 17.1   UML usecase diagram.

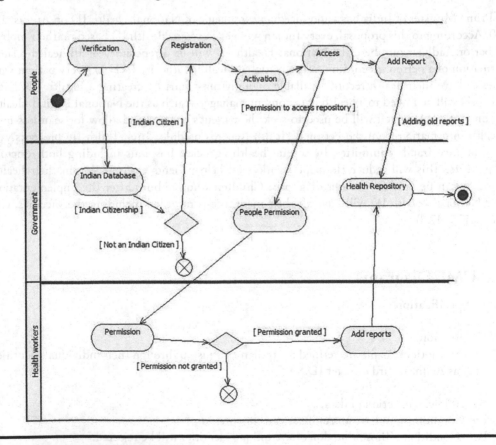

Figure 17.2   UML activity diagram.

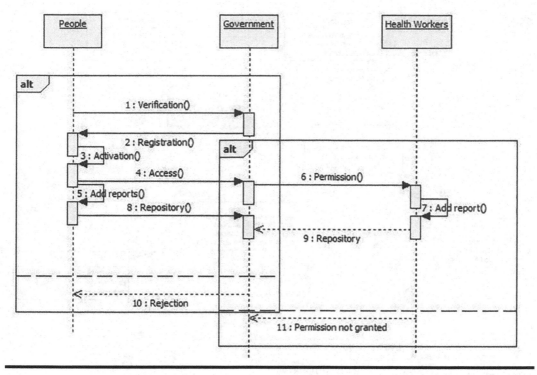

Figure 17.3   UML sequence diagram.

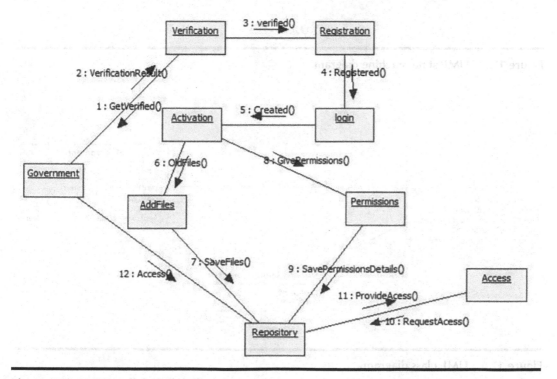

Figure 17.4   UML collaboration diagram.

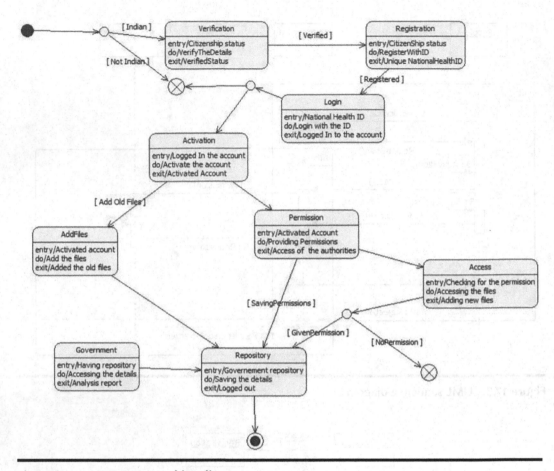

Figure 17.5   UML state machine diagram.

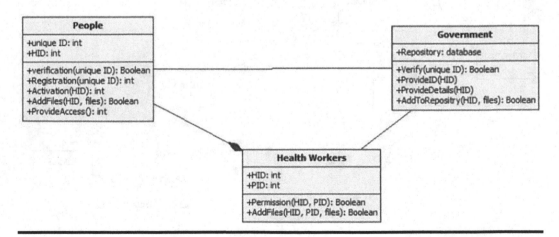

Figure 17.6   UML class diagram.

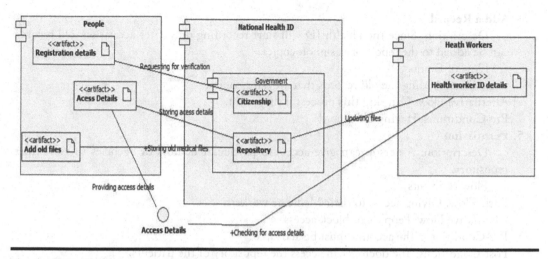

Figure 17.7   UML component diagram.

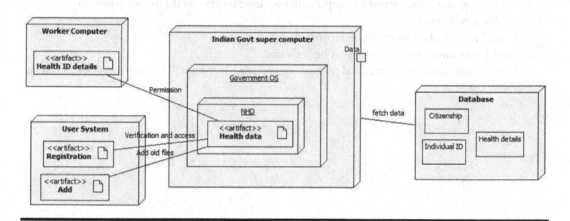

Figure 17.8   UML deployment diagram.

2. **Registration**

Description: People will be registered in the NHD repository to generate the unique National Health ID for each and everyone.

Flow of Events

Basic Flow: Registration through Aadhaar.

Alternative Flow: Registration can also be done with a Phone number.

Pre-Conditions: Verification as Indian Citizen.

Post-Conditions: To activate the account.

3. **Activation**

Description: Everyone should activate the account with their unique Health ID.

Flow of Events

Basic Flow: To activate the account that has been created.

Pre-Conditions: To have a unique Health ID.

Post-Conditions: To use the ID during all the medical transactions to keep the record.

4. **Add a Record**
   Description: Since the Health ID will start recording only after activation, old records can be added to the repository as photocopies.
   Flow of Events
   Basic Flow: Adding the old records that are hard copies.
   Alternative Flow: Can skip this process if they want.
   Pre-Conditions: Having old records.

5. **Permission**
   Description: A person can give access to particular doctors or agencies to view their repository.
   Flow of Events
   Basic Flow: Giving access to their Medicare workers.
   Alternative Flow: People can block access.
   Pre-Conditions: The account must be activated.
   Post-Conditions: The doctors can access the repository of the patients.

6. **Health Repository**
   Description: The record of people is maintained by the NHD in this repository.
   Flow of Events
   Basic Flow: A place to store the records.
   Pre-Conditions: The account must be activated.
   Post-Conditions: All the medical transactions after activation will be stored in the repository.

Chapter 18

Design of UML Diagrams for Device Handout System

18.1 Problem Statement

Amidst this pandemic period, students are being educated through online education platforms on smartphones and other similar devices. Many underprivileged children are unable to get access to such devices. Also, the people who are willing to help aren't able to reach the needy due to lockdown. The ultimate aim of this system is to help such children by giving the collected devices from the people who were willing to help them. This system requests the donors to enter the details regarding the device they are willing to donate. It also requests the address details of the donor in order to reach them. On successful entry of such details, the user has to wait for the approval of the device. The admin has to verify the details of the device and assign it to a pickup executive for collection. This system also allows the volunteers to join the team. So that they could be helped by picking up the devices in their locality (Figures 18.1–18.12).

18.2 UML Diagrams

Usecase Specification

1. **New Donor**
   Description: The person in the case, being a new donor gives his personal details.
   Flow of Events
   Basic Flow: Registers with the system.
   Alternative Flow: Having already registered proceeds as an old donor.
2. **Contact Details**
   Description: Being new to the system, having given the personal details, proceeds with the collection of contact details from the donor.
   Flow of Events
   Basic Flow: Registering with the system.
   Pre-Conditions: Has given the personal details.

DOI: 10.1201/9781003287124-18

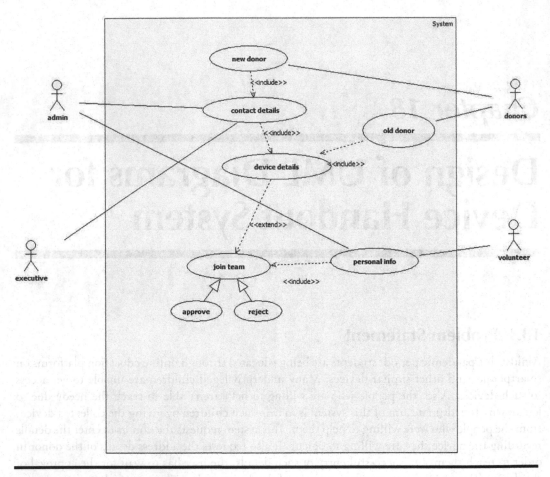

Figure 18.1   UML usecase diagram.

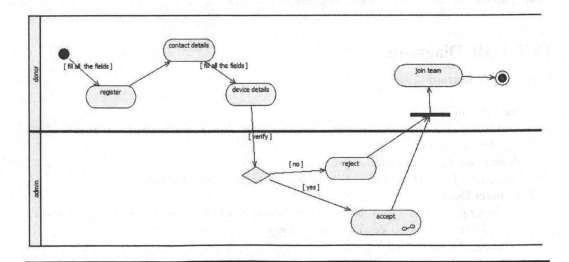

Figure 18.2   UML activity diagram (part 1).

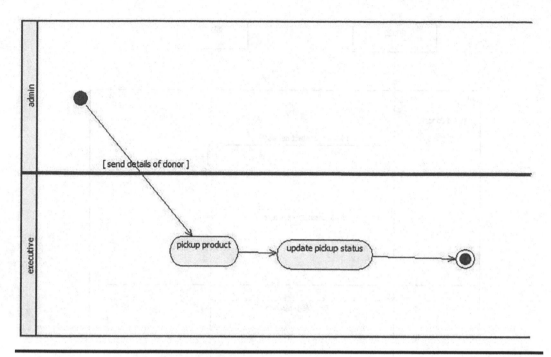

Figure 18.3   UML activity diagram (part 2).

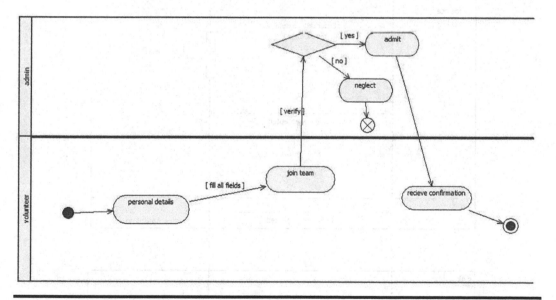

Figure 18.4   UML activity diagram (part 3).

3. **Device Details**

Description: Gives the details and model of the device the donor donates.

Flow of Events

Basic Flow: Donating a device.

Pre-Conditions: Registration with the system.

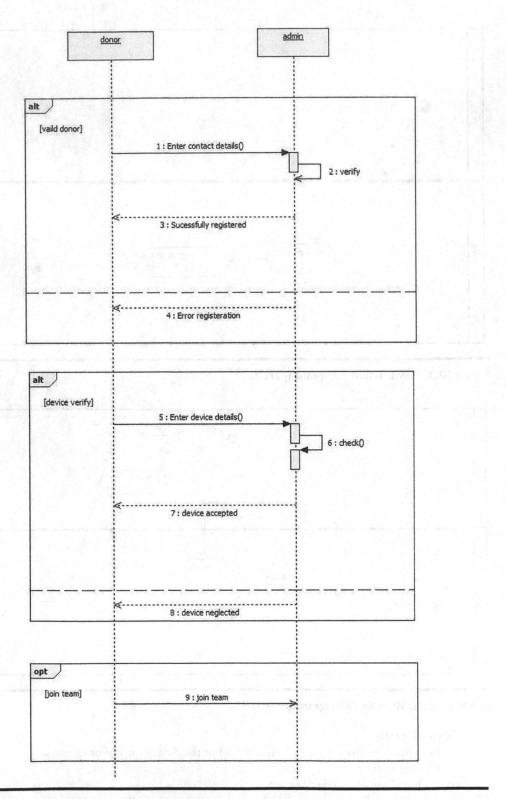

Figure 18.5 UML sequence diagram (part 1).

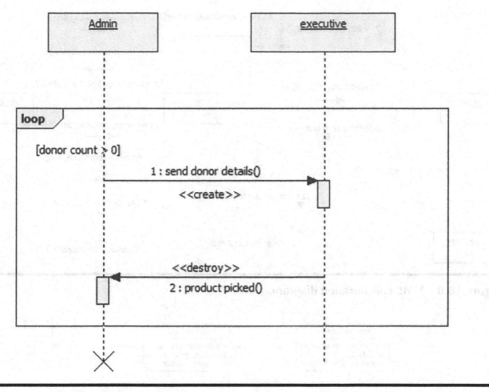

Figure 18.6   UML sequence diagram (part 2).

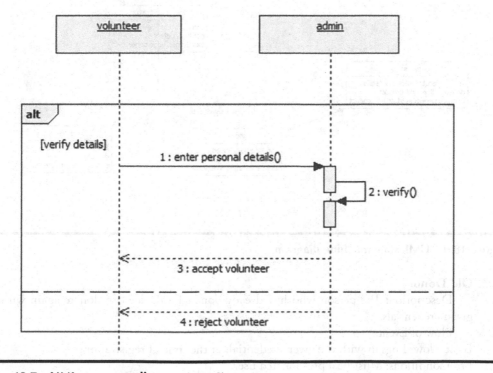

Figure 18.7   UML sequence diagram (part 3).

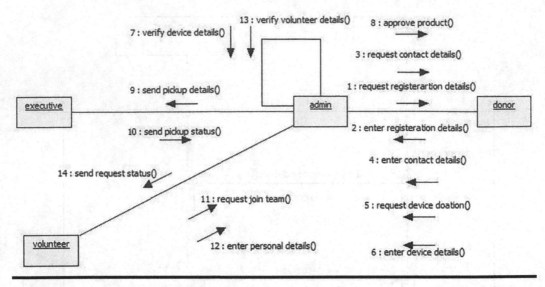

Figure 18.8   UML collaboration diagram.

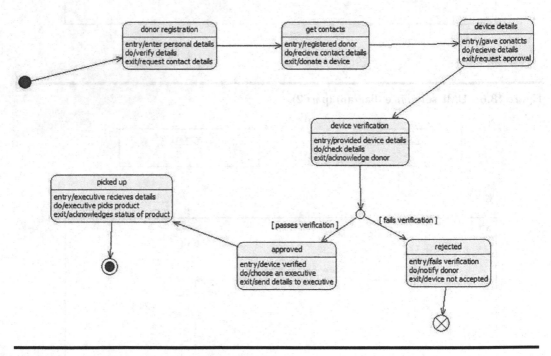

Figure 18.9   UML state machine diagram.

4. **Old Donor**

   Description: The person who has already donated a device can donate again with the given credentials.

   Flow of Events

   Basic Flow: Logs in with the given credentials at the time of registration.

   Pre-Conditions: Must be a pre-donated user.

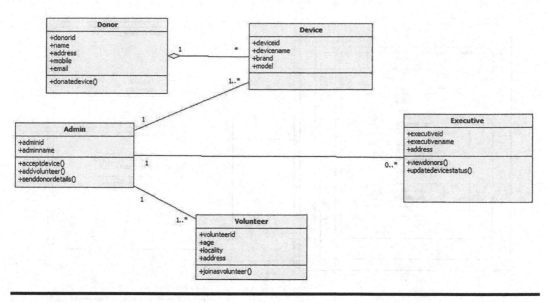

Figure 18.10   UML class diagram.

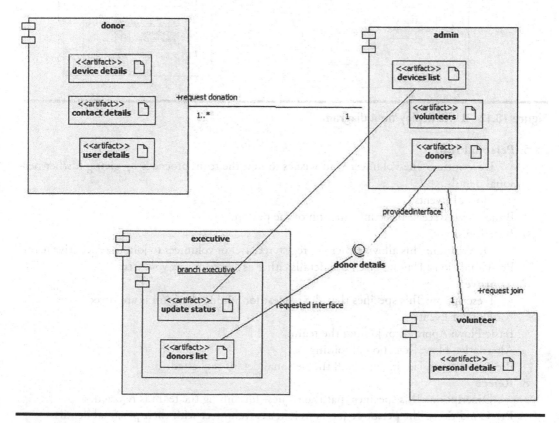

Figure 18.11   UML component diagram.

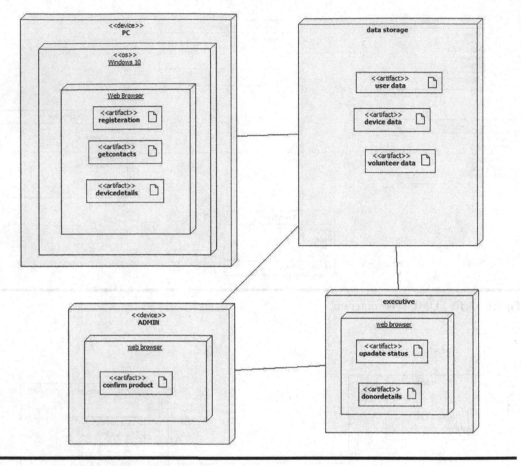

Figure 18.12 UML deployment diagram.

5. **Personal Info**

Description: The volunteer who wishes to join the team proceeds by giving his/her personal details.

Flow of Events

Basic Flow: Receive basic information of the person.

6. **Join Team**

Description: This allows either the registered user or volunteer to join the executive team.

Pre-Conditions: Having given the details either as a user or as a volunteer.

7. **Approve**

Description: This specifies that the request for joining the team is approved.

Flow of Events

Basic Flow: Approval of joining the team.

Alternative Flow: Rejection of joining

Pre-Conditions: Having given all the personal details requested.

8. **Reject**

Description: This specifies that the request for joining the team is rejected.

Pre-Conditions: The person requests to join as a volunteer with their personal details.

Chapter 19

Design of UML Diagrams for Online College Magazine System

19.1 Problem Statement

College magazines provide an authoritative, recognizable and artistic platform of expression to the student body. However, paperback college magazines narrow the scope for a more extensive audience and are lavish of important resources like paper, especially when the magazines are printed seasonally on campus year after year. Consequently, many students may not be able to make it to the print media of the college. To subdue these shortcomings, an online college magazine system can be developed. This system will enable students of the college to liberally generate content for and about the college. Anyone in any part of the world can read and rate articles being published in the online magazine. Resource usage is much more minimal, but the experience is as efficient as in paperback magazines. With the help of this software, they will be able to read, write, draft, edit and publish all forms of content like articles, essays, op-eds, photography, poetry, etc. Selected students and faculty can regularly write and post articles for the magazine. Contributors (like alumni) can write for the magazine occasionally. Guests or readers can read, comment on and rate articles. Guests can also act as contributors if interested. Moderators will review articles before publishing to decide the pertinence of content. Articles will be organized based on categories appropriate to the workflow of the college. Thus, the implementation of this system will benefit all members of the college by providing consistent campus-related news and also by improving the literary and technical insight of faculty and students who write for the magazine (Figures 19.1–19.8).

DOI: 10.1201/9781003287124-19

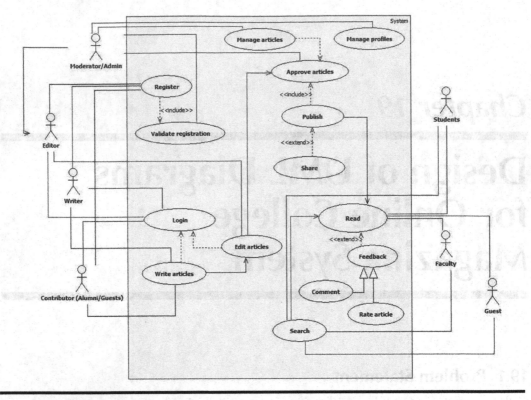

Figure 19.1 UML usecase diagram.

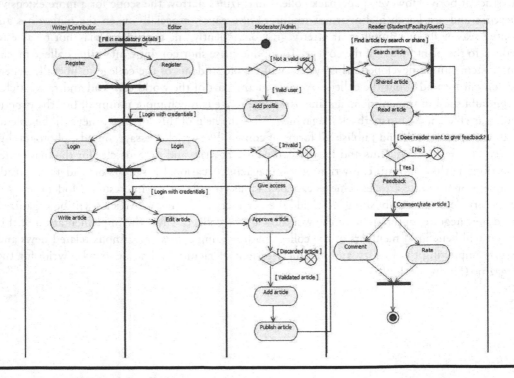

Figure 19.2 UML activity diagram.

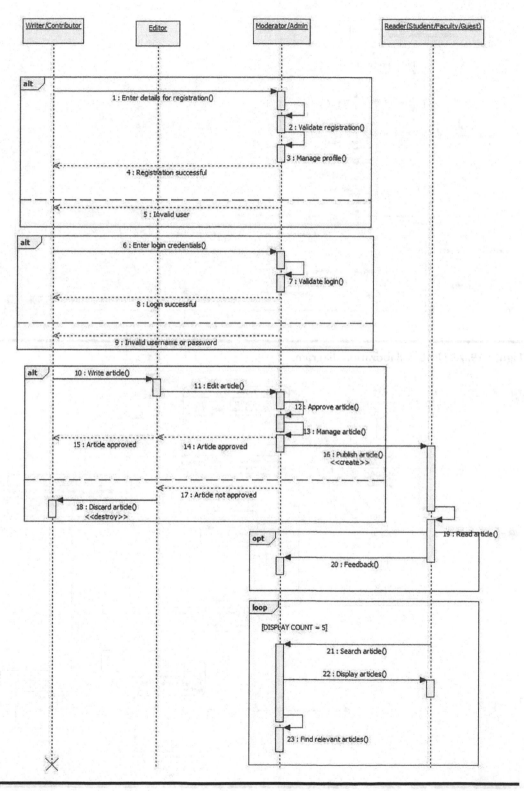

Figure 19.3 UML sequence diagram.

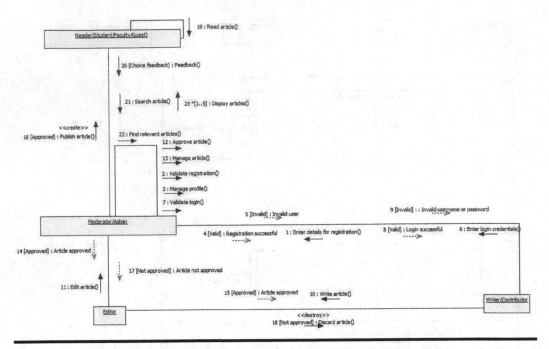

Figure 19.4   UML collaboration diagram.

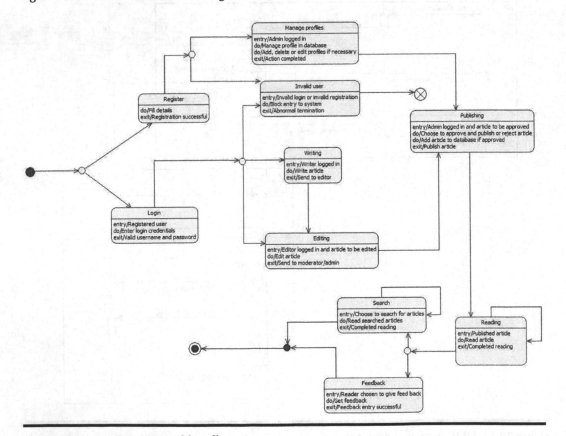

Figure 19.5   UML state machine diagram.

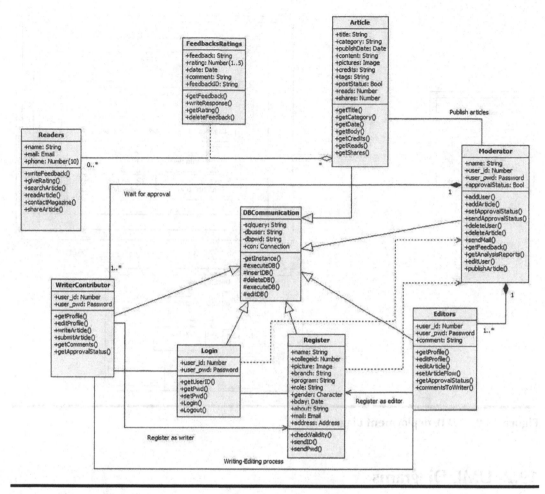

Figure 19.6   UML class diagram.

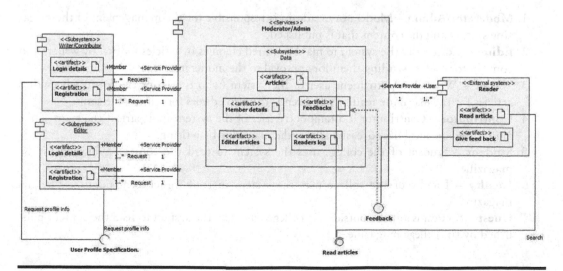

Figure 19.7   UML component diagram.

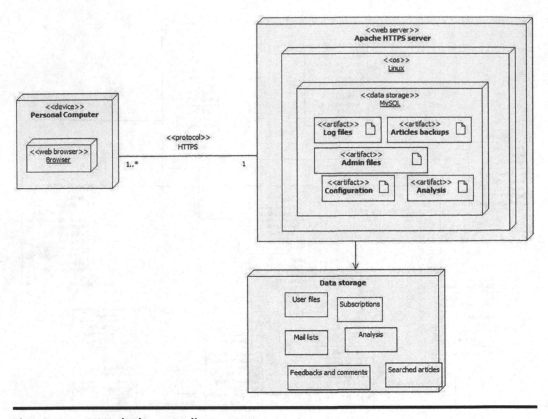

Figure 19.8 UML deployment diagram.

19.2 UML Diagrams

Actor Specification

1. **Moderator/Admin** – Moderator or admin is responsible for the management of the magazine system and the content that is published.
2. **Editor** – Editor uses the system to make required changes in articles written by writers and contributors before sending them for approval to the moderator.
3. **Writer** – Writer is a permanent user of the system (who is part of the team) who writes articles for the magazine regularly and sends them to editors for editing the same.
4. **Contributor** – Contributor is a temporary user of the system (not part of the team – like alumni) who contributes occasionally to the magazine by writing.
5. **Student** – Student of the college uses the system to read the content published by the magazine.
6. **Faculty** – Faculty of the college uses the system to read the content published by the magazine.
7. **Guest** – A guest is anyone outside the college who uses the system to read the content published by the college magazine.

Usecase Specification

1. Register

Description: Functionality involves registering into the system with relevant details.
Flow of Events

Basic Flow: Register into the system with details like name, mail ID, phone, etc.

Alternative Flow: Nil.

Pre-Conditions: The registering candidate must be a student, faculty or alumnus of the college.

Post-Conditions: The registration request is sent to the moderator/admin for validation.

2. Validate Registration

Description: Functionality involves the admin validating the request for registration from the user after confirming legitimacy.
Flow of Events

Basic Flow: If requested registration is from a writer or editor of the magazine or from an alumnus, the admin validates the registration.

Alternative Flow: If the requested registration is not from a legitimate user, the admin does not validate the registration.

Pre-Conditions: The user seeking registration must be a student or faculty in the team or alumnus of the college.

Post-Conditions: After validation, the user's profile is created successfully.

3. Login

Description: Refers to changing an existing information in the system to fix errors or enhance functionality and deleting outdated information and updating of new data into the system.
Flow of Events

Basic Flow: Modifying and updating of the database based on the various criteria.

Pre-Conditions: Status of each company/seeker.

Post-Conditions: Based on the feedback received from recruiters/seekers.

4. Manage Articles

Description: Functionality involves organizing approved articles, adding and deleting articles in the system's database by the moderator/admin.
Flow of Events

Basic Flow: The articles approved by the moderator/admin is added to the database under appropriate categories.

Alternate Flow: Prevalent articles can be modified or deleted.

Pre-Conditions: The article must be approved by the admin/moderator.

Post-Conditions: The article is available for publishing.

5. Manage Profiles

Description: Functionality involves managing writers, editors and contributors of the system by the moderator with appropriate access, adding, editing and deleting profiles, etc.
Flow of Events

Basic Flow: Validated registrations are added to the database as writer, editor or contributor profiles.

Alternate Flow: Prevalent profiles can be modified or deleted by the admin.

Pre-Conditions: The registered profiles must be validated by the admin.

Post-Conditions: The profile is given appropriate access to the system.

6. **Write Articles**

Description: Functionality involves writing articles in the system by writers and contributors.

Flow of Events

Basic Flow: The writer writes an article in the system.

Pre-Conditions: The writer must have logged in to the system.

Post-Conditions: The article is sent to an editor for editing.

7. **Edit Articles**

Description: Functionality involves editing written articles in the system by editors.

Flow of Events

Basic Flow: Editor edits an article written by a writer or contributor.

Alternative Flow: Article is sent back to the writer for redrafting.

Pre-Conditions: Editor must have logged in to the system.

Post-Conditions: The edited article is sent to admin/moderator for approval.

8. **Approve Articles**

Description: Functionality involves the moderator approving articles after editors edit them.

Flow of Events

Basic Flow: Admin/moderator reads and approves edited articles.

Alternate Flow: Article is sent back to the editor for re-editing.

Pre-Conditions: Article must have been edited at least once.

Post-Conditions: Approved article is added to database.

9. **Publish**

Description: Functionality involves the moderator publishing articles in the magazine after approval.

Flow of Events

Basic Flow: Approved article is published in the magazine.

Alternate Flow: Nil.

Pre-Conditions: Article must have been approved by admin.

Post-Conditions: Article can be shared across social media.

10. **Share**

Description: Functionality involves sharing published articles in the magazine to social media subscribers.

Flow of Events

Basic Flow: Published articles are shared via mail, Instagram, Facebook and other social media platforms.

Alternate Flow: Published articles are shared only within the college.

Pre-Conditions: Article must have been published.

Post-Conditions: Nil.

11. **Read**

Description: Functionality involves students. Faculty and guest readers reading the published articles.

Flow of Events

Basic Flow: Readers like students, faculty and guests read published articles.

Alternative Flow: Nil.

Pre-Conditions: Article must be published and/or shared.

Post-Conditions: Article can receive feedback from readers or readers can search for more articles in the system.

12. **Search**

Description: Functionality involves readers searching for a particular article in the magazine system.

Flow of Events

Basic Flow: Reader searches for a particular article or category of articles in the system.

Alternative Flow: Nil.

Pre-Conditions: The searched article must have been published in the system.

Post-Conditions: The searched article can be read and shared.

13. **Feedback**

Description: Functionality involves readers giving feedback for articles they read in the magazine system.

Flow of Events

Basic Flow: Reader chooses to give feedback on an article he/she reads.

Alternative Flow: Reader searches for a new article in the system.

Pre-Conditions: Reader reads the article.

Post-Conditions: Feedback is sent to the writer, editor and moderator.

14. **Comment**

Description: Functionality involves feedback from the readers as comments.

Flow of Events

Basic Flow: Reader writes a comment on the article he/she reads.

Alternative Flow: Nil.

Pre-Conditions: Reader reads the article.

Post-Conditions: The writer, editor or admin can respond to the comment.

15. **Rating**

Description: Functionality involves feedback from the readers in the form of star ratings.

Flow of Events

Basic Flow: Reader can rate an article he/she reads on 5 stars.

Alternative Flow: Nil.

Pre-Conditions: Reader reads the article.

Post-Conditions: The rating is recorded in the database.

Chapter 20

Design of UML Diagrams for Crime Bureau

20.1 Problem Statement

Rules and regulations are paramount to all aspects of life. Certain proponents have asserted that crime which is a violation against laws of the society, is integral to the human nature and hence the society can never be completely free from it. In the existing system, all work is done on papers, so it is very difficult to secure crime reports data. This system needs more manpower to track the records of crimes and it lacks security. Modern society is characterized by increasing levels of risk posed by internal and external security threats. This poses the importance to develop an automated crime management system to keep a record of the crime and the criminals involved. The proposed crime bureau is a database system in which the police keeps the record of criminals who have been arrested, to be arrested, or escaped and the complaints. This will help the police department in enhanced management of information. The main entities in the whole process include; the petitioner (the person who files a First Incident Report (FIR)), victim, accused or criminal, case and investigating officer. The proposed crime record management system can overcome all the limitations of the existing system. This system provides proper security and reduces the manual work. This project helps to maintain a database through which the entire crime activities in the state can be monitored (Figures 20.1–20.8).

20.2 UML Diagrams

Usecase Specification

1. **Login**
   Description: Officials are provided with a username and password, through which they can log into the crime bureau.
   Flow of Events
   Basic Flow: Opens the crime bureau website.
   Alternative Flow: NIL.

DOI: 10.1201/9781003287124-20

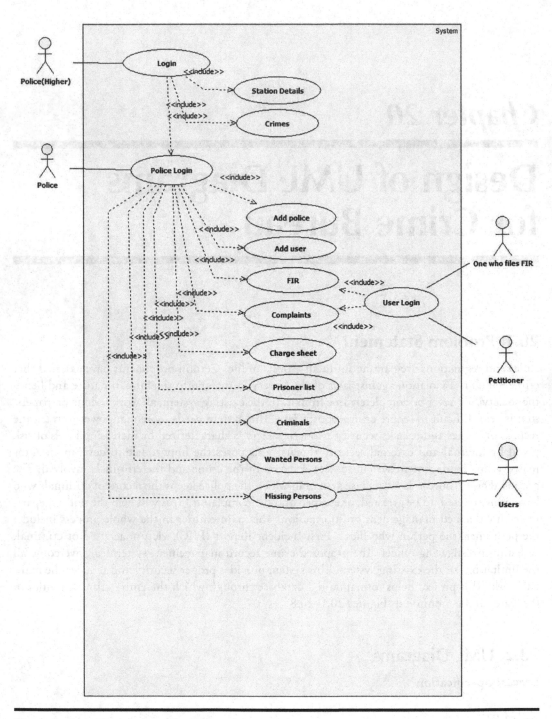

Figure 20.1   UML usecase diagram.

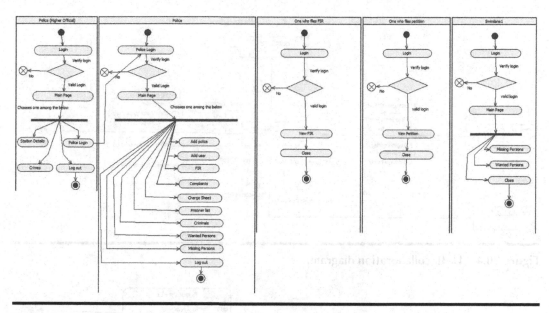

Figure 20.2   UML activity diagram.

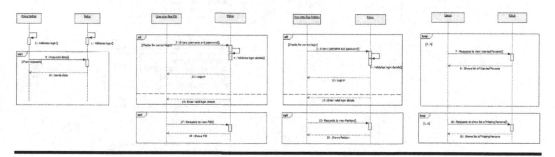

Figure 20.3   UML sequence diagram.

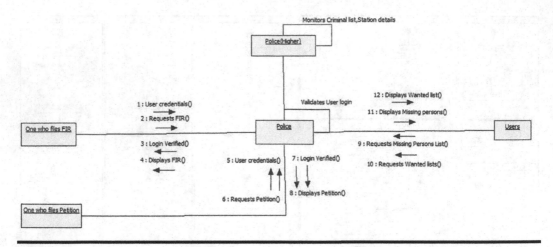

Figure 20.4 UML collaboration diagram.

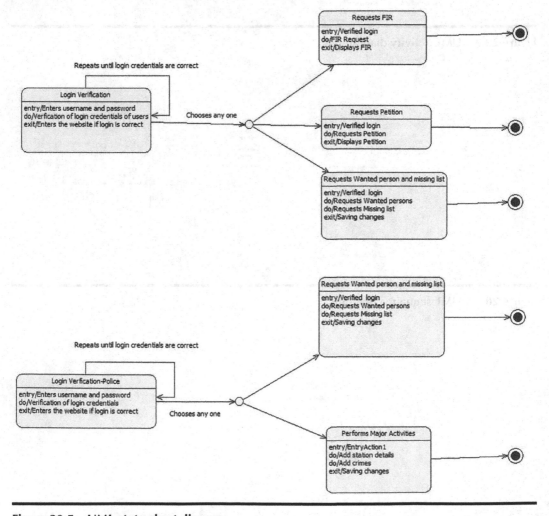

Figure 20.5 UML state chart diagram.

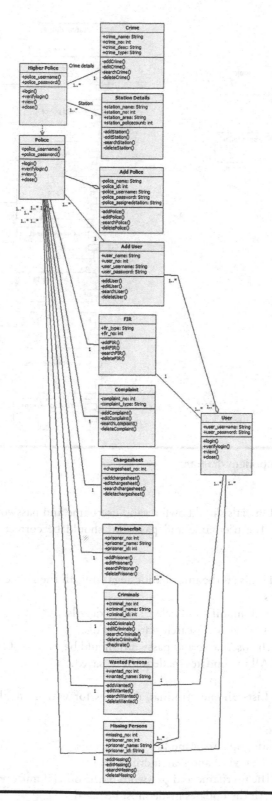

Figure 20.6   UML class diagram.

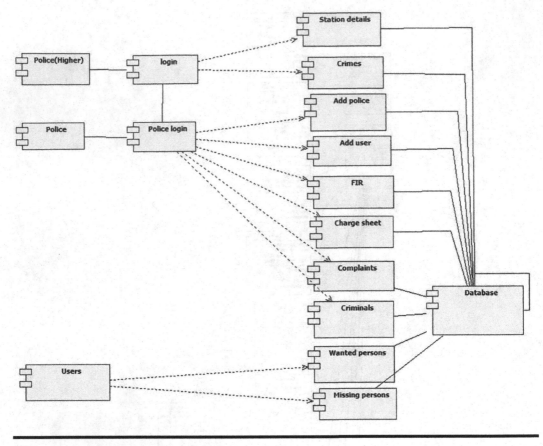

Figure 20.7 UML component diagram.

Pre-Conditions: Officials should own a valid username and password.

Post-Conditions: The username and password should be correct for accessing the crime bureau.

2. **Station Details**

Description: Holds all the information regarding all the police stations in the state.

Flow of Events

Basic Flow: Can add, modify and delete station details.

Alternative Flow: Can view or search station details.

Pre-Conditions: The username and password should be valid and correct.

Post-Conditions: All the updates made must be saved.

3. **Crimes**

Description: Lists all the criminal activities for which an FIR or complaint can be filed.

Flow of Events

Basic Flow: Can add, update or modify crime details.

Alternative Flow: Can view and search crime details.

Pre-Conditions: The username and password of the official must be correct.

Post-Conditions: All the updates made must be saved.

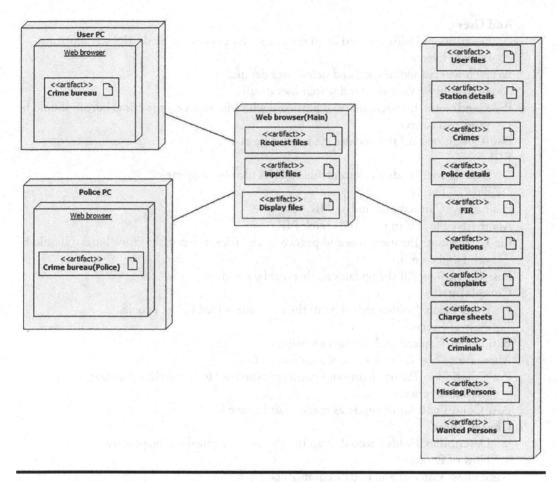

Figure 20.8   UML deployment diagram.

4. **Police Login**

Description: Officials are provided with a username and password, through which they can log into the crime bureau.

Flow of Events

Basic Flow: Opens the crime bureau website.

Alternative Flow: NIL.

Pre-Conditions: The police officers should have a valid username and login.

Post-Conditions: The username and password should be correct for accessing the crime bureau.

5. **Add Police**

Description: Holds a record of all the police officers.

Flow of Events

Basic Flow: Can add, update and delete police officer details.

Alternative Flow: Can view and search the police officer details.

Pre-Conditions: The username and password who tries to access the crime bureau should be valid and correct.

Post-Conditions: All the updates made must be saved.

6. **Add User**

   Description: Holds a record of all the users who either have filed FIR or complaints.
   Flow of Events

   Basic Flow: Can add, update and delete user details.

   Alternative Flow: Can view and search user details.

   Pre-Conditions: The username and password who tries to access the crime bureau should be valid and correct.

   Post-Conditions: All the updates made must be saved.

7. **FIR**

   Description: Holds a record of all the FIRs filed by the people.
   Flow of Events

   Basic Flow: Can add and update FIR.

   Alternative Flow: Can view and search FIR.

   Pre-Conditions: The username and password who tries to access the crime bureau should be valid and correct.

   Post-Conditions: All the updates made must be saved.

8. **Complaints**

   Description: Holds a record of all the complaints filed by the people.
   Flow of Events

   Basic Flow: Can add and update complaints.

   Alternative Flow: Can view and search complaints.

   Pre-Conditions: The username and password who tries to access the crime bureau should be valid and correct.

   Post-Conditions: All the updates made must be saved.

9. **Charge Sheet**

   Description: Holds a record of all the charge sheets filed by the people.
   Flow of Events

   Basic Flow: Can add and update complaints.

   Alternative Flow: Can view and search complaints.

   Pre-Conditions: The username and password who tries to access the crime bureau should be valid and correct.

   Post-Conditions: All the updates made must be saved.

10. **Prisoner List**

    Description: Holds a list of all the prisoners.
    Flow of Events

    Basic Flow: Can add, update or delete prisoners.

    Alternative Flow: Can view and search prisoners.

    Pre-Conditions: The username and password who tries to access the crime bureau should be valid and correct.

    Post-Conditions: All the updates made must be saved.

11. **Criminals**

    Description: Holds a list of all the criminals.
    Flow of Events

    Basic Flow: Can add, update or delete criminals.

    Alternative Flow: Can view and search criminals.

    Pre-Conditions: The username and password who tries to access the crime bureau should be valid and correct.

    Post-Conditions: All the updates made must be saved.

12. **Wanted Persons**

> Description: Holds a list of wanted persons.
> Flow of Events

Basic Flow: Can add, update or delete wanted persons.

Alternative Flow: Can view and search wanted persons.

Pre-Conditions: The username and password who tries to access the crime bureau should be valid and correct.

Post-Conditions: All the updates made must be saved.

13. **Missing Persons**

> Description: Holds a list of missing persons.
> Flow of Events

Basic Flow: Can add, update or delete missing persons.

Alternative Flow: Can view and search missing persons.

Pre-Conditions: The username and password who tries to access the crime bureau should be valid and correct.

Post-Conditions: All the updates made must be saved.

14. **User Login**

> Description: Login page for the users
> Flow of Events

Basic Flow: Opens the crime bureau website.

Alternative Flow: NIL.

Pre-Conditions: The user must own a valid username and password issued by the police officers.

Post-Conditions: The username and password must be valid and correct.

Chapter 21

Design of UML Diagrams for Smart Traffic Management System

21.1 Problem Statement

In our modern metropolitan city, people don't follow the traffic rules. The outcome of it is unfortunate. In India, 64.4% of the total deaths are accounted by road accidents. As the automobiles get revolutionized the number of vehicles keep increasing. Conventional traffic signals are not efficient and strict. Smart traffic system aims in minimizing the risks of accidents by precautionary taking actions on people who violate the traffic rules. Cameras to monitor the roads with high traffic levels in order to facilitate the traffic signal. Helmet and seat belt detection using image processing to warn the drivers. Details of the driver are submitted to the traffic police, when he/she violates the law more than two times via the number plate which is captured by cameras. Street lights are operated based on the population density on road at night, thereby saving electricity. License will be cancelled as penalty, if the law is violated. Details of the driver will be passed on to successive signals on account of speeding. Automated traffic lights regulate the traffic flow in order to avoid congestions (Figures 21.1–21.8).

21.2 UML Diagrams

Actor Specification

1. **Driver** – Driver refers to all the citizens who drive any type of vehicle and who doesn't follow the traffic rules.
2. **RTO Server** – RTO Server is the Database that holds the information (Addresses, vehicle details) of all registered vehicles, monitors the traffic signals.
3. **Traffic Police** – Police officers who regulate the traffic on the ground, patrol cars and road safety officers.

DOI: 10.1201/9781003287124-21

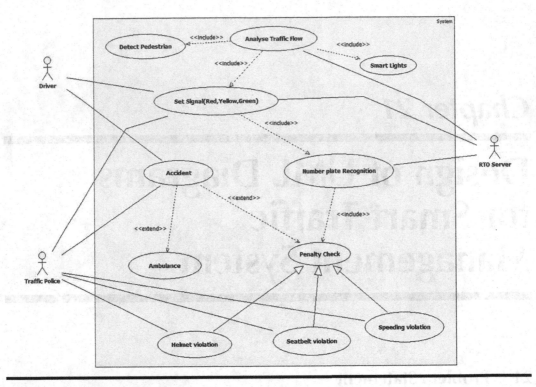

Figure 21.1   UML usecase diagram.

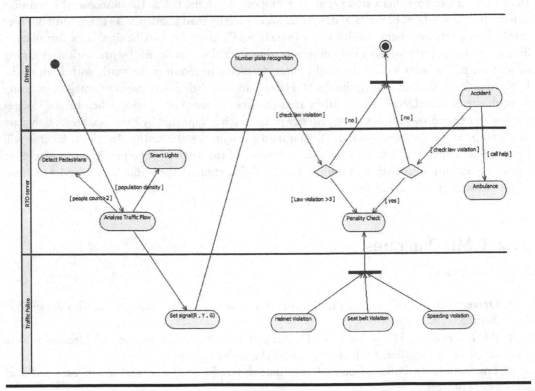

Figure 21.2   UML activity diagram.

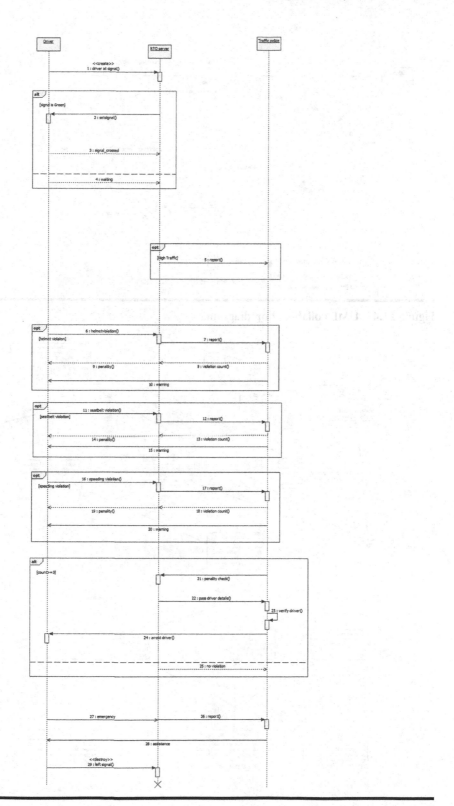

Figure 21.3   UML sequence diagram.

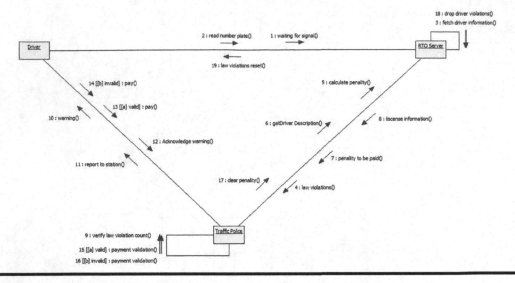

Figure 21.4   UML collaboration diagram.

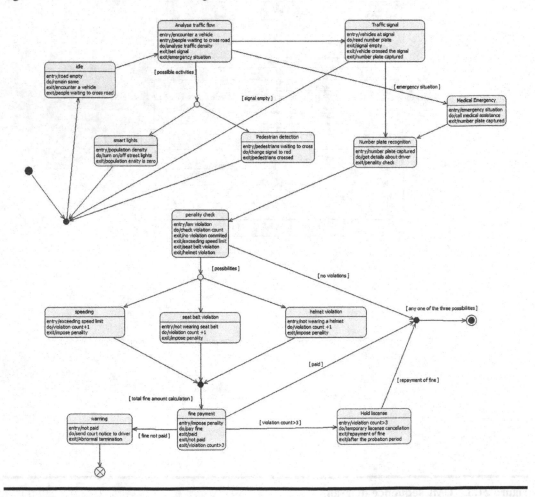

Figure 21.5   UML state chart diagram.

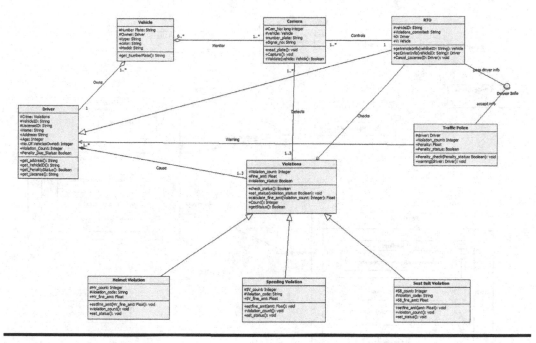

Figure 21.6   UML class diagram.

Usecase Specification

1. **Accident**
    Description: Cameras positioned check for any kind of undesirable events.
    Flow of Events
    Basic Flow: Automatically call an ambulance to the desired spot, charge a penalty based on the violation.
    Alternative Flow: Nil.
    Pre-Conditions: An undesirable event like an accident must take place.
    Post-Conditions: Based on law violation impose a penalty on the driver.
2. **Ambulance**
    Description: 24/7 Emergency service equipped for taking sick or injured people to and from the hospital, especially in emergencies.
    Flow of Events
    Basic Flow: Provide an ambulance vehicle to the desired location specified from the cameras.
    Alternative Flow: Nil.
    Pre-Conditions: An emergency call.
    Post-Conditions: Nil.
3. **Analyse Traffic Flow**
    Description: Monitors the traffic intensity on roads and based on population density set the signal lights to ease traffic flow.
    Flow of Events
    Basic Flow: Pass on data about population density and maintain the smart lights on the system.
    Alternative Flow: Nil.
    Pre-Conditions: Nil.
    Post-Conditions: Sets the desired signal with green light.

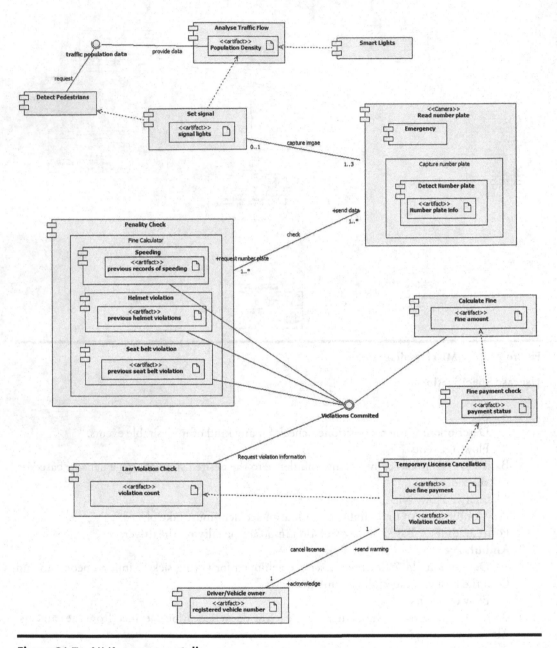

Figure 21.7 UML component diagram.

4. **Detect Pedestrian**

Description: Checks for civilians to crossroad and indicate the traffic light to trigger appropriate signal.

Flow of Events

Basic Flow: Pedestrian walking signal is enabled.

Alternative Flow: Nil.

Pre-Conditions: Group of civilians (minimum of 3) waiting to cross the road.

Post-Conditions: Nil.

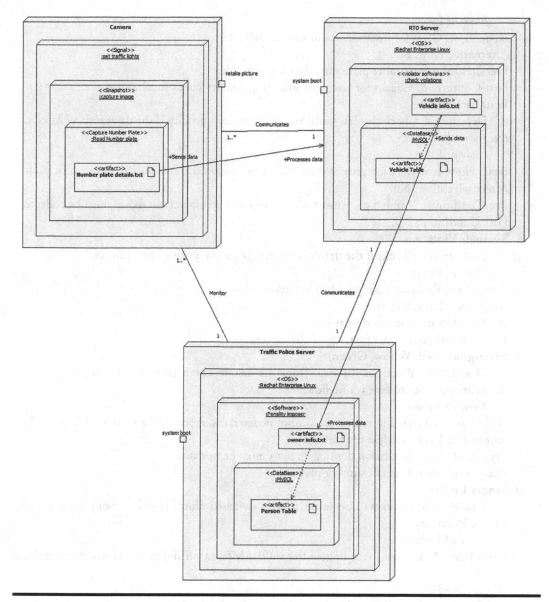

Figure 21.8   UML deployment diagram.

5. **Helmet Violation**
    Description: Checks for drivers who are not wearing a helmet and imposes a penalty.
    Flow of Events
Basic Flow: Recognition of helmet violation.
Alternative Flow: Nil.
Pre-Conditions: Violating the law by not wearing a helmet.
Post-Conditions: Impose a penalty on the driver.
6. **Number Plate Recognition**
    Description: Reads the number plate and gathers information about the driver from the RTO Server.

Flow of Events

Basic Flow: Gives information about vehicle owners.

Alternative Flow: Nil.

Pre-Conditions: Number plate must be clearly visible.

Post-Conditions: Checks for law violation using penalty check mechanism.

7. **Penalty Check**

Description: Checks for law violation and imposes a penalty if the driver has violated the law more than thrice.

Flow of Events

Basic Flow: Law violation greater than 3, pass information about the driver to traffic police.

Alternative Flow: Nil.

Pre-Conditions: Number plate must be read and information about driver must be collected.

Post-Conditions: Nil.

8. **Seatbelt Violation**

Description: Checks if the driver is wearing a seat belt using the cameras.

Flow of Events

Basic Flow: Recognition of seat belt violation.

Alternative Flow: Nil.

Pre-Conditions: Absence of seat belt.

Post-Conditions: Impose penalty on the driver.

9. **Set Signal (Red, Yellow, Green)**

Description: Based on the data from the system about population density the traffic lights are operated to ease traffic flow.

Flow of Events

Basic Flow: Set signal to red on account of pedestrians, green to the road with high traffic.

Alternative Flow: Analyse the traffic.

Pre-Conditions: Population density on road must be updated.

Post-Conditions: Detects number plates.

10. **Smart Lights**

Description: Lights will be automatically switched on/off based on population density to save electricity.

Flow of Events

Basic Flow: Switch on street lights after 6.00 AM/turn off lights on areas without vehicle flow.

Alternative Flow: Nil.

Pre-Conditions: Population density must be updated.

Post-Conditions: Nil.

11. **Speeding Violation**

Description: Captures images of drivers speeding in signals exceeding the speed limit.

Flow of Events

Basic Flow: Takes a snap shot of the vehicle along with the number plate.

Alternative Flow: Nil.

Pre-Conditions: Exceeding the speed limit.

Post-Conditions: Impose penalty on the driver.

Chapter 22

Design of UML Diagrams for Job Seeker Portal System

22.1 Problem Statement

Job seekers work hard to gain the right skills and knowledge to give them an edge over others in the role they seek. However, at times, despite their best efforts, one may find it difficult to move a step closer to this sought-after job. Hence a platform for listing out the availability of jobs irrespective of the field is required. Furthermore, a job site serves a dual purpose. On one hand, it lists out the availability of jobs to candidates, and on the other, it serves as a database of registered candidate's profiles for companies to shortlist. The objective is to develop a software solution to predict the availability of jobs based on location, sectors, package, platform, interest and eligibility. As it is important to keep the candidates engaged during their job search, it is important to provide facets on the above-mentioned criteria so that they can narrow down to the jobs of their choice (Figures 22.1–22.8).

22.2 UML Diagrams

Actor Specification

1. **Admin** – Verifies the company/seeker and maintains the system.
2. **Recruiter** – Posts job vacancies and its requirements.
3. **Seeker** – Can apply for a job posting.

Usecase Specification

1. **Approve New Companies**
     Description: Checks the credibility of the company and admits the company into the system.
     Flow of Events
Basic Flow: Verifies the Company's information.
Pre-Conditions: Checking the proofs submitted.
Post-Conditions: Background checks.

DOI: 10.1201/9781003287124-22

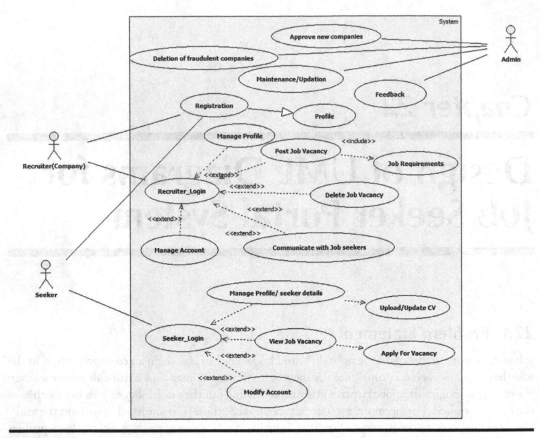

Figure 22.1   UML usecase diagram.

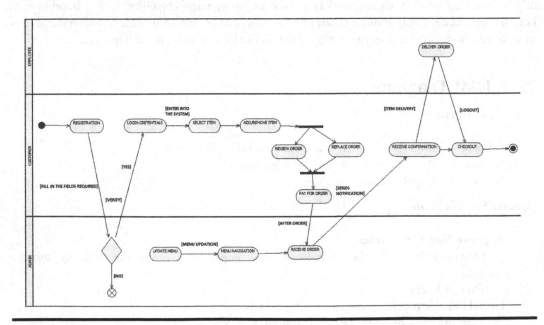

Figure 22.2   UML activity diagram.

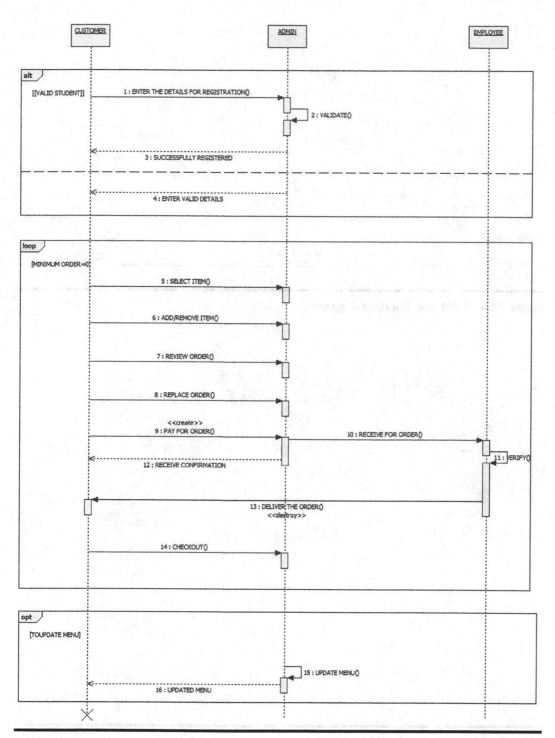

Figure 22.3 UML sequence diagram.

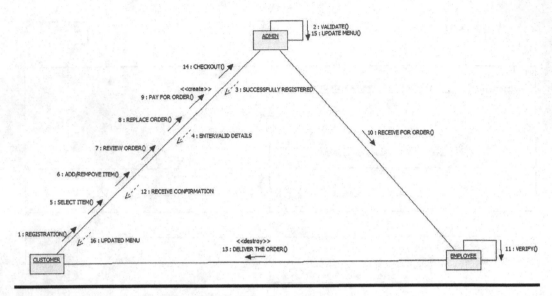

Figure 22.4 UML collaboration diagram.

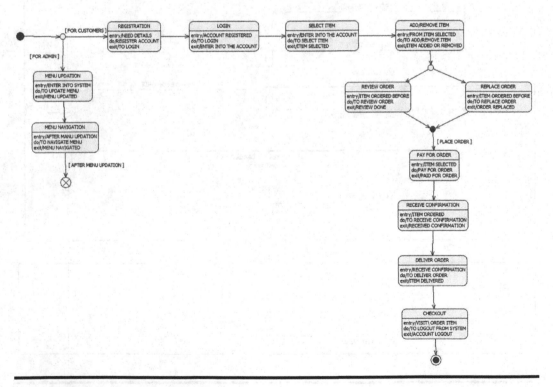

Figure 22.5 UML state machine diagram.

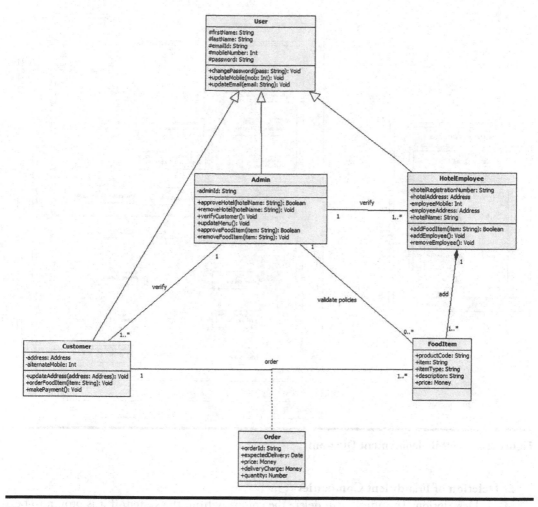

Figure 22.6   UML class diagram.

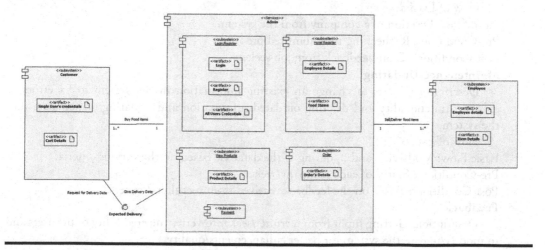

Figure 22.7   UML component diagram.

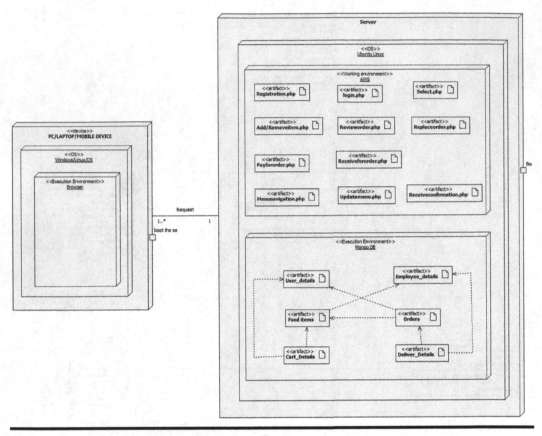

Figure 22.8   UML deployment Diagram.

2. **Deletion of Fraudulent Companies**

   Description: The admin can delete the company from the system if it is proven to be a false/fraudulent company.

   Flow of Events

   Basic Flow: Deletion of a company from the system.

   Pre-Conditions: Rechecking the submitted proof.

   Post-Conditions: From feedback from job seekers.

3. **Maintenance/Updating**

   Description: Refers to change an existing information in the system to fix errors or enhance functionality and deleting outdated information and updating of new data into the system.

   Flow of Events

   Basic Flow: Modifying and updating of the database based on the various criteria.

   Pre-Conditions: Status of each company/seeker.

   Post-Conditions: Based on the feedback received from recruiters/seekers.

4. **Feedback**

   Description: Getting input from recruiter/seeker to verify the credibility of the users and to modify/update the system for better enhancements/quality.

   Flow of Events

Basic Flow: Input from both recruiter and seeker.

Pre-Conditions: The feedback collected must be from the registered users of the system.

Post-Conditions: Nil.

5. **Registration**

Description: Every recruiter/seeker must first register to avail the opportunity to use the system.

Flow of Events

Basic Flow: Every user must submit the needed requirements for registration.

Pre-Conditions: The proofs/ID must be credible.

Post-Conditions: Nil.

6. **Profile**

Description: This contains the information which will be displayed to all other users of the system.

Flow of Events

Basic Flow: The information available in the profile should be credible.

Pre-Conditions: Only required information to be displayed.

Post-Conditions: Additional information can be added.

7. **Recruiter Login**

Description: The recruiter/company login through a separate login page.

Flow of Events

Basic Flow: Login into the system using the recruiter password.

Alternative Flow: Logins through alternate means provided by admin (Forgot_password).

Pre-Conditions: Username and password must be correct.

Post-Conditions: Can change username/password.

8. **Manage Profile**

Description: Displays the information about the company.

Flow of Events

Basic Flow: Display Company information.

Pre-Conditions: Can input the credible information about the company.

Post-Conditions: Update the required information.

9. **Post Job Vacancy**

Description: Can post a job vacancy and the required information about the field, category and salary and so on about the job.

Flow of Events

Basic Flow: Post a job vacancy with the required details.

Pre-Conditions: Should post all the details that the seeker must know.

Post-Conditions: Can post what is needed from the seeker for the required post.

10. **Job Requirements**

Description: Displays the information of the job posted.

Flow of Events

Basic Flow: Job requirement information.

Pre-Conditions: Information about what is to be expected from the seeker.

Post-Conditions: Additional requirements along with the existing information from the company.

11. **Delete Job Vacancy**

Description: If a job vacancy is filled or if it's no longer needed, the company could delete the job posting from the system.

Flow of Events

Basic Flow: Deletion of job posting if the post is filled.

Alternative Flow: Deletion of job post if it's no longer needed.

Pre-Conditions: The recruiter should only delete the job posting for an appropriate reason.

Post-Conditions: Can notify the admin after the change is made.

12. **Communicate with Job Seeker**

Description: If a job seeker applies for a job vacancy, the recruiter should communicate with the seeker to provide the information such as interview date, company test and so on.

Flow of Events

Basic Flow: Communication between recruiter and seeker through the system.

Alternative Flow: Nil.

Pre-Conditions: The seeker must satisfy the required job specification for the posting.

Post-Conditions: Nil.

13. **Manage Account**

Description: This detail actions such as change/update username and password and deletion of the account of the recruiter.

Flow of Events

Basic Flow: Updation/deletion of account.

Alternative Flow: Nil.

Pre-Conditions: Must be a registered user.

Post-Conditions: Nil.

14. **Seeker Login**

Description: The job seeker logins through a separate login page.

Flow of Events

Basic Flow: Seeker login through password.

Alternative Flow: Logins through alternate means provided by admin (Forgot_password).

Pre-Conditions: Username and password must be correct.

Post-Conditions: Can change username/password.

15. **Manage Profile/Seeker Details**

Description: Displays the information of the seeker provided during registration.

Flow of Events

Basic Flow: Information about seeker.

Alternative Flow: Nil.

Pre-Conditions: Nil.

Post-Conditions: Nil.

16. **Upload/Update CV**

Description: The CV/resume, submitted in the profile section is a requirement for applying for jobs.

Flow of Events

Basic Flow: Upload/update resume.

Alternative Flow: Nil.

Pre-Conditions: Only credible information must be presented in the resume.

Post-Conditions: Can update the resume whenever it's required.

17. **View Job Vacancy**

Description: A job seeker can browse through various job postings, based on category and field and further constraints.

Flow of Events

Basic Flow: Browsing job vacancies.

Alternative Flow: Nil.

Pre-Conditions: Must be a registered user.

Post-Conditions: Nil.

18. **Apply for Job Vacancy**

Description: A job seeker, if interested in a certain job posting, can apply for that posting.

Flow of Events

Basic Flow: Applying for job vacancy.

Alternative Flow: Nil.

Pre-Conditions: Should meet the required requirements of the posting.

Post-Conditions: Upload CV.

19. **Modify Account**

Description: This detail actions such as change/update username and password and deletion of the account of the job seeker.

Flow of Events

Basic Flow: Account modification/updation.

Alternative Flow: Nil.

Pre-Conditions: Must be a registered user.

Post-Conditions: Nil.

Chapter 23

Design of UML Diagrams for AAROGYA SETU – Health Care APP

23.1 Problem Statement

Coronavirus pandemic is spreading in large numbers. Experts suggest that social distancing has been used for a long time as one of the methods to reduce the spike in diseases and infectious illnesses. In India alone, the cases have sharply spiked up in the past two weeks, which has led to imposing even tougher measures. By identifying 'hotspots', necessary mapping can help deal with the problem of community transmission, i.e., when cases start

Spreading within the population in such a way that people don't know how they were exposed to the contagion. This is known as 'Stage 3' of an outbreak. The Aarogya Setu app, which is a coronavirus tracker of sorts works on the basis of contact tracing and can help a user identify possible coronavirus 'hotspot' around his or her area. It can help people stay safe and adopt necessary precautions in some areas where there are cases and accordingly, help stop or prevent community transmission to an extent. On the basis of geotagging, it can also alert a specific user about their proximity to a nearby infection case or hotspot. The app also helps users self-identify their risk and monitor their health assessment, considering the times when it can get difficult (and most of all, is not particularly safe to step out and visit health clinics).

Aarogya Setu app also helps people identify the symptoms, alert them about the best safety precautions and other relevant information concerning the spread of COVID-19. While this is a noble initiative, the app also lists down basic quarantine measures for those who are considered to be in the 'high-risk' category. It can also help people, who have had a travel history self-quarantine and prevent any risk of transmission (Figures 23.1–23.8).

DOI: 10.1201/9781003287124-23

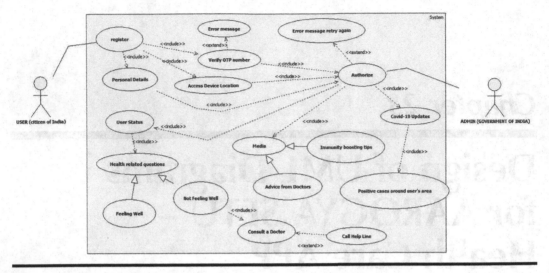

Figure 23.1   UML usecase diagram.

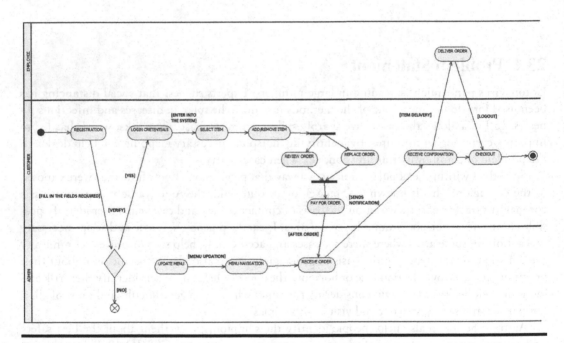

Figure 23.2   UML activity diagram.

23.2 UML Diagrams

Actor Specification

1. **User** – User has to register by giving personal details and the verification process.
2. **Admin** – Admin provides authorization to the user by the verification process.

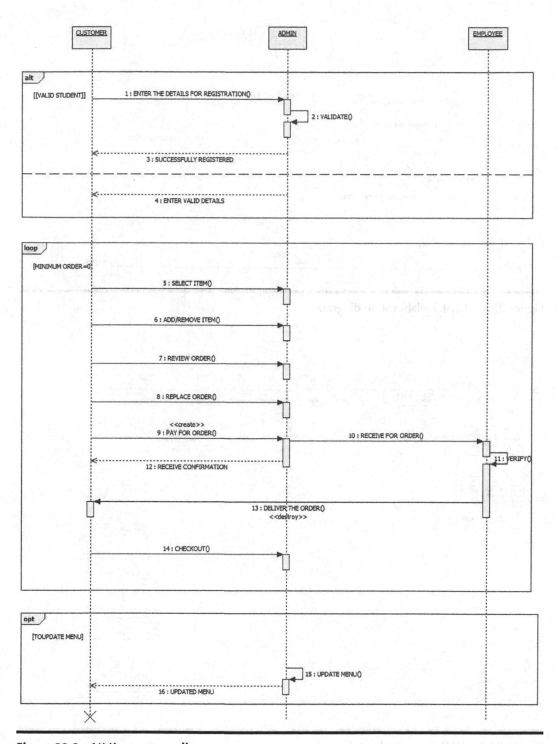

Figure 23.3   UML sequence diagram.

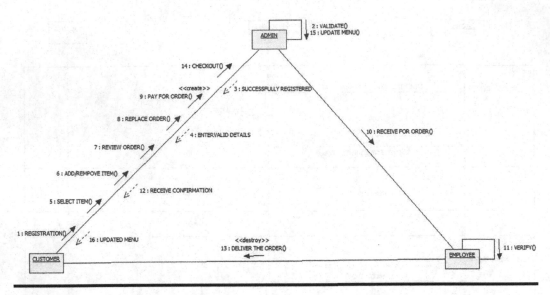

Figure 23.4   UML collaboration diagram.

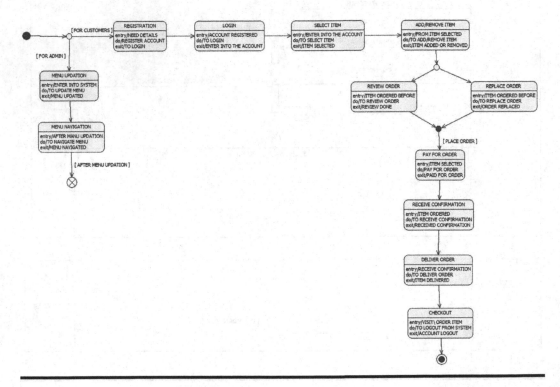

Figure 23.5   UML state machine diagram.

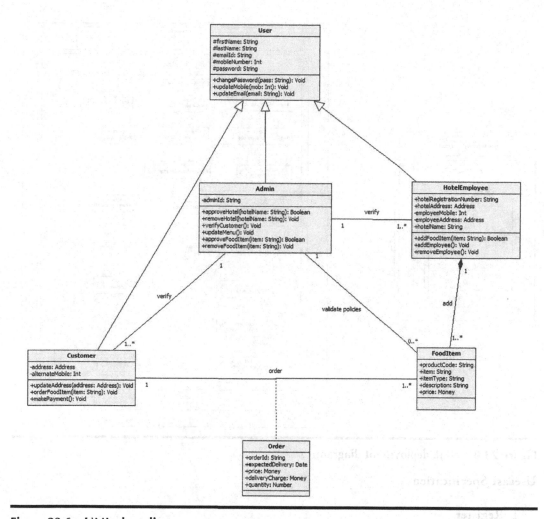

Figure 23.6   UML class diagram.

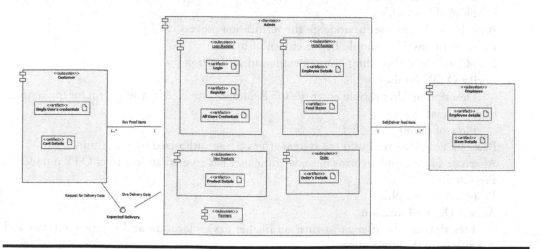

Figure 23.7   UML component diagram.

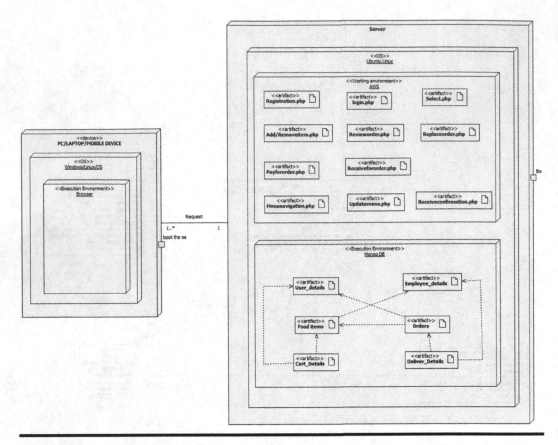

Figure 23.8   UML deployment diagram.

Usecase Specification

1. **Register**
    Description: User should register to get access to the application.
    Flow of Events
    Basic Flow: Allows user to undergo the verification process.
    Pre-Conditions: User should be the citizen of India.
    Post-Conditions: Providing proper details and verification process.
2. **Verify OTP Number**
    Description: User should enter the OTP number provided by the system for the verification process.
    Flow of Events
    Basic Flow: Allows user into the system after getting authorized by the admin.
    Alternate Flow: Displays error message if the user has entered an incorrect OTP number.
    Pre-Conditions: Nil.
    Post-Conditions: Nil.
3. **Access Device Location**
    Description: The user must turn on his/her device location and accept the terms and conditions of the application.
    Flow of Events

Basic Flow: Allows user into the system after getting authorized by the admin.
Alternate Flow: Displays error message if the location is not turned on.
Pre-Conditions: Users location should be in India.
Post-Conditions: Nil.

4. **Personal Details**
   Description: Users should provide all the necessary personal details asked by the system.
   Flow of Events
   Basic Flow: Allows user into the system after getting authorized by the admin.
   Alternate Flow: Displays an error message if the provided details are wrong.
   Pre-Conditions: Nil.
   Post-Conditions: Nil.

5. **Error Message**
   Description: If the entered user's OTP number is wrong.
   Flow of Events
   Basic Flow: Gets out of the system.
   Alternate Flow: Nil.
   Pre-Conditions: User should enter the correct OTP number.
   Post-Conditions: Nil.

6. **Authorize**
   Description: Admin authorizes the user into the system after the verification process.
   Flow of Events
   Basic Flow: Allows into the system.
   Alternate Flow: Displays an error message if the verification process gets failed.
   Pre-Conditions: Verification process should be done correctly by the user.
   Post-Conditions: Nil.

7. **Error Message Retry Again**
   Description: If the admin did not authorize the user, users should retry again.
   Flow of Events
   Basic Flow: Gets out of the system.
   Alternative Flow: Nil.
   Pre-Conditions: Authorization should be done properly.
   Post-Conditions: Nil.

8. **User Status**
   Description: To check the users' health conditions.
   Flow of Events
   Basic Flow: Allows user to take a self-analysis test.
   Alternate Flow: Nil.
   Pre-Conditions: The admin should authorize the user.
   Post-Conditions: User should answer the health care questions correctly.

9. **Media**
   Description: The System provides the users with advices, healthcare tips and trending videos.
   Flow of Events
   Basic Flow: Allows user too many categories of videos provided by the system.
   Alternate flow: Nil.
   Pre-Conditions: The admin should authorize the user.
   Post-Conditions: Nil.

10. **Covid-19 Updates**

   Description: The system provides the users with a daily number of positive cases.

   Flow of Events

   Basic Flow: Allows users to know the number of cases around their area.

   Alternate Flow: Nil.

   Pre-Conditions: The admin should authorize the user.

   Post-Conditions: Nil.

11. **Health-Related Questions**

   Description: The user should answer the health care questions in order to check their health condition.

   Flow of Events

   Basic Flow: Splits the users into feeling well and not feeling well categories accordingly.

   Alternative Flow: Nil.

   Pre-Conditions: The admin should authorize the user.

   Post-Conditions: If the user is not feeling well, he/she should consult a doctor.

12. **Feeling Well**

   Description: The system provides the users with the output of the self-analysis test as feeling well.

   Flow of Events

   Basic Flow: Nil.

   Alternative Flow: Nil.

   Pre-Conditions: The users must take the self-analysis test.

   Post-Conditions: Nil.

13. **Not Feeling Well**

   Description: The system provides the users with the output of the self-analysis test as not feeling well.

   Flow of Events

   Basic Flow: Suggests users to consult a doctor.

   Alternative Flow: Nil.

   Pre-Conditions: The users must take the self-analysis test.

   Post-Conditions: Nil.

14. **Consult Doctor**

   Description: If the users are not feeling well, the system suggests the users to consult a doctor.

   Flow of Events

   Basic Flow: Suggests users to call healthcare members.

   Alternative Flow: Nil.

   Pre-Conditions: The users must take the self-analysis test.

   Post-Conditions: Nil.

15. **Call Helpline**

   Description: In case if the users are not feeling well, the system suggests the users to call helpline.

   Flow of Events

   Basic Flow: Nil.

   Alternative Flow: Nil.

   Pre-Conditions: The users must take the self-analysis test.

   Post-Conditions: Nil.

16. **Advice from Doctors**

Description: The system provides the users with many advising videos of doctors.

Flow of Events

Basic Flow: The system provides many health-related videos to the users.

Alternative Flow: Nil.

Pre-Conditions: The admin must authorize the user.

Post-Conditions: Nil.

17. **Immunity-Boosting Tips**

Description: The system provides many immunity-boosting tips to the users.

Flow of Events

Basic Flow: Nil.

Alternative Flow: Nil.

Pre-Conditions: The Admin must authorize the user.

Post-Conditions: Nil.

18. **Positive Cases around User's Surroundings**

Description: The system provides the number of positive corona cases around users' area.

Flow of Events

Basic Flow: Nil.

Alternative Flow: Nil.

Pre-Conditions: The admin should authorize the users.

Post-Conditions: Nil.

Chapter 24

Design of UML Diagrams for Online Pharmacy Management System

24.1 Problem Statement

The customer goes to the shop and purchases the medicine required. So a lot of time is wasted and the person gets tired. If he wants to exchange the product, once again he goes to the shop and replaces them. The complete process depends on the physical interactions. The Online Pharmacy is easy to use and order. The customer selects the required medicines and orders them with a single click. Before it, the customer needs to create a login account and fill all the details like name, address, any id no, etc. The client can able to view the status of the medicines. The business goal for the application is to provide the medicines to all the people and admin will provide the supplier details (Figures 24.1–24.20).

24.2 UML Diagrams

Actor Specification

1. **Customer** – He/she can create an account to order/view medicines online.
2. **Admin** – He/she can view, update medicines availability based on the needs. He/she can view customer details and can update delivery man attendance.
3. **Delivery Man** – He can view the address to be delivered, he can update/view his profile his attendance.

Usecase Specification

1. **Login**
   Description: It allows the customer to login into the page.
   Flow of Events

DOI: 10.1201/9781003287124-24

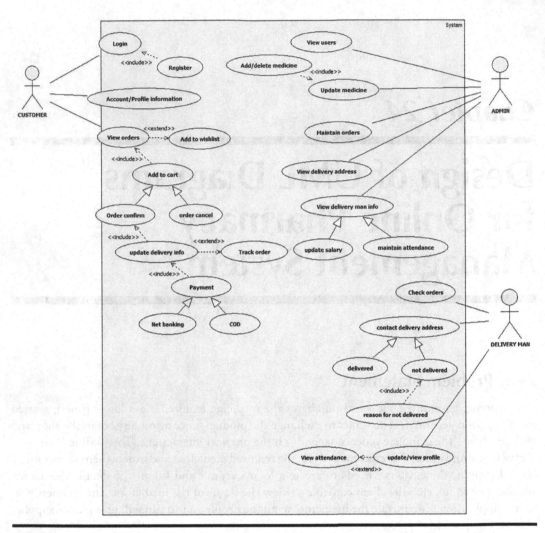

Figure 24.1 UML usecase diagram.

Basic Flow: Login into the page.
Alternate Flow: Requests to create a login for the new customers.
Pre-Conditions: The customer should already have an account to login.
Post-Conditions: It directs to the home page.

2. **Register**
    Description: It allows the customer to create an account.
    Flow of Events
Basic Flow: Creates an account.
Alternate Flow: Already registered customers can login directly.
Pre-Conditions: All the required details should be mentioned to create an account.
Post-Conditions: After registration, it directs to the login page.

3. **Account/Profile Information**
    Description: Customer can edit their information.
    Flow of Events

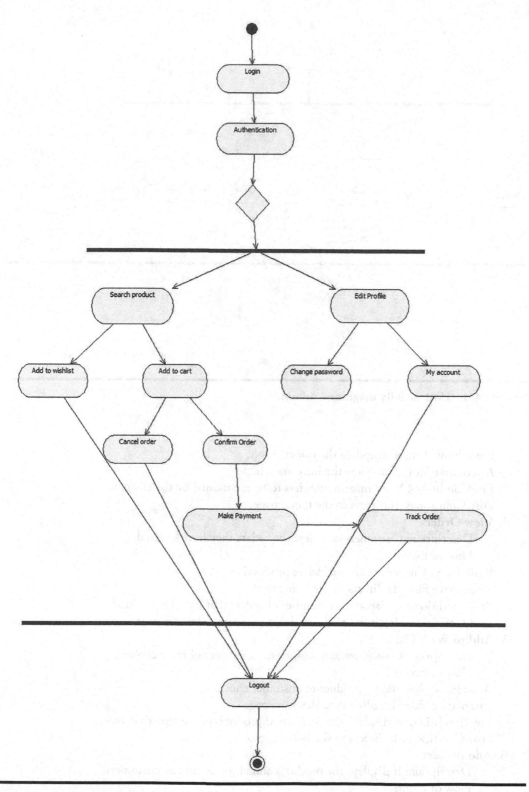

Figure 24.2   UML activity diagram – User.

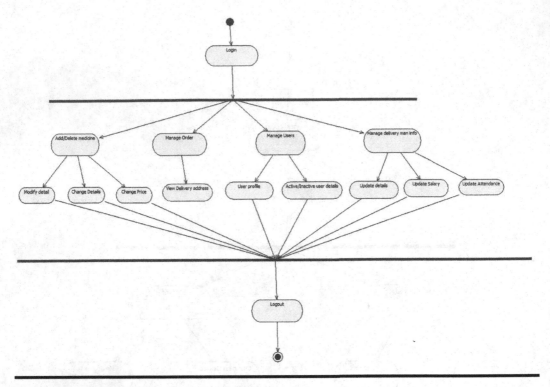

Figure 24.3 UML activity diagram – Admin.

Basic Flow: Can edit/update the information.
Alternative Flow: Can view the information.
Pre-Conditions: Valid information has to be mentioned by the customers.
Post-Conditions: It directs to the home page.

4. **View Orders**
    Description: Customers can view the orders they have selected.
    Flow of Events
Basic Flow: Customer can add/delete products.
Alternative Flow: It directs to the homepage.
Pre-Conditions: It displays the number of orders that have been added.
Post-Conditions: It directs to the wish list page or to the cart page.

5. **Add to Wish List**
    Description: Customers can wish to list a product of their choice.
    Flow of Events
Basic Flow: Wish lists a product of customer choice.
Alternative Flow: It redirects to the homepage.
Pre-Conditions: It displays the wish-listed products of customer's choice.
Post-Conditions: It directs to the home page.

6. **Add to Cart**
    Description: It displays the products added to the cart by customers.
    Flow of Events

Basic Flow: It displays the product in the cart.

Alternative Flow: It redirects to the view orders page.

Pre-Conditions: Items must be added to the cart to order them.

Post-Conditions: It directs to the view orders page or to the order confirm or order cancel option.

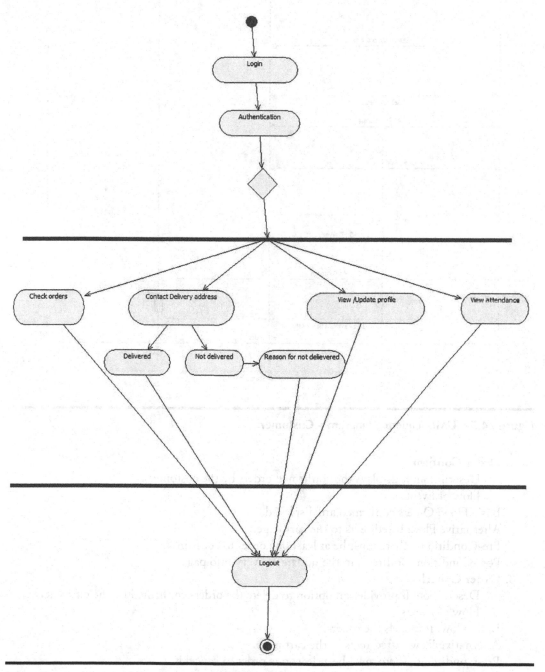

Figure 24.4　UML activity diagram – Delivery Man.

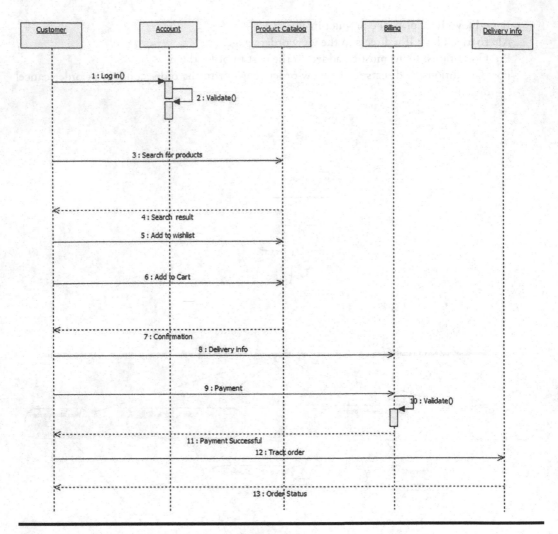

Figure 24.5   UML sequence diagram – Customer.

7. **Order Confirm**
   Description: It displays the confirmed orders by the customers.
   Flow of Events
   Basic Flow: Orders confirmed are displayed.
   Alternative Flow: It redirects to the cart page.
   Pre-Conditions: There must be at least one order to confirm it.
   Post-Conditions: It directs to the update delivery info page.
8. **Order Cancel**
   Description: It provides an option to delete the orders confirmed by the customers.
   Flow of Events
   Basic Flow: It cancels the orders.
   Alternative Flow: It redirects to the cart page.
   Pre-Conditions: There must be at least one order to cancel it.
   Post-Conditions: It directs to the cart page.

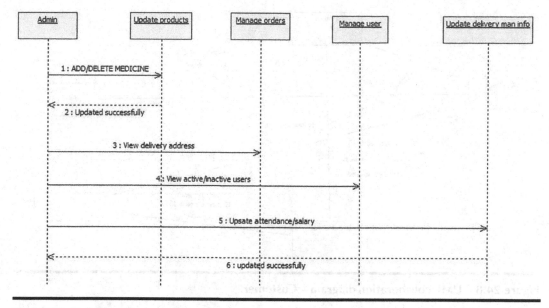

Figure 24.6   UML sequence diagram – Admin.

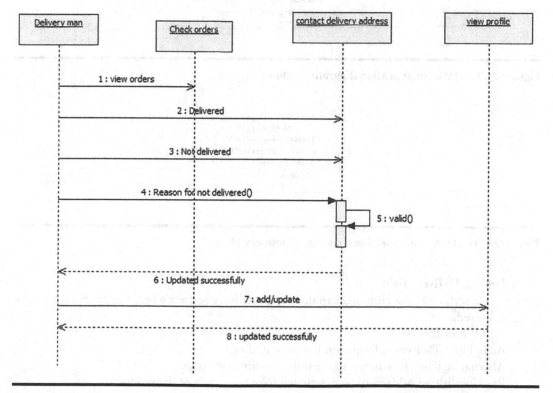

Figure 24.7   UML sequence diagram – Delivery Man.

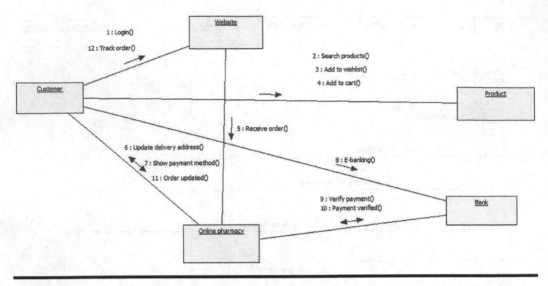

Figure 24.8   UML collaboration diagram – Customer.

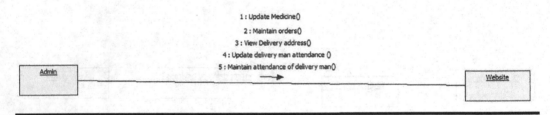

Figure 24.9   UML collaboration diagram – Admin.

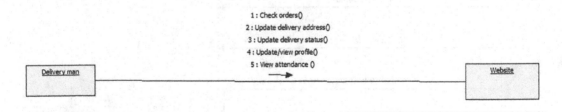

Figure 24.10   UML collaboration diagram – Delivery Man.

9. **Update Delivery Info**

Description: The customer can update the delivery address where the products are to be delivered.

Flow of Events

Basic Flow: Delivery information has to be updated.

Alternative Flow: It redirects to the order confirmation page.

Pre-Conditions: Address to be mentioned in order to deliver the products.

Post-Conditions: It directs to the track order/payment page.

Figure 24.11   UML state machine diagram – Customer.

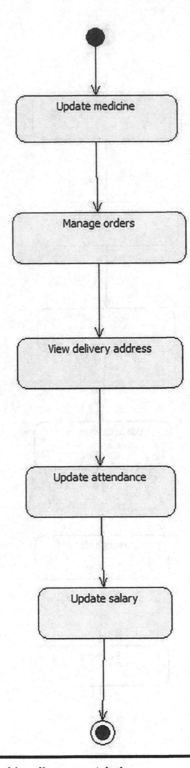

Figure 24.12   UML state machine diagram – Admin.

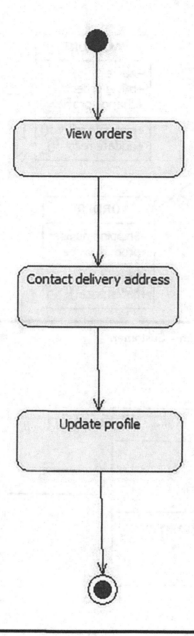

Figure 24.13   UML State machine diagram – Delivery Man.

10. **Track Orders**
      Description: This page allows the customer to track their orders.
      Flow of Events
    Basic Flow: It requires the order to display the tracking option.
    Alternative Flow: It directs to the payment/update delivery info page.
    Pre-Conditions: It requires order to track them.
    Post-Conditions: It directs to the update delivery info page.

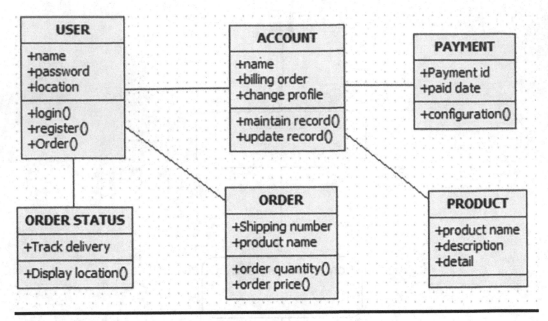

Figure 24.14 UML class diagram – Customer.

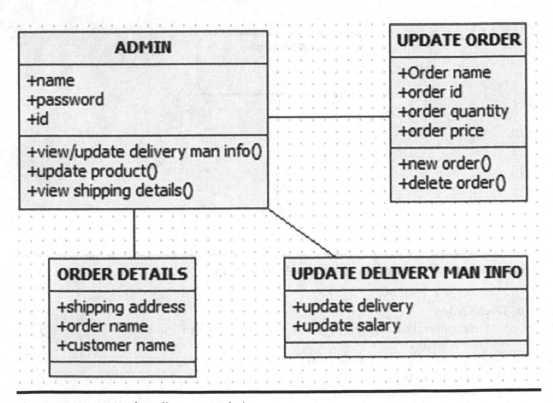

Figure 24.15 UML class diagram – Admin.

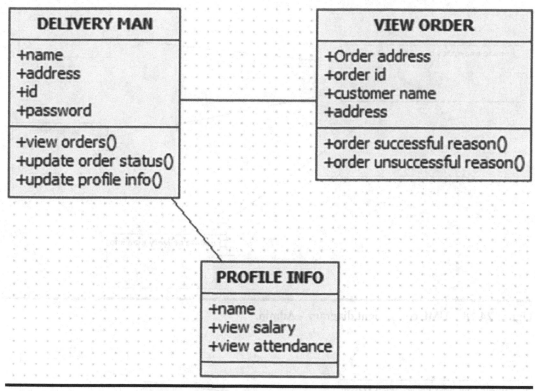

Figure 24.16 UML class diagram – Delivery Man.

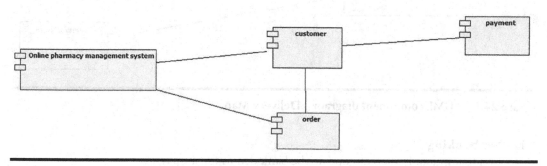

Figure 24.17 UML component diagram – Customer.

11. **Payment**

Description: This page allows the customer to pay for the ordered products.
Flow of Events
Basic Flow: It requires the payment details.
Alternative Flow: It directs to update delivery info page.
Pre-Conditions: It requires payment details to proceed.
Post-Conditions: It directs to the Net banking or COD page.

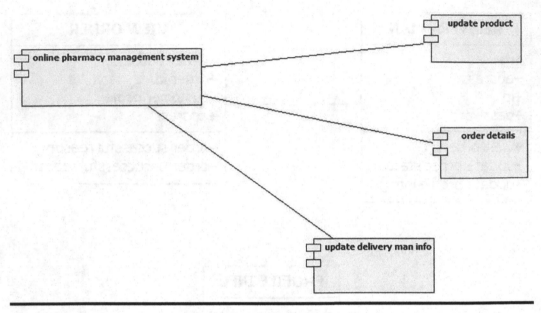

Figure 24.18   UML component diagram – Admin.

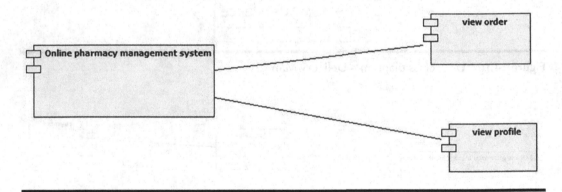

Figure 24.19   UML component diagram – Delivery Man.

12. **Net Banking**
      Description: It allows to update the bank details for the payment.
      Flow of Events
   Basic Flow: It requires bank details.
   Alternative Flow: It directs to the payment page.
   Pre-Conditions: It requires bank details.
   Post-Conditions: Once payment is successful, it directs to the homepage.
13. **COD**
      Description: It provides an option for the customers to pay at the time of delivery.
      Flow of Events
   Basic Flow: It provides an option for pay on delivery.
   Alternative Flow: It directs to the payment page.
   Pre-Conditions: It requires confirmation on orders in order to pay on delivery.
   Post-Conditions: It directs to the payment page.

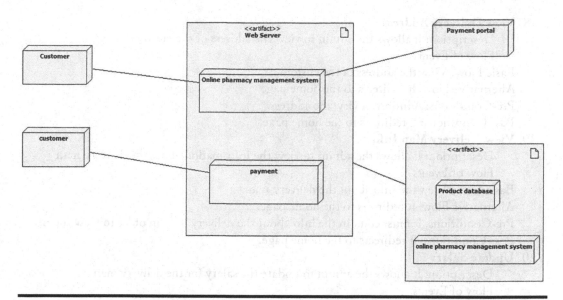

Figure 24.20   UML deployment diagram.

14. **View Users**
> Description: Admin can view the users who logged in into the page.
> Flow of Events

Basic Flow: It allows to view the users who are currently logged in into the system.
Alternative Flow: It directs to the home page.
Pre-Conditions: He/she must be an admin to view the users.
Post-Conditions: It directs to the home page.

15. **Update Medicine**
> Description: Admin can view the number of medicines available and update them on
the website.
> Flow of Events

Basic Flow: Allows to update the medicine.
Alternative Flow: It directs to the home page.
Pre-Conditions: Update the medicines.
Post-Conditions: It directs to the home page.

16. **Add/Delete Medicine**
> Description: It allows the admin to add/delete medicines based on the quantity available.
> Flow of Events

Basic Flow: Adding/deleting the medicines.
Alternative Flow: It redirects to the update medicine page.
Pre-Conditions: It adds/deletes the medicines.
Post-Conditions: It redirects to the update medicine page.

17. **Maintain Orders**
> Description: It allows the admin to maintain orders.
> Flow of Events

Basic Flow: Admin maintains the orders ordered by the customer.
Alternative Flow: It redirects to the home page.
Pre-Conditions: There must be some orders to maintain them.
Post-Conditions: It redirects to the home page.

18. **View Delivery Address**

    Description: It allows the admin to view the address of the customers.
    Flow of Events

    Basic Flow: View the address of the customers.

    Alternative Flow: It redirects to the home page.

    Pre-Conditions: Admin can view the address.

    Post-Conditions: It redirects to the home page.

19. **View Delivery Man Info**

    Description: It allows the admin to view the information about the delivery man.
    Flow of Events

    Basic Flow: View the info about the delivery man.

    Alternative Flow: It redirects to the home page.

    Pre-Conditions: It must contain the info about the delivery man in order to view them.

    Post-Conditions: It redirects to the home page.

20. **Update Salary**

    Description: It allows the admin to update the salary for the delivery man.
    Flow of Events

    Basic Flow: Updating salary for the delivery man.

    Alternative Flow: It redirects to the view delivery man info page.

    Pre-Conditions: There must be delivery man info to update salary to them.

    Post-Conditions: It redirects to the view delivery man info page.

21. **Maintain Attendance**

    Description: It allows the admin to maintain attendance for the delivery man.
    Flow of Events

    Basic Flow: Allows to maintain attendance based on their working days.

    Alternative Flow: It redirects to the view delivery man info page.

    Pre-Conditions: There must be delivery man info to maintain attendance for them.

    Post-Conditions: It redirects to the view delivery man info page.

22. **Check Orders**

    Description: It allows the delivery man to check orders in order to deliver them.
    Flow of Events

    Basic Flow: It must allow to check orders in order to deliver.

    Alternative Flow: It redirects to the home page.

    Pre-Conditions: There must be orders in order to check them to deliver.

    Post-Conditions: It redirects to the home page.

23. **Contact Delivery Address**

    Description: It allows the delivery man to contact the address of the customers to deliver them.
    Flow of Events

    Basic Flow: Allows to view address in order to deliver them.

    Alternative Flow: It redirects to the home page.

    Pre-Conditions: Address must be mentioned correctly to deliver them.

    Post-Conditions: It redirects to the home page.

24. **Delivered**

    Description: Delivery mentions the status that he delivered the order to the customer.
    Flow of Events

    Basic Flow: Order must be delivered in order to mention the status delivered.

Alternative Flow: It redirects to the contact delivery address page.
Pre-Conditions: Order must be delivered in order to mention the status delivered.
Post-Conditions: It redirects to the contact delivery address page.

25. **Not Delivered**
    Description: It allows the delivery man to update the status of not delivered.
    Flow of Events
Basic Flow: It allows the delivery man to update not delivered status.
Alternative Flow: It redirects to the contact delivery address page.
Pre-Conditions: It allows the delivery man to update not delivered status.
Post-Conditions: It redirects to the contact delivery address page.

26. **Reason for Not Delivered**
    Description: It allows the delivery man to mention why the order has not been delivered.
    Flow of Events
Basic Flow: Allow to mention the reason for not delivered.
Alternative Flow: It redirects to the not delivered page.
Pre-Conditions: Allow to mention the reason for not delivered.
Post-Conditions: It redirects to the not delivered page.

27. **Update/View Profile**
    Description: It allows the delivery man to edit/view his profile.
    Flow of Events
Basic Flow: It allows to edit profile.
Alternative Flow: It redirects to the home page.
Pre-Conditions: It allows to edit profile.
Post-Conditions: It redirects to the home page.

28. **View Attendance**
    Description: It allows the delivery man to view attendance.
    Flow of Events
Basic Flow: Allows to view attendance.
Alternative Flow: It redirects to the update/view profile page.
Pre-Conditions: Allows to view attendance.
Post-Conditions: It redirects to the update/view profile page

Chapter 25

Design of UML Diagrams for EQUIHEALTH

25.1 Problem Statement

This case study mainly focusses on developing an application to address the health disparities among the various classes of patients and the appropriate medical interventions in order to achieve health equity for every individual. The target users of the application are patients, caretakers, healthcare providers, medical professionals and government officials. One of the main functionalities of the system is a patient classification based on social determinants such as economic backgrounds, health insurance amount received, medical allowances, demographics, age, type of disability and hereditary health information. It has to be ensured that appropriate treatment is administered for the people of all categories in an equitable manner. The patient should be able to feed health details into the application that will be corroborated by the details furnished by the healthcare providers and the patient's public health records. Another important functionality is to notify the patients about the relevant medical events and health schemes available based on the system's categorization of the patient's data. The system also must provide personal health-tracking facilities for the patients by means of assessing the patients' individual medical records. The next function is to enable the healthcare providers such as hospitals and clinics to plan and schedule health worker activity based on the patient's need. Consequently, the application should make available the analysis of these data to the government, thereby assisting in the implementation of significant intervention schemes to offer medical facilities without any conflicts and eliminate the health discrepancies. Thus, with a holistic approach, the application should allow patients to register and upload social and medical data which get classified based on criteria that are then used by the healthcare providers and governments to extend healthcare to all individuals without any disparities.

Functionalities:

- Registration: The users of the application are registered with unique credentials and categorized as patients, health workers or a government authority.
- Login: The login section is for the users to login to the application using the unique credentials provided during the registration phase.
- Logout: The logout option is included in the user's user interface enabling the user to log out of the application at any time the user wants to.
- Data Entry: A section to enter all the medical details as well as the various social and economic details including unique identification details for the patient user and registered identification details for the health workers.
- Validation of Medical Data: The details entered by the patient will be corroborated by the details furnished by the respective hospital medical records of the patients.
- Patient Dashboard: A catered dashboard for every patient user with articles relating to the patient's present medical conditions and the possible ailments that the patient may be prone to, obtained by analysis of the patient's medical records. It also incorporates a search bar to search for specific articles relating to a medical term.
- Health Worker Dashboard: A dashboard for every health worker belonging to every registered medical institution that provides informative articles pertaining to the worker's area of specialization.
- Health Tracking: A section that provides a health-tracking facility by means of detailed analytics of the patient's individual health records furnished by the patient as well as the healthcare establishments from where the patient receives active treatment. This section also has provisions to synchronize the data from other health monitoring applications in the user's device and include them for health tracking.
- Alerts: Alerts are scheduled for all the users and dispatched to the patients whenever an activity is due such as a health checkup or a medical camp and dispatched to the health workers to catch up on a scheduled activity.
- Activity Scheduling: Activities of the health workers are scheduled according to the analysed requirements of the patients based on various medical and social factors and the progress of these planned activities can be tracked.
- Analytics: All the exhaustive data that goes into the application is analysed for patterns of medical disparities based on family and community issues and socio-economic determinants and a holistic report of this data is presented in the dashboard accessible to the authorized government authority to be used to bring about the appropriate health interventions.
- Health Financing: Using the application's analytics data, the government should be able to implement substantial schemes to bring forth health equity for all the affected individuals by initiating health financing schemes with various state-level agencies through an authorized section in the application (Figures 25.1–25.12).

25.2 System Architecture

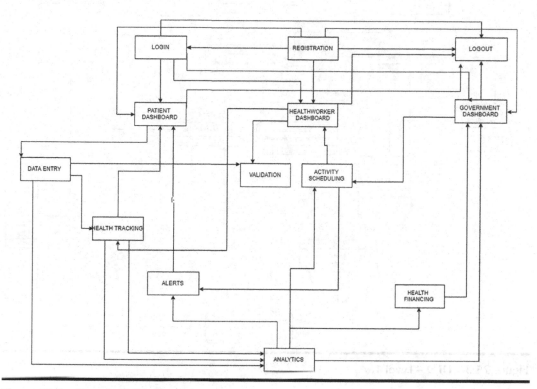

Figure 25.1   System architecture.

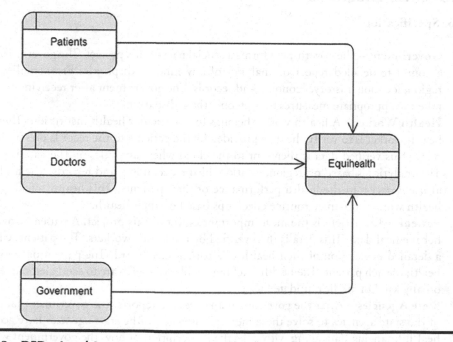

Figure 25.2   DFD – Level 0.

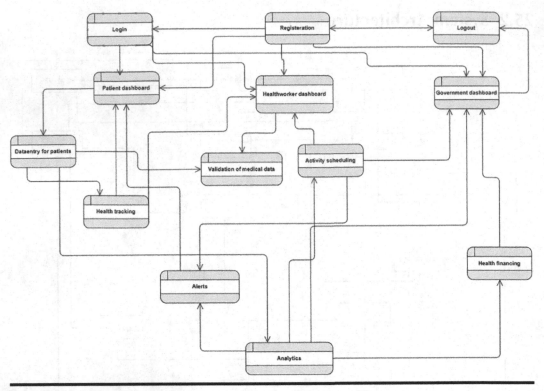

Figure 25.3   DFD – Level 1.

25.3 UML Diagrams

Actor Specification

1. **Government** – The government forms a crucial part of this project. The government receives a complete detailed report of analytics of any kind of disparities or anomalies based on region, location, history, economy and records. The government after receiving the data will take the appropriate measures to overcome these disparities.
2. **Health Worker** – A health worker belongs to a particular health institution. The job of the health worker is to verify the data provided by the patients to the records present in the hospital. This verified data is then sent to the cloud where analytics on the data is performed. The analytics is based on region, location, history, economy and records. The health worker also has access to the health performance of their patients. This health tracking helps the health workers organize routine check-ups based on their health.
3. **Patient** – The patient is the most important aspect of this project. A patient provides his or her medical data. This data is then verified by the health workers. The patient will be given a detailed description of their health in a patient dashboard. The patient dashboard tracks health of each patient. The health tracking enables the software to send alerts to the patients on any kind of medical update.
4. **State Agencies** – After the government analyses the reports, the government takes the help of the state agencies to solve these medical disparities. The state agencies have access to the health financing data along with a detailed description of how the government wants them to help. The state agencies have no access to the private data of the patient.

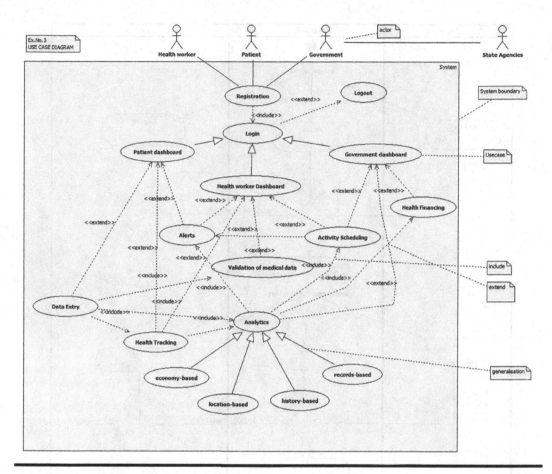

Figure 25.4   UML usecase diagram.

Usecase Specification

1. **Activity Scheduling**
       Description: This usecase is used to schedule activity for the health workers on the basis of the analyzed information in order to remove disparities'.
       Flow of Events
   Basic Flow: The activity scheduling usecase makes use of data from analytics usecase and generates a health worker schedule accordingly.
   Pre-Conditions: Data Entry and Analytics usecases should have been invoked.
   Post-Conditions: The activity schedule is displayed on the health worker dashboard.
2. **Alerts**
       Description: Alerts are scheduled for all the users and dispatched to the patients whenever an activity is due such as a health checkup or a medical camp and dispatched to the health workers to catch up on a scheduled activity.
       Flow of Events
   Basic Flow: Based upon the activity schedule and the data analytics, appropriate alerts are sent to the users.
   Pre-Conditions: Activity Scheduling and Analytics usecases must be invoked.
   Post-Conditions: The alerts are displayed on the patient or the health worker's dashboard.

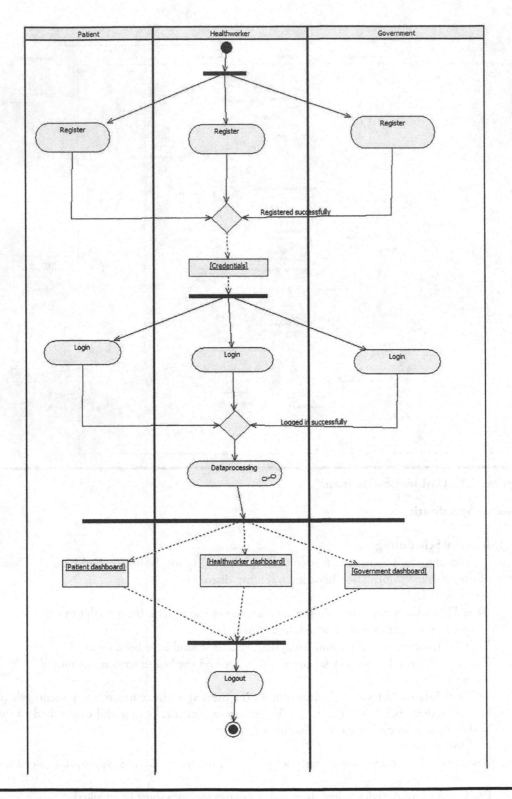

Figure 25.5 UML activity diagram – Part (1).

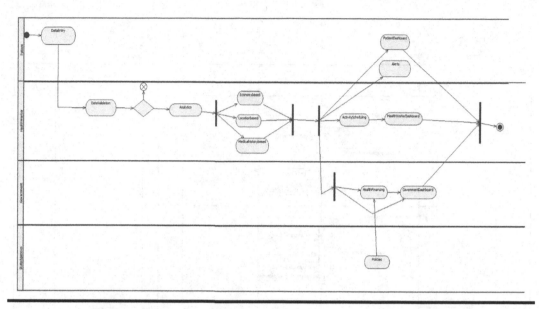

Figure 25.6   UML activity diagram – Part (2).

3. **Analytics**

Description: All the exhaustive data that goes into the application is analyzed for patterns of medical disparities based on family and community issues and socio-economic determinants.

Flow of Events

Basic Flow: The data entered into the application is analyzed and categorized based on several factors and sent to the other usecases and results from those usecases are combined to obtain a holistic report.

Alternate Flow: The data is categorized into Economy-, Location-, History- and Records-based classifications.

Pre-Conditions: Data Entry and Health Tracking usecases must be invoked.

Post-Conditions: The report of the analyzed data is sent for activity scheduling and health financing alerts and the report details are displayed on the government dashboard.

4. **Data Entry**

Description: A section to enter all the medical details as well as the various social and economic details including unique identification details for the patient user and for registered identification details for the health workers.

Flow of Events

Basic Flow: Various fields are provided for the user to feed the medical data into the application.

Pre-Conditions: Login and Registration usecases must be invoked.

Post-Conditions: The data collected from the patients are sent for validation and following the validation, the data is given to health tracking and analytics usecases.

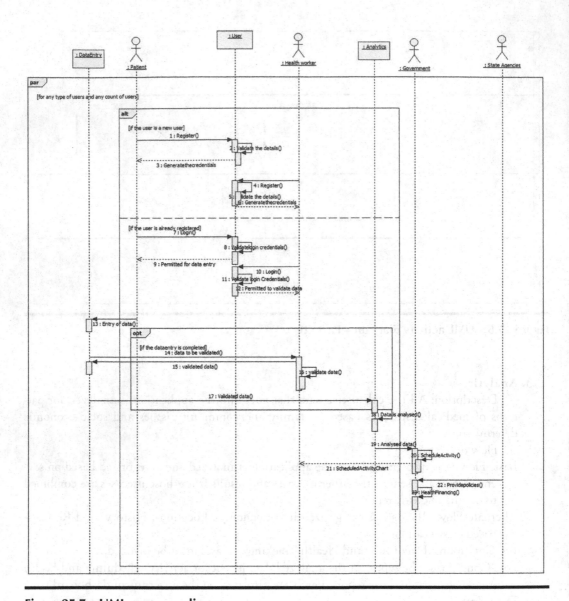

Figure 25.7   UML sequence diagram.

5. **Government Dashboard**

Description: A holistic report of the analyzed data is presented in the dashboard accessible to the authorized government authority to be used to bring about the appropriate health interventions.

Flow of Events

Basic Flow: The analyzed data is illustrated with graphical representations in the interface for the government that can be used to implement the appropriate health intervention schemes.

Pre-Conditions: Data Entry and Analytics usecases must be invoked.

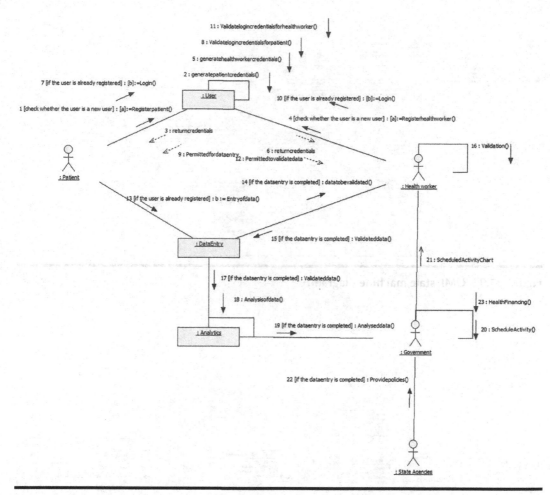

Figure 25.8   UML collaboration diagram.

6. **Health Financing**

   Description: Using the application's analytics data, the government should be able to implement substantial schemes to bring forth health equity for all the affected individuals by initiating health financing schemes with various state-level agencies through an authorized section in the application.

   Flow of Events

   Basic Flow: Provides the options for implementing health financing schemes for the government in collaboration with state agencies.

   Pre-Conditions: Data Entry and Analytics usecases must be invoked.

   Post-Conditions: The various health financing requirements are displayed in the government dashboard.

7. **Health Tracking**

   Description: A section that provides a health-tracking facility by means of detailed analytics of the patient's individual health records furnished by the patient as well as the healthcare establishments from where the patient receives active treatment.

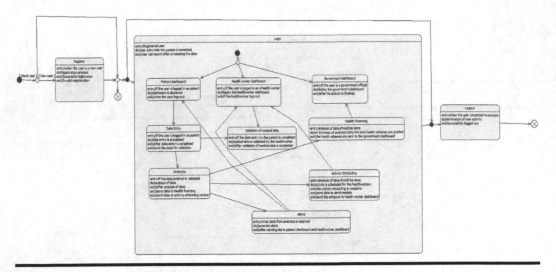

Figure 25.9 UML state machine diagram.

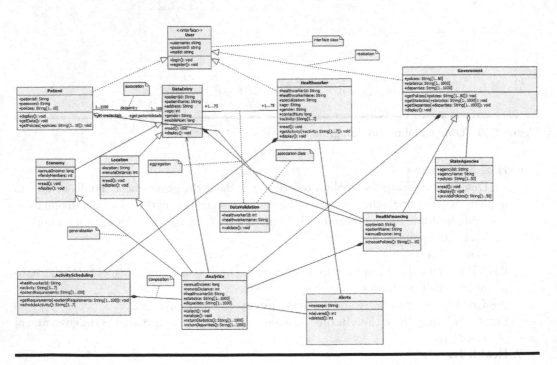

Figure 25.10 UML class diagram.

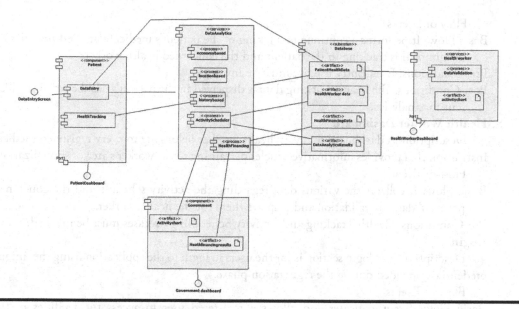

Figure 25.11   UML component diagram.

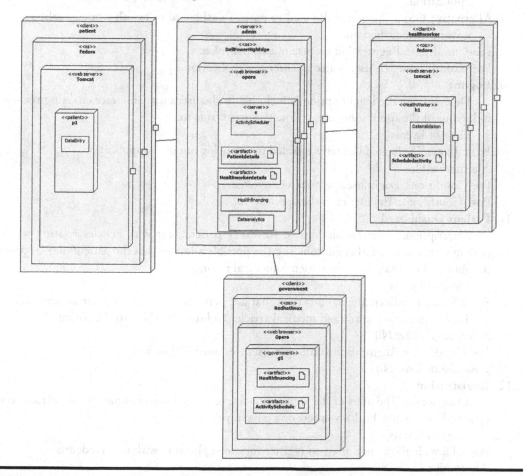

Figure 25.12   UML deployment diagram.

Flow of Events

Basic Flow: It performs a continuous tracking of the patient's medical data and provides an insight of this tracking to the patient and the concerned health workers.

Pre-Conditions: Data Entry usecase must be invoked.

Post-Conditions: The health-tracking data is displayed in the patient's dashboard and is also sent for analytics.

8. **Health Worker Dashboard**

Description: A dashboard for every health worker belonging to every registered medical institution that provides informative articles pertaining to the worker's area of specialization.

Flow of Events

Basic Flow: It collects the various data regarding the activity schedule and the concerned patients' data for validation and displays them for the health worker.

Pre-Conditions: Health Tracking and Activity Scheduling usecases must be invoked.

9. **Login**

Description: The login section is for the users to login to the application using the unique credentials provided during the registration phase.

Flow of Events

Basic Flow: It authenticates and allows a registered user to access the facilities of the application.

Alternative Flow: The user is directed to patient dashboard or health worker dashboard or government dashboard.

Pre-Conditions: Registration usecase must be invoked.

Post-Conditions: The user is able to enter the application.

10. **Logout**

Description: The logout option is included in the user's user interface enabling the user to log out of the application at any time the user wants to.

Flow of Events

Basic Flow: The logged in user is enabled to safely log out of the application.

Alternative Flow: Nil.

Pre-Conditions: Login usecase must be invoked.

Post-Conditions: The user exits the application.

11. **Patient Dashboard**

Description: A catered dashboard for every patient user with articles relating to the patient's present medical conditions and the possible ailments that the patient may be prone to, obtained by analysis of the patient's medical records.

Flow of Events

Basic Flow: It collects the various data that are pertinent to the particular patient such as health-tracking records and medical articles and displays them to the patient.

Alternative Flow: Nil.

Pre-Conditions: Registration and Login usecases must be invoked.

Post-Conditions: Nil.

12. **Registration**

Description: The users of the application are registered with unique credentials and categorized as patients, health workers or a government authority.

Flow of Events

Basic Flow: It allows new users to register for the application with new credentials.

Alternative Flow: Nil.

Pre-Conditions: Internet connectivity is required.

Post-Conditions: The user is directed to the login page.

13. **Validation of Medical Data**

    Description: The details entered by the patient will be corroborated by the details furnished by the respective hospital medical records of the patients.

    Flow of Events

    Basic Flow: The data obtained from the patients is validated by the health workers using the patient's medical records.

    Alternative Flow: Nil.

    Pre-Conditions: Data entry usecase must be invoked.

    Post-Conditions: The validated medical data is sent to the analytics and health-tracking modules.

14. **Economy-based**

    Description: This usecase is used to do a deep data analysis based on the economic data provided by the user.

    Flow of Events

    Basic Flow: Here, the data are classified based on the user's annual income, money previously spent on medical treatments and parent's income.

    Alternative Flow: Nil.

    Pre-Conditions: Data entry usecase must be invoked.

    Post-Conditions: The report of the analysis is sent to the analytics usecase.

15. **History-based**

    Description: This usecase analyses data based on the medical history of the patient.

    Flow of Events

    Basic Flow: Here, the data is analyzed based on patient's medical data along with the hereditary medical data of their family members.

    Alternative Flow: Nil.

    Pre-Conditions: Data entry usecase must be invoked.

    Post-Conditions: The report of the analysis is sent to the analytics usecase.

16. **Location-based**

    Description: This usescase analyses the data based on the geographical location of the patients.

    Flow of Events

    Basic Flow: Here a detailed analysis is done based on the demographic details of the patients.

    Alternative Flow: Nil.

    Pre-Conditions: Data entry usecase must be invoked.

    Post-Conditions: The report of the analysis is sent to the analytics usecase.

17. **Records-based**

    Description: This usescase analyses the data based on the present medical data of the patients.

    Flow of Events

    Basic Flow: Here a collective analysis is done based on the current medical data of the patients.

    Alternative Flow: Nil.

    Pre-Conditions: Data entry usecase must be invoked.

    Post-Conditions: The report of the analysis is sent to the analytics usecase.

Chapter 26

Design of UML Diagrams for an OTT-Based System – MINI REEL

26.1 Problem Statement

An over-the-top (OTT) media service is a streaming media service offered directly to viewers via the internet. The OTT media can be streamed anywhere with just the use of an internet connection. The scope of this project lies in the maximised use of the internet by the current generation. The system aims at providing a fun-filled and informative services that they would be able to access easily from their place. This system includes streaming of shows and movies that could be viewed by the users and an administrator governing the updates in the OTT based on the schedule of the show or movie release. Users can have a trial package of the services offered for 1 month and further subscriptions are based on the amount paid categorised as normal users and premium users. Creating an account involves payment to the services provided. Hence the trial users could use the trial package for a month and create an account for them maintaining a secret password that makes their account safe from other people accessing it. The premium users have the privilege of providing suggestions of the shows in the discussion room. All the users should be provided with the facility of a chat room where the users can chat and express their views and comments. The administrator will have control over the shows broadcasted and maintain a proper timeline of the shows, movies and live shows. News feeds highlighting the recent updates in the world will also be available in MINIREELS in a brief format. Users can also add their favourite videos to LIKES list and watch them whenever needed (Figures 26.1–26.8).

DOI: 10.1201/9781003287124-26

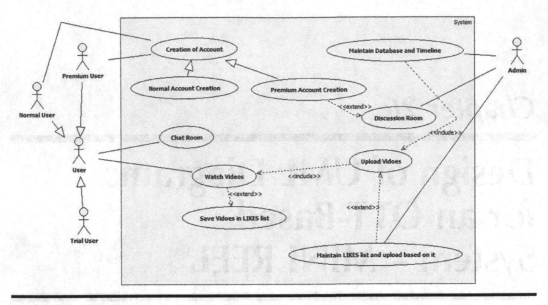

Figure 26.1 UML usecase diagram.

26.2 UML Diagrams

Actor Specification

1. **Administrator** – Takes care of all updates of shows and movies along with database maintenance.
2. **Normal User** – Watch shows and movies streamed upon creation of an account by paying a specified amount.
3. **Trial User** – Watch shows and movies streamed without account creation and use the trial service for a month.
4. **Premium User** – Watch shows and movies streamed upon creation of an account by paying amount higher than the normal user.
5. **User** – Premium user, trial user and normal user are generalized as users who can watch movies, show and use chat room.

Usecase Specification

1. **Maintain Database and Follow Timeline Scheduled**
   Description: Maintain a proper database and schedule the update of shows, movies, etc.
   Flow of Events
   Basic Flow: Maintain the database.
   Alternative Flow: Nil.
   Pre-Conditions: Nil.
   Post-Conditions: Update shows and movies based on the database.
2. **Discussion Room**
   Description: A chat room where only premium users can provide suggestions or complaints to the administrator directly.
   Flow of Events
   Basic Flow: Discussion Room.

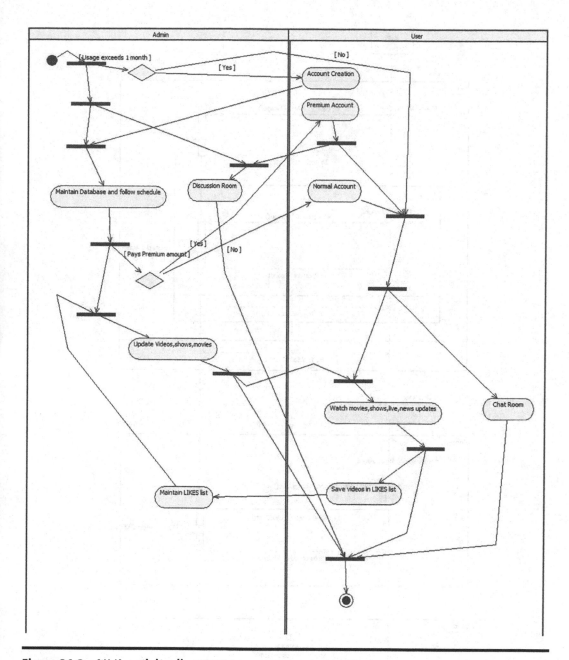

Figure 26.2   UML activity diagram.

Alternative Flow: Nil.

Pre-Conditions: Creation of Premium Account.

Post-Conditions: Nil.

3. **Update Shows, Movies, Live Stream and Recent News**

Description: Update the shows, movies or news based on a schedule maintained so that users can watch it.

Flow of Events

Basic Flow: Update of shows and movies.

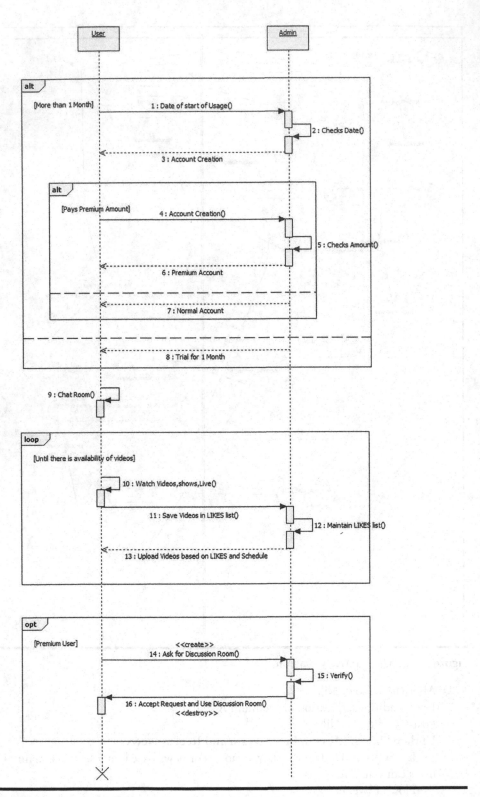

Figure 26.3   UML sequence diagram.

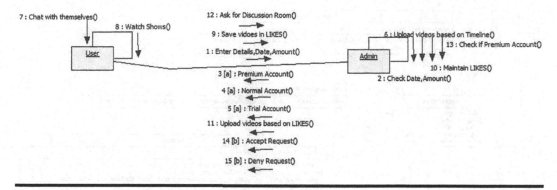

Figure 26.4 UML collaboration diagram.

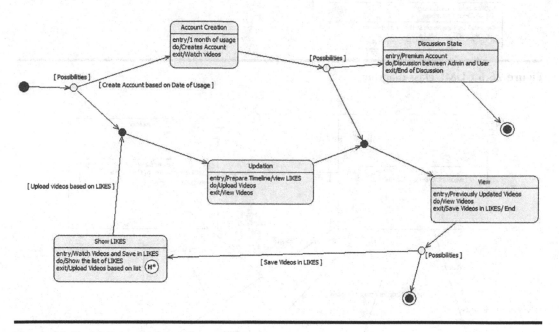

Figure 26.5 UML state chart diagram.

Alternative Flow: Nil.

Pre-Conditions: Maintain a proper database and schedule the updates.

Post-Conditions: Users watch the updated shows, movies, news, etc.

4. **Maintain LIKES List for Every User and Upload Videos Based on It**

Description: Maintain a LIKES list for every user and upload videos based on it so that it would interest the users.

Flow of Events

Basic Flow: Maintain LIKES list.

Alternative Flow: Normal Update of shows, movies, etc.

Pre-Conditions: Users save videos in the LIKES list.

Post-Conditions: Update of videos.

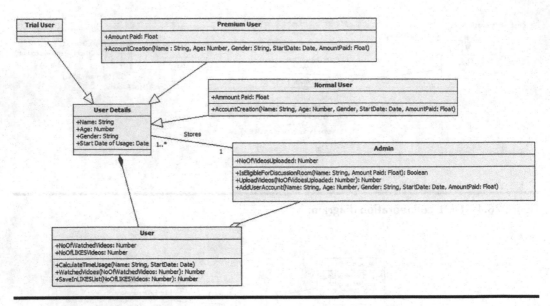

Figure 26.6   UML class diagram.

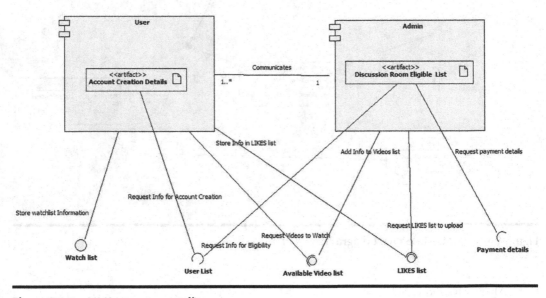

Figure 26.7   UML component diagram.

5. **Creation of Account**

   Description: Normal and premium users create a account by paying a specified amount and enjoy the services.

   Flow of Events

   Basic Flow: Creation of account.

   Alternative Flow: For 1 month, no account need to be created. Users can use the trial version.

   Pre-Conditions: Nil.

   Post-Conditions: Users can watch videos and use chat room.

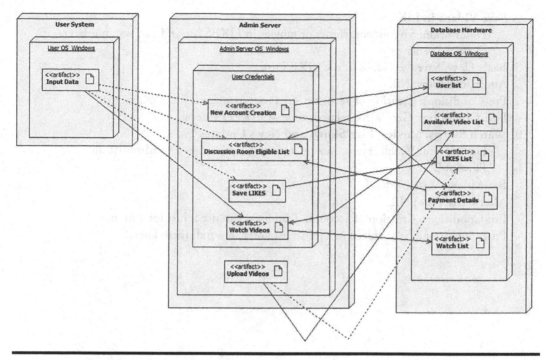

Figure 26.8 UML deployment diagram.

6. **Premium Account Creation**

   Description: Creates an account for premium users by paying an amount higher than the normal user.

   Flow of Events

   Basic Flow: Creation of Premium account.

   Alternative Flow: Nil.

   Pre-Conditions: Nil.

   Post-Conditions: Watch videos and can use discussion rooms where they can discuss about suggestions and complaints.

7. **Normal Account Creation**

   Description: Creates an account for normal users by paying a specified amount.

   Flow of Events

   Basic Flow: Normal account creation.

   Alternative Flow: Nil.

   Pre-Conditions: Nil.

   Post-Conditions: Watch videos and use chat room to chat with other users.

8. **Chat Room**

   Description: A room where users can chat among themselves.

   Flow of Events

   Basic Flow: Chat room.

   Alternative Flow: Nil.

   Pre-Conditions: Nil.

   Post-Conditions: Creation of account. Trial users can enjoy it only for a month.

9. **Save Videos in LIKES**

   Description: Save videos, shows or movies in LIKES list and can watch it later.
   Flow of Events

   Basic Flow: Save the videos in the LIKES list.

   Alternative Flow: Nil.

   Pre-Conditions: Creation of account. Trial users can use it just for a month.

   Post-Conditions: Get videos related to those LIKED videos.

10. **Watch Shows, Movies, Live Shows and News Updates**

    Description: Watch shows, movies and news updated by the administrator.
    Flow of Events

    Basic Flow: Watch videos.

    Alternative Flow: Nil.

    Pre-Conditions: Creation of account. Trial users can use it just for a month.

    Post-Conditions: Save videos in LIKES list and can watch them later.

Chapter 27

Design of UML Diagrams for e-Med Medical Assistance Tool

27.1 Problem Statement

e-Med is your perfect medical friend. We often see our grandparents forgetting to take their medicines or getting tensed when they run out of medical supplies. In this fast-paced world with unhealthy lifestyles, a number of young people also have some medical issues. e-Med is a tool that helps keep track of and address all your personal medical needs. Once the data is fed regarding the schedule of intake of medicines, this tool will provide reminders for taking the medicines. It will also send notifications to restock the medicines. It is also programmed to schedule monthly or yearly appointments regularly with the family doctor. Another interesting feature of this tool is that during critical situations, pressing the emergency button will automatically contact your near and dear ones whose contacts are in your emergency contact list. The tool helps in keeping a record of your medical history such as your blood sugar levels, pressure levels, etc. by using the Medical Notes feature. e-Med is an indispensable tool for people of all ages with medical issues to help maintain a good health routine (Figures 27.1–27.8).

27.2 UML Diagrams

Actor Specification

1. **Customers/Users** – The users of this tool are people of all ages with chronic health issues who need to take medicines regularly to keep themselves healthy. Users must record their medical history and update medical history whenever required. The users can schedule appointments regularly with their doctor. They can press the emergency button when a critical situation arises. They can also write and update medical notes.

DOI: 10.1201/9781003287124-27

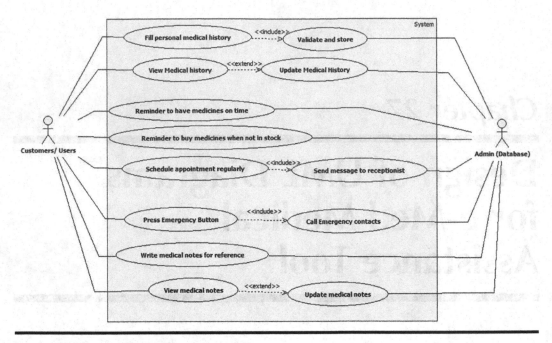

Figure 27.1   UML usecase diagram.

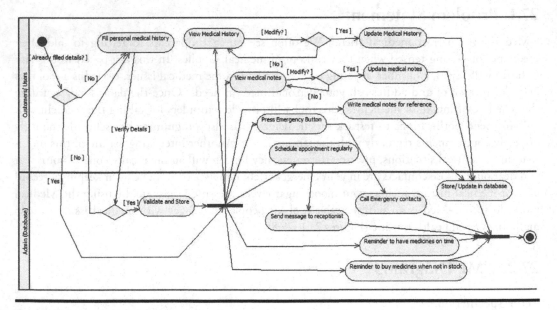

Figure 27.2   UML activity diagram.

2. **Admin (Database)** – The database stores all the information about the users, their medical history, notes, etc. It initiates operations like sending notifications when it is time for the users to take their medicine or restock medicines. It also sends a message to the receptionist to schedule an appointment and calls the emergency contacts as soon as the emergency button is pressed.

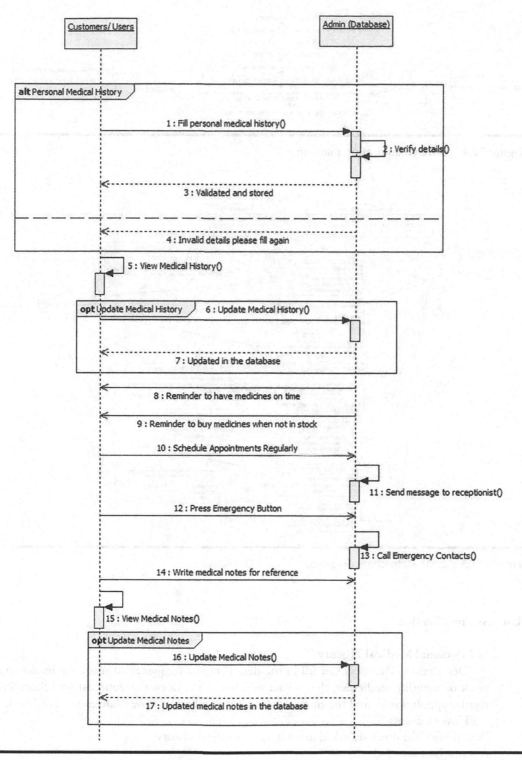

Figure 27.3   UML sequence diagram.

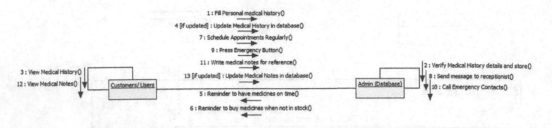

Figure 27.4   UML collaboration diagram.

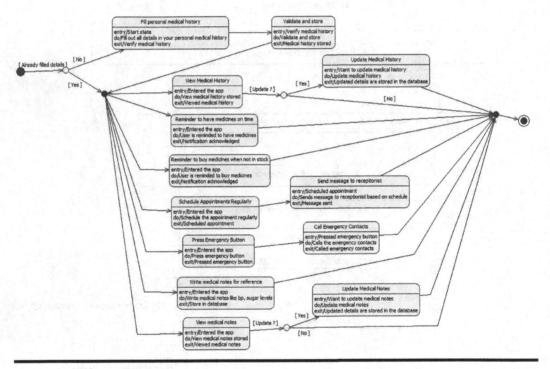

Figure 27.5   UML state chart diagram.

Usecase Specification

1. Fill Personal Medical History

Description: The users can fill in the details of the frequency of medicine intake, the stock of monthly medicines, the contact number of the doctor/receptionist for scheduling regular appointments and the emergency contact numbers of close relatives and neighbours.

Flow of Events

Basic Flow: The users are asked to fill in their medical history.

Alternative Flow: Nil.

Pre-Conditions: Nil.

Post-Conditions: The details entered by the user must be validated.

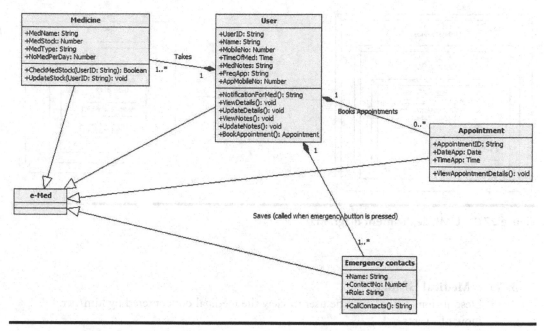

Figure 27.6   UML class diagram.

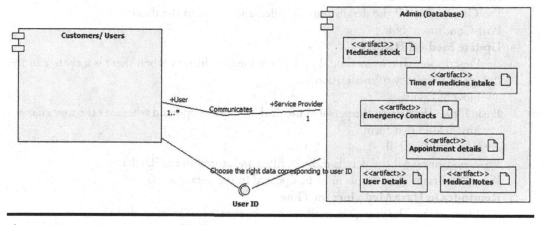

Figure 27.7   UML component diagram.

2. **Validate and Store**

Description: The personal medical history of the user is validated and stored in the database.

Flow of Events

Basic Flow: The details entered by the user in their personal medical history are validated and stored in the database.

Alternative Flow: If the details are incorrect, the user has to re-enter the data in the fields with incorrect data.

Pre-Conditions: All the required details must be filled and verified before storing them in the database.

Post-Conditions: Nil.

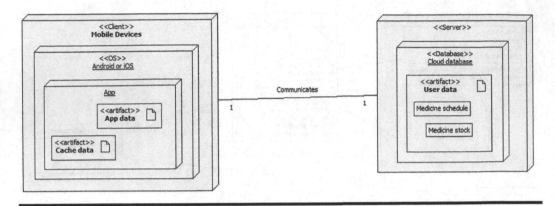

Figure 27.8 **UML deployment diagram.**

3. **View Medical History**
   Description: This allows the user to view the medical data entered by him/her.
   Flow of Events
Basic Flow: The user can view the details that he/she filled in their medical history.
Alternative Flow: Nil.
Pre-Conditions: All the details must be filled and stored in the database.
Post-Conditions: Nil.

4. **Update Medical History**
   Description: The users should update the medical history when there is a change in the dosage or frequency of medication.
   Flow of Events
Basic Flow: The data in the personal medical history are updated whenever the user changes any field in that form.
Alternative Flow: Nil.
Pre-Conditions: All the details must be filled and stored in the database.
Post-Conditions: The details must be updated in the database.

5. **Reminder to Have Medicines on Time**
   Description: The app gives notifications for timely intake of medicines.
   Flow of Events
Basic Flow: The users are reminded to have their medicines on time.
Alternative Flow: Nil.
Pre-Conditions: The user must have filled the details regarding the schedule of intake of medicines in his/her personal medical history.
Post-Conditions: Nil.

6. **Reminder to Buy Medicines When Not in Stock**
   Description: The app tracks the stock of medicines and reminds the user to restock the medicines that would not last for more than a few days.
   Flow of Events
Basic Flow: The users are reminded to buy medicines when they are out of stock.
Alternative Flow: Nil.

Pre-Conditions: The user must have filled in the details regarding the stock of medicines at the moment and the number of medicines he/she takes daily in his/her personal medical history.

Post-Conditions: Nil.

7. **Schedule Appointments Regularly**

Description: e-Med schedules appointment regularly with the doctor.

Flow of Events

Basic Flow: The app schedules appointments after a fixed period of time by sending a message to the doctor/receptionist.

Alternative Flow: Nil.

Pre-Conditions: The number of appointments with the doctor in a year (like once in 6 months, once a month, etc.) must be stored

Post-Conditions: Message should be sent to the doctor/receptionist to book an appointment.

8. **Send Messages to Receptionist**

Description: It regularly sends a message to the receptionist for the booking of appointments.

Flow of Events

Basic Flow: The app sends a message to the receptionist/doctor to book appointments.

Alternative Flow: Nil.

Pre-Conditions: The receptionist/doctor's contact number must be saved in the app.

Post-Conditions: Nil.

9. **Press Emergency Button**

Description: The users can press the emergency button when in serious condition.

Flow of Events

Basic Flow: When an emergency situation arises, the users can press this button to call for help immediately.

Alternative Flow: Nil.

Pre-Conditions: Nil.

Post-Conditions: The app should call the emergency contacts right after the button is pressed.

10. **Call Emergency Contacts**

Description: As soon as the emergency button is pressed, the app calls all the emergency contacts.

Flow of Events

Basic Flow: The emergency contacts are called after the emergency button is pressed.

Alternative Flow: Nil.

Pre-Conditions: The contact numbers of close relatives and neighbours must be saved as emergency contacts.

Post-Conditions: Nil.

11. **Write Medical Notes for Reference**

Description: Medical notes such as sugar levels, pressure levels etc. can be recorded here.

Flow of Events

Basic Flow: Users can write any medical details that they wish to keep track of in the medical notes.

Alternative Flow: Nil.

Pre-Conditions: Nil.

Post-Conditions: It must be stored in the database as soon as the notes are saved.

12. **View Medical Notes**

    Description: Users can view the medical notes to monitor sugar or pressure levels.

    Flow of Events

Basic Flow: The user can view the details that he/she wrote in their medical notes.

Alternative Flow: Nil.

Pre-Conditions: All the details written by the user in the medical notes must be stored in the database.

Post-Conditions: Nil.

13. **Update Medical Notes**

    Description: Users may update medical notes after taking another sugar level or pressure level reading.

    Flow of Events

Basic Flow: The data in the medical notes are updated whenever the user changes it.

Alternative Flow: Nil.

Pre-Conditions: All the details written by the user in the medical notes must be stored in the database.

Post-Conditions: The updated notes must be stored in the database.

Chapter 28

Design of UML Diagrams for Diet Care

28.1 Problem Statement

Health is wealth. Health plays a major role in everyone's life. People consume unhealthy food and ruin their diet. Some medication results in side effects. This application benefits people with rich nutrients to improve their health. The application provides recommendations of nutrients they need. Users can provide their daily diet cycle and get good recommendations to improve it. They can also provide their medical reports to get nutrients according to their medical state. The user also gets the privilege to enter the disease name and get the nutrient benefit for fighting that disease. Users can ping professional nutritionists for more clarification. Users are authenticated and recommendation is provided by a trained machine learning model (Figures 28.1–28.10).

28.2 UML Diagrams

Actor Specification

1. **Data Base** – A system that maintains the collection of organized data.
2. **Professional Nutritionist** – A person who is an expert in nutrition science and can solve user's issues.
3. **System** – An Interface that accepts user's request and provides the result to user.
4. **Trained Model** – Machine learning model that can suggest the healthy diet.
5. **User** – People who are making use of this application.

Usecase Specification

1. **Analysis**
   Description: Finding the malnutrition and disease/deficiency from users' data.
   Flow of Events
   Basic Flow: Scan user input and find terms that match malnutrition food or any disease name.

DOI: 10.1201/9781003287124-28

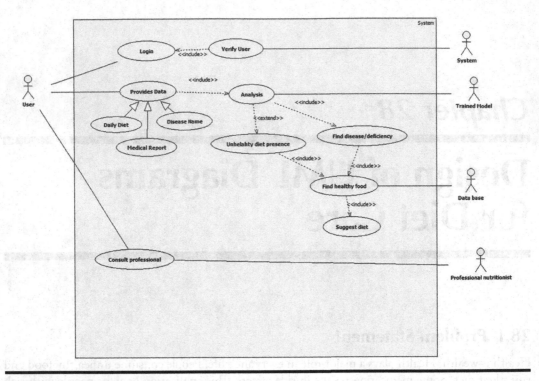

Figure 28.1 UML usecase diagram.

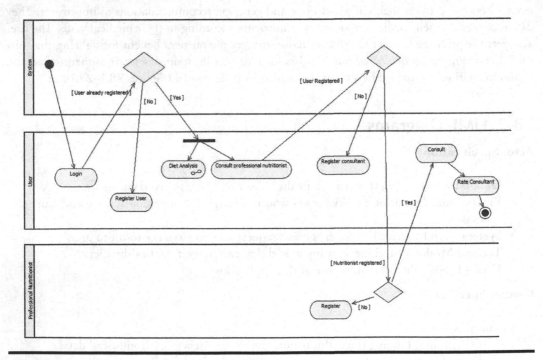

Figure 28.2 UML activity diagram – Scenario 1.

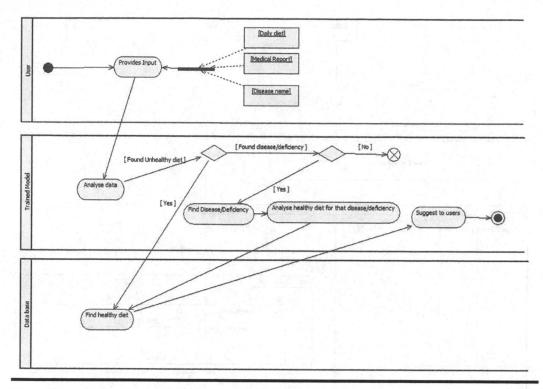

Figure 28.3 UML activity diagram – Scenario 2.

Alternative Flow: Nil.
Pre-Conditions: Valid user's data must be present.
Post-Conditions: Analyse data and find malnutrition or disease/deficiency terms.

2. **Consult Professional Nutritionist**
    Description: Getting to know more about nutrition topics.
    Flow of Events
   Basic Flow: User can contact any professionals through user's ID.
   Alternative Flow: Nil.
   Pre-Conditions: User's should be registered, and professionals have to be available.
   Post-Conditions: User can rate/thank professionals.

3. **Daily Diet**
    Description: User's routine diet.
    Flow of Events
   Basic Flow: User inputs his/her daily diet.
   Alternative Flow: Nil.
   Pre-Conditions: Nil.
   Post-Conditions: Data is processed for analysis.

4. **Disease Name**
    Description: Provide the name of any disease for medication.
    Flow of Events
   Basic Flow: Enter disease name.

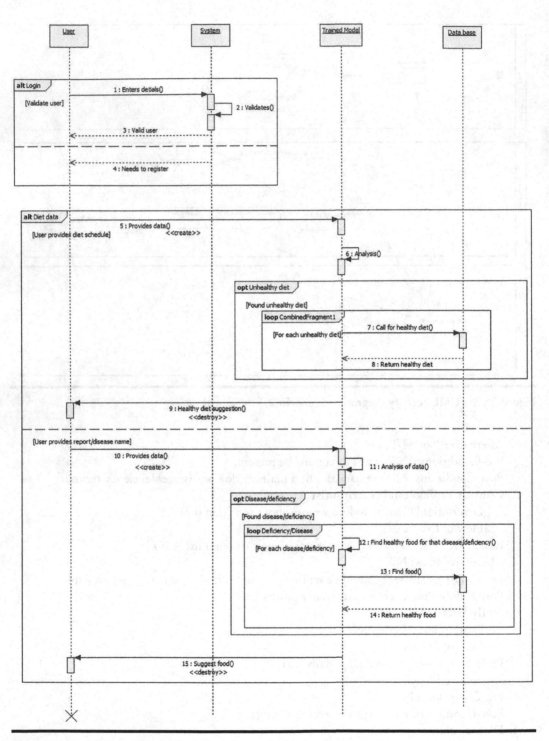

Figure 28.4   UML sequence diagram – Scenario 1.

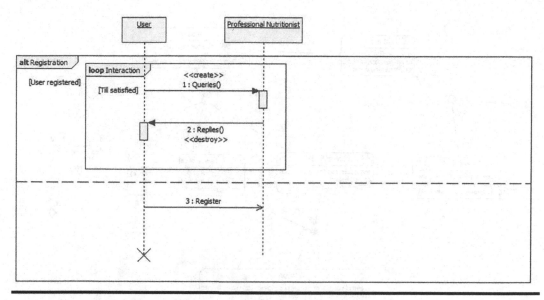

Figure 28.5   UML sequence diagram – Scenario 2.

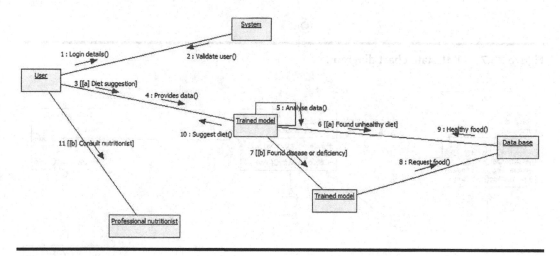

Figure 28.6   UML collaboration diagram.

Alternative Flow: Nil.
Pre-Conditions: Nil.
Post-Conditions: Data are processed for analysis.

5. **Find Disease/Deficiency**
    Description: Find the name of disease/deficiency from user's analyzed data.
    Flow of Events
Basic Flow: Find the name of disease/deficiency from user's analyzed data.
Alternative Flow: Nil.
Pre-Conditions: User's data have to be analyzed, disease/deficiency should be present.
Post-Conditions: Suggest a healthy diet.

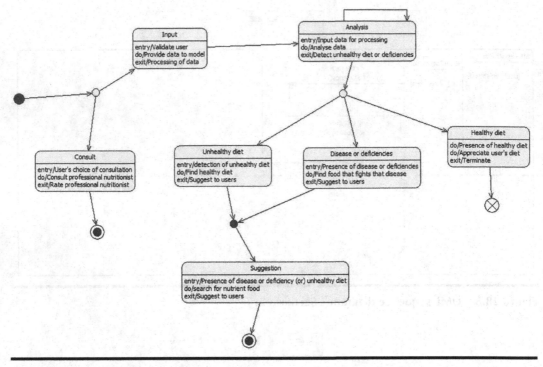

Figure 28.7   UML state chart diagram.

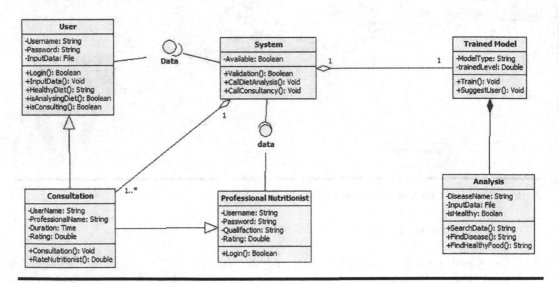

Figure 28.8   UML class diagram.

6. **Find Healthy Food**

Description: Find healthy food that fights corresponding disease or deficiency.

Flow of Events

Basic Flow: Searched food with specific nutrition to fight that disease/deficiency.

Alternative Flow: Nil.

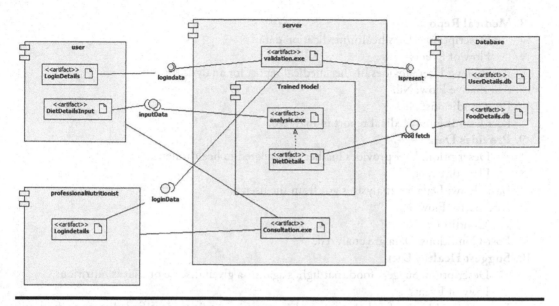

Figure 28.9   UML component diagram.

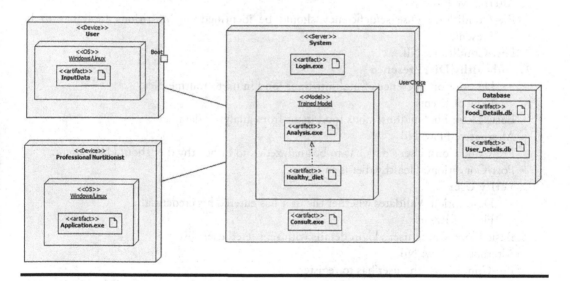

Figure 28.10   UML deployment diagram.

Pre-Conditions: Presence of disease or deficiency or unhealthy diet.
Post-Conditions: Suggest to users.

7. **Login**

Description: Identification of user.
Flow of Events

Basic Flow: User enters his/her credentials.
Alternative Flow: Register user.
Pre-Conditions: Nil.
Post-Conditions: User is assigned an identification.

8. **Medical Report**
   Description: User's health/medication data.
   Flow of Events
   Basic Flow: User provides his/her medical report for analysis.
   Alternative Flow: Nil.
   Pre-Conditions: Nil.
   Post-Conditions: Medical report is analyzed.

9. **Provides Data**
   Description: User provides his/her data related to health/diet.
   Flow of Events
   Basic Flow: Data for analysis is got from the user.
   Alternative Flow: Nil.
   Pre-Conditions: Nil.
   Post-Conditions: Data are analyzed.

10. **Suggest Healthy Diet**
    Description: Suggest food that fight's against a given disease or that is nutritious.
    Flow of Events
    Basic Flow: Identify food that is good in nutrition against identified disease or find any healthy food in place of malnutritious food.
    Alternative Flow: Nil.
    Pre-Conditions: Disease/deficiency should be identified, malnutritious food has to be present.
    Post-Conditions: Nil.

11. **Unhealthy Diet Presence**
    Description: Presence of malnutritious food in user's routine diet.
    Flow of Events
    Basic Flow: Find malnutritious food items from analyzed data.
    Alternative Flow: Nil.
    Pre-Conditions: User's data has to be analyzed, and unhealthy diet should be present.
    Post-Conditions: Healthy diet is suggested.

12. **Verify User**
    Description: Validates whether the user has entered his credentials.
    Flow of Events
    Basic Flow: Check user's login details with registered users list.
    Alternative Flow: Nil.
    Pre-Conditions: The user has to register.
    Post-Conditions: User can get diet suggestion or user can interact with professionals.

Chapter 29

Design of UML Diagrams for Student Counselling Management System

29.1 Problem Statement

The first phase of a person's life is confined mainly by education and training. Hence, counselling is an important aspect for the students of the current technological generation as an individual counsellor may remain in contact with all individual students as well as parents. Student Counselling Management System will simplify the process and reduce the manual paperwork. It is used to smoothen the work of each counsellor who is facing problems currently, and making complete atomization of manual process to computerized system. The main objective of the Student Counselling Management System is to design a system to rationalize the admission to particular courses in a university/institution. Through this system, the student will be able to register for counselling if he is eligible. If the student is qualifying the criteria then he will get the information regarding the colleges and the universities in which he can apply. The main features are online admission, report generation based on student's merit list and keeping track of counselling procedures and finally publishing results. A student can also get the information regarding how many seats have been booked and vacant seats available in the institution (Figures 29.1–29.8).

29.2 UML Diagrams

Actor Specification

1. **Student** – Student is the one who initiates the process by registering and filling choices.
2. **Admin Team** – Admin Team is the one that responds to students' submissions of forms and choice sheets and is also responsible for seat allotment.
3. **College** – College is the one that collects admit letters from admin team and decides whether or not to accept the student.

DOI: 10.1201/9781003287124-29

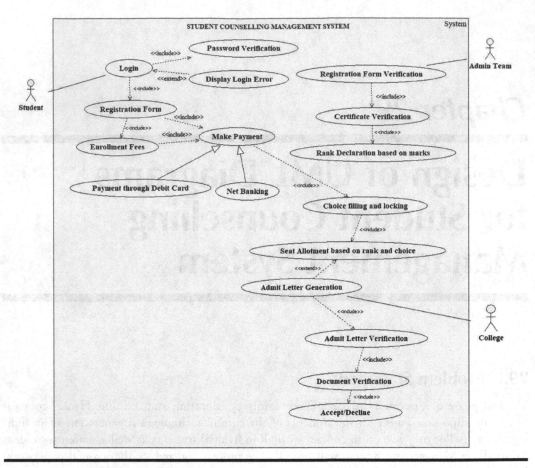

Figure 29.1   UML usecase diagram.

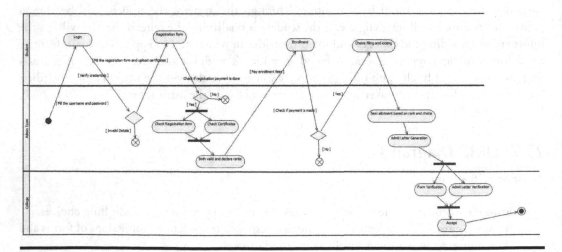

Figure 29.2   UML activity diagram.

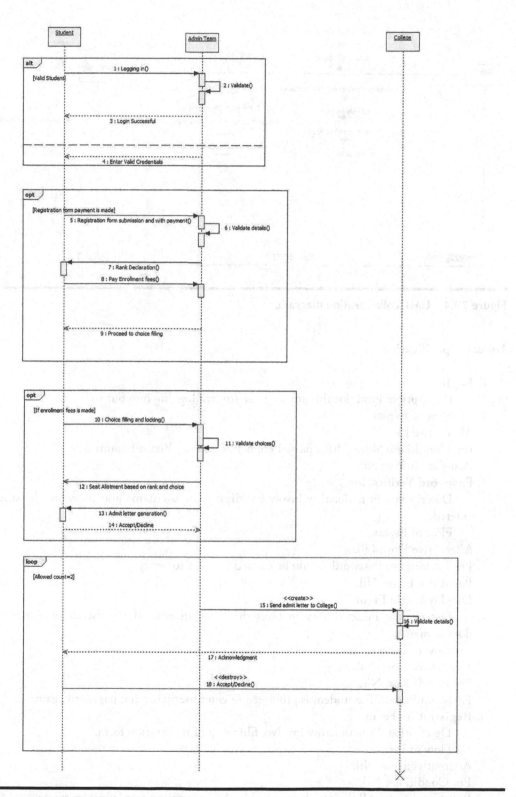

Figure 29.3 UML sequence diagram.

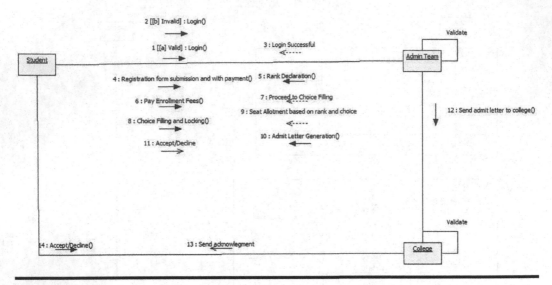

Figure 29.4 UML collaboration diagram.

Usecase Specification

1. **Login**
   Description: Functionality involves the student logging into our website.
   Flow of Events
   Alternative Flow: Nil.
   Pre-Conditions: Should have passed Higher Secondary Board Examinations.
   Post-Conditions: Nil.

2. **Password Verification**
   Description: Functionality involves verifying the username and password the student entered.
   Flow of Events
   Alternative Flow: Nil.
   Pre-Conditions: Password should be entered in order to verify.
   Post-Conditions: Nil.

3. **Display Login Error**
   Description: Functionality involves throwing an error if the username or password doesn't match.
   Flow of Events
   Alternative Flow: Nil.
   Pre-Conditions: Nil.
   Post-Conditions: The student is prompted to enter username and password again.

4. **Registration Form**
   Description: Functionality involves filling up of registration form.
   Flow of Events
   Alternative Flow: Nil.
   Pre-Conditions: Nil.
   Post-Conditions: All the details specified in the registration form must be entered.

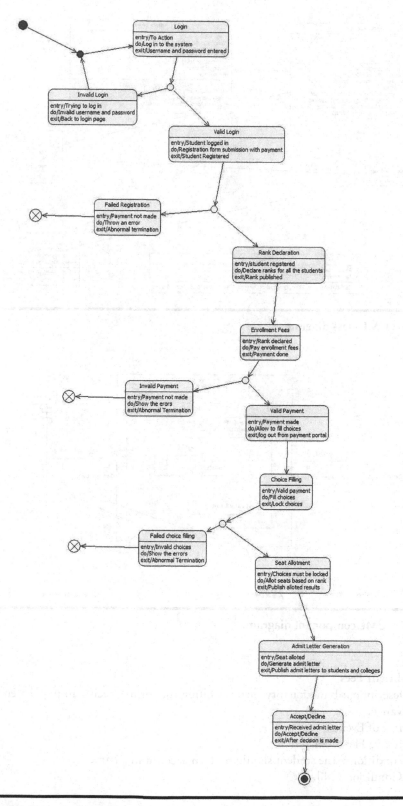

Figure 29.5 UML state chart diagram.

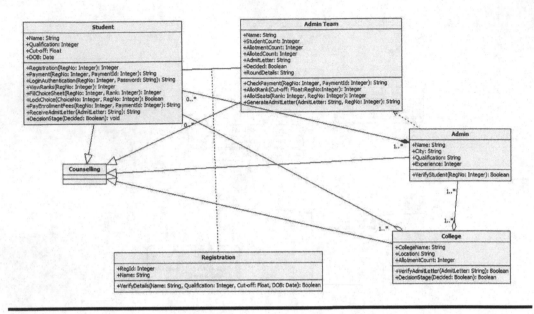

Figure 29.6   UML class diagram.

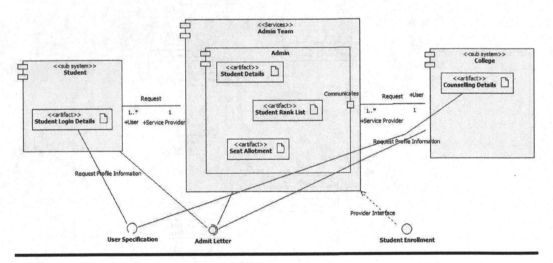

Figure 29.7   UML component diagram.

5. **Enrolment Fees**
      Description: Functionality involves filling the form agreeing to pay the enrolment fees in advance.
      Flow of Events
Alternative Flow: Nil.
Pre-Conditions: The student should have an account in a bank.
Post-Conditions: Nil.

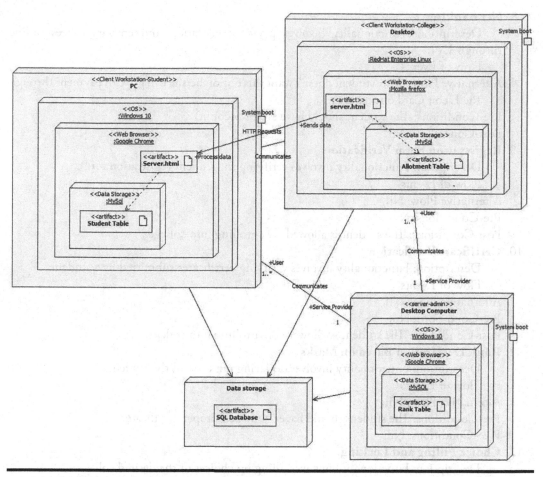

Figure 29.8   UML deployment diagram.

6. **Make Payment**

   Description: Functionality involves making payment for registration and enrolment forms.

   Flow of Events

   Alternative Flow: If the payment failed, make another payment.

   Pre-Conditions: Nil.

   Post-Conditions: The student is eligible to fill the choice sheet.

7. **Payment through Debit Card**

   Description: Functionality involves paying registration and enrolment fees through Debit Card.

   Flow of Events

   Alternative Flow: If the student doesn't want this option he can go with the net banking option.

   Pre-Conditions: The student must specify the Debit Card details correctly.

   Post-Conditions: Nil.

8. **Net Banking**

    Description: Functionality involves paying registration and enrolment fees online through UPI.

    Flow of Events

    Alternative Flow: If the student doesn't want this option he/she can go with payment through the Debit Card option.

    Pre-Conditions: The student should have a UPI account.

    Post-Conditions: Nil.

9. **Registration Form Verification**

    Description: Functionality involves verifying the student registration form.

    Flow of Events

    Alternative Flow: Nil.

    Pre-Conditions: Nil.

    Post-Conditions: The student is allowed for enrolling into college.

10. **Certificate Verification**

    Description: Functionality involves verifying certificates submitted by a student.

    Flow of Events

    Alternative Flow: Nil.

    Pre-Conditions: Nil.

    Post-Conditions: The student is allowed for enrolling into college.

11. **Rank Declaration Based on Marks**

    Description: Functionality involves declaring rank for all the students.

    Flow of Events

    Alternative Flow: Nil.

    Pre-Conditions: The student should have submitted proper certificates.

    Post-Conditions: Nil.

12. **Choice Filling and Locking**

    Description: Functionality involves filling up choices of the desired college.

    Flow of Events

    Alternative Flow: The student can opt not to fill choices if he is not interested.

    Pre-Conditions: The student should have paid enrolment fees.

    Post-Conditions: Nil.

13. **Seat Allotment Based on Rank and Choice**

    Description: Functionality involves allotting seats to students in college based on choice and rank.

    Flow of Events

    Alternative Flow: If the student didn't fill the choice sheet, the seat is not allotted.

    Pre-Conditions: The student should have paid enrolment fees.

    Post-Conditions: Nil.

14. **Admit Letter Generation**

    Description: Functionality involves generating admit letters for students.

    Flow of Events

    Alternative Flow: Nil.

    Pre-Conditions: Nil.

    Post-Conditions: The admit letter will be passed to the corresponding college.

15. **Admit Letter Verification**

    Description: Functionality involves verifying the admit letter given by the admin team.
    Flow of Events

    Alternative Flow: Nil.

    Pre-Conditions: Nil.

    Post-Conditions: The student has to approach the college with admit letter generated.

16. **Document Verification**

    Description: Functionality involves verifying documents submitted by a student.
    Flow of Events

    Alternative Flow: Nil.

    Pre-Conditions: Nil.

    Post-Conditions: The student can accept or decline the offer from the college.

17. **Accept/Decline**

    Description: Functionality involves accepting/declining the student from the college side.
    Flow of Events

    Alternative Flow: Nil.

    Pre-Conditions: The student should have passed all eligibility criteria.

    Post-Conditions: Nil.

Chapter 30

Design of UML Diagrams for E-Visa Processing and Follow-Up System

30.1 Problem Statement

A visa is a document issued by a country giving a certain individual permission to enter a country for a given period of time for certain purposes. It is received after several verifications through offline mode. It requires the applicant to go to the Passport Verification Centre for the verification of documents. Sometimes even the cost of getting the visa will be high as there may be middlemen involved in it. It takes anywhere from two weeks to two months to receive the visa if applied in offline mode. With the use of an online visa processing system, the middlemen entry in getting the visa gets reduced and the process of application of visa becomes easier. The overall aim of the system is that the applicant can apply for the visa from anywhere and at any time. The applicant can apply for the visa and submit it online. It provides more flexibility to the applicant compared to the existing system. There are certain types of visas that the applicant can apply for such as employment visa, study visa, resident visa, H1 visa, business visa, etc. People who apply for the visa for work, education, etc will be benefitted a lot from this system. The applicant should register by providing a valid email and a password. The applicant has to log in to apply for the visa. The credentials are checked for correctness and the applicant to allow to log in. Once the applicant logs in, he/she will be shown the application form which asks the applicant to provide the necessary details and asks him/her to attach the necessary documents. It also provides a list of visas to choose from. He/she can also view the details of fair to visa for each country. The applicant can view, modify and delete the details applied. The system will have a provision for the administrator to view the details of what types of visas are required by the applicant. The administrator will also be able to update and delete the details of the applicants. The administrator will have a facility to interact with the Visa Consultant Officer. The Visa Consultant Officer can be able to view and check the document proofs (valid passport, Demand Draft Visa Fee I-20 form, letter of admission, aid letter, etc.) submitted by the applicant and can be able to view the purpose of application of visa. He/She has the authority to accept/reject the visa application applied by the applicant (Figures 30.1–30.9).

DOI: 10.1201/9781003287124-30

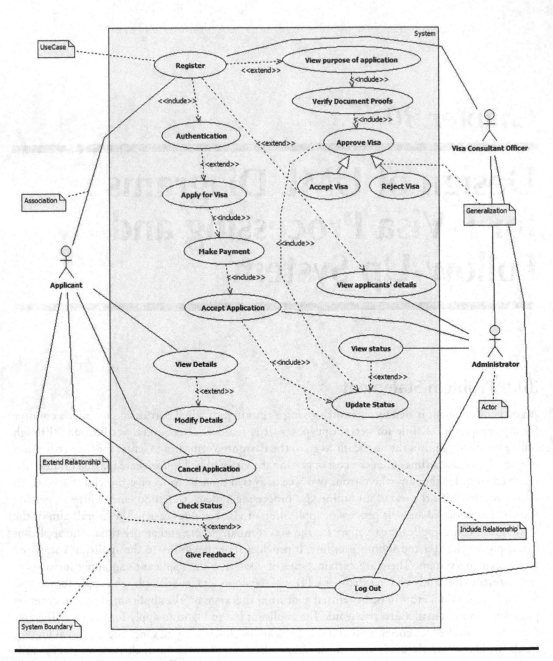

Figure 30.1   UML usecase diagram.

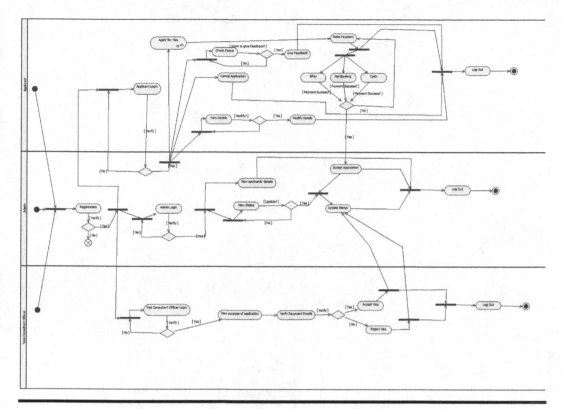

Figure 30.2   UML activity diagram – Scenario 1.

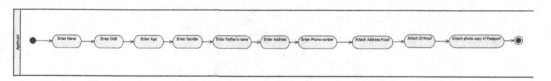

Figure 30.3   UML activity diagram – Scenario 2.

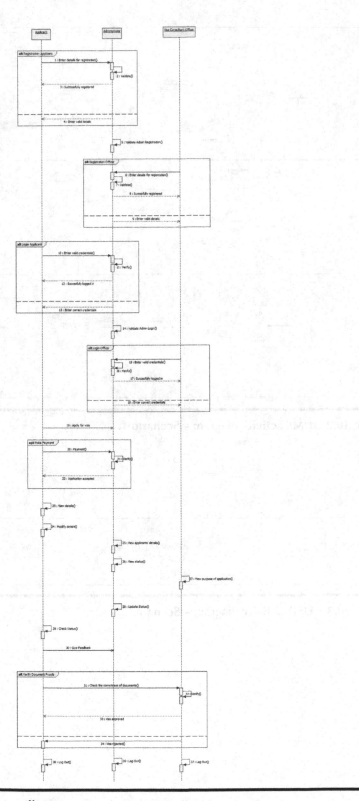

Figure 30.4 UML sequence diagram.

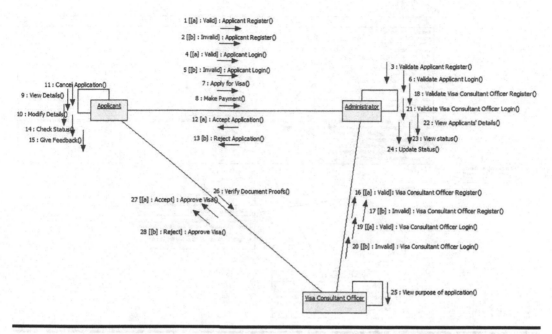

Figure 30.5   UML collaboration diagram.

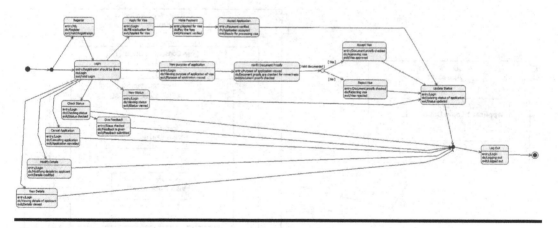

Figure 30.6   UML state chart diagram.

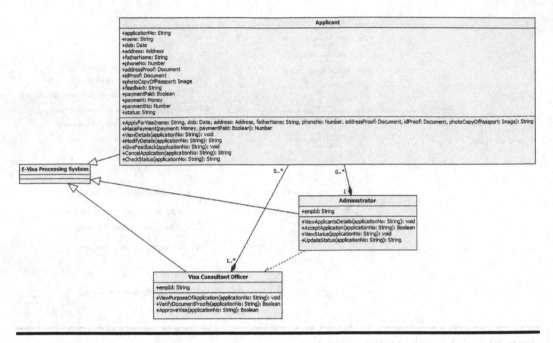

Figure 30.7   UML class diagram.

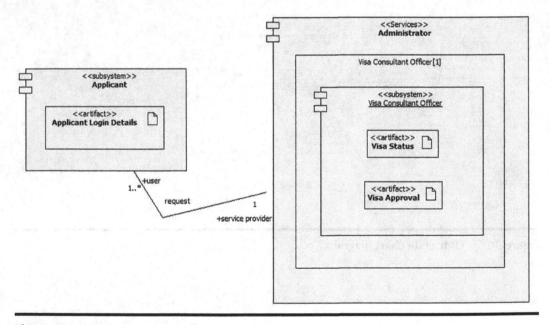

Figure 30.8   UML component diagram.

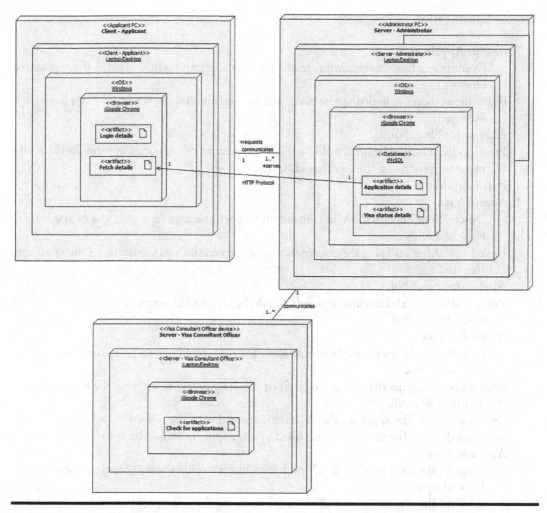

Figure 30.9 UML deployment diagram.

30.2 UML Diagrams

Actor Specification

1. **Administrator** – The administrator can view applicants' details, accept applications, view and update the status of the visa.
2. **Applicant** – The applicant can apply for a visa, view details, modify details, cancel the application, check the status and give feedback (optional).
3. **Visa Consultant Officer** – The Visa Consultant Officer views the purpose of the application, verifies the document proofs and accepts or rejects the visa.

Usecase Specification

1. **Accept Application**

   Description: Enables the administrator to accept applications submitted by the applicants.
   Flow of Events

   Basic Flow: After submitting the form online and making payment, the application is accepted.

   Alternative Flow: Nil.

   Pre-Conditions: The details should be filled correctly in the application form and the payment for processing the visa should be made.

   Post-Conditions: Nil.

2. **Accept Visa**

   Description: Enables the Visa Consultant Officer to accept (approve) visa of applicants.
   Flow of Events

   Basic Flow: After verifying the documents to be correct, the Visa Consultant Officer accepts the visa.

   Alternative Flow: Nil.

   Pre-Conditions: Valid document proofs should be attached correctly.

   Post-Conditions: Nil.

3. **Apply for Visa**

   Description: Helps the applicants to apply for a visa by filing an application form online.
   Flow of Events

   Basic Flow: Set of details that are to be filled correctly before submitting the form online.

   Alternative Flow: Nil.

   Pre-Conditions: The applicant should have registered with the system.

   Post-Conditions: The details that are filled by the applicant should be correct.

4. **Approve Visa**

   Description: Enables the Visa Consultant Officer to either accept or reject the visa.
   Flow of Events

   Basic Flow: The visa consultant officer, after verifying the document proofs that are submitted accepts or rejects the visa.

   Alternative Flow: Nil.

   Pre-Conditions: The document proofs should be checked for correctness.

   Post-Conditions: If the documents are verified to be correct, the visa is accepted. Otherwise, it is rejected.

5. **Authentication**

   Description: Used to verify the credentials when an actor logs in.
   Flow of Events

   Basic Flow: The actor is asked to enter a valid username and a password.

   Alternative Flow: The actor is redirected to the login page.

   Pre-Conditions: The user should have entered valid credentials.

   Post-Conditions: The credentials should be correct.

6. **Cancel Application**

   Description: Enables the user to cancel his/her application.
   Flow of Events

   Basic Flow: The applicant is given an option to cancel his/her application if he/she no longer has to apply for the visa.

Alternative Flow: Nil.

Pre-Conditions: The application form should be submitted earlier.

Post-Conditions: Nil.

7. **Check Status**

Description: Enables the applicant to check the status of his/her application.

Flow of Events

Basic Flow: The applicant can check the status of his/her application (in progress, approved, rejected).

Alternative Flow: Nil.

Pre-Conditions: Nil.

Post-Conditions: The application should be submitted.

8. **Give Feedback**

Description: Enables the user to give feedback about the visa that is being processed.

Flow of Events

Basic Flow: After checking the status, the applicant can give optional feedback.

Alternative Flow: Nil.

Pre-Conditions: The status should be checked.

Post-Conditions: Nil.

9. **Log Out**

Description: enables all the actors to log out of the system.

Flow of Events

Basic Flow: After performing all the operations that the actor wants, he/she can log out of the system.

Alternative Flow: Nil.

Pre-Conditions: The user should have signed in.

Post-Conditions: Nil.

10. **Make Payment**

Description: Enables the applicant to make payment.

Flow of Events

Basic Flow: The applicant will pay for the processing of the visa.

Alternative Flow: The applicant will be redirected to the home page.

Pre-Conditions: The application form should be submitted.

Post-Conditions: The amount paid is checked.

11. **Modify Details**

Description: Enables the applicant to modify the details that were given in the application form.

Flow of Events

Basic Flow: If the applicant feels that he/she has given the wrong details, he/she can modify the details.

Alternative Flow: Nil.

Pre-Conditions: The application should be submitted.

Post-Conditions: The modifications are to be done in the database.

12. **Register**

Description: Enables a user to register with the system.

Flow of Events

Basic Flow: The actor registers with the system by entering a valid username and a password.

Alternative Flow: Nil.

Pre-Conditions: Nil.

Post-Conditions: The user should enter a valid credentials (email and password).

13. **Reject Visa**

Description: Enables the Visa Consultant Officer to reject the visa.

Flow of Events

Basic Flow: The visa consultant officer rejects the visa if the document proofs submitted are not verified to be correct.

Alternative Flow: The applicant is shown the next date when he/she can reapply.

Pre-Conditions: The document proofs submitted should be invalid.

Post-Conditions: Nil.

14. **Update Status**

Description: Updating the status of the visa as per the process being carried out.

Flow of Events

Basic Flow: The administrator updates the status of the applicant's visa application after each stage is completed.

Alternative Flow: Nil.

Pre-Conditions: The application form should be submitted.

Post-Conditions: Nil.

15. **Verify Document Proofs**

Description: The document proofs submitted by the applicant are verified for correctness by the Visa Consultant Officer.

Flow of Events

Basic Flow: The visa consultant officer verifies whether the document proofs submitted are valid and correct.

Alternative Flow: Nil.

Pre-Conditions: The purpose of the application should be checked by the Visa Consultant Officer.

Post-Conditions: The document proofs submitted should not be invalid.

16. **View Details**

Description: Enables the applicant to view the details which he/she gave in the form.

Flow of Events

Basic Flow: The applicant can view the details that he/she provided in the application form.

Alternative Flow: Nil.

Pre-Conditions: The form should be submitted.

Post-Conditions: Nil.

17. **View Applicants' Details**

Description: Enables the Administrator to view the details provided by the applicants.

Flow of Events

Basic Flow: The administrator views the applicants' details.

Alternative Flow: Nil.

Pre-Conditions: The application should be accepted.

Post-Conditions: It is checked whether the applicants have provided all the details.

18. **View Purpose of Application**

Description: The Visa Consultant Officer can view the purpose of visa application (tourist visa, study visa, etc.).

Flow of Events

Basic Flow: The visa consultant officer views the purpose of the application to check what documents to verify.

Alternative Flow: Nil.

Pre-Conditions: The application should be accepted by the administrator.

Post-Conditions: The documents needed for getting the particular type of visa should be checked.

19. **View Status**

Description: Enables the administrator can view the status of the visa of the applicants.

Flow of Events

Basic Flow: The administrator views the status of all the applications.

Alternative Flow: Nil.

Pre-Conditions: The application should be accepted by the administrator.

Post-Conditions: The status should be updated if the processing of the visa moves to the next state.

Chapter 31

Design of UML Diagrams for Placement Automation System

31.1 Problem Statement

Placement provides the opportunity for the students to gain Specific Subject skills as well as Real work employability skills. Placement Offices play a crucial role in providing students the necessary training and various opportunities where the students can effectively evidence their various skills and abilities on their resume. Hence, the Automation of Placement office provides a more smooth placement process for both the companies and the students. This System mainly focuses on flows between the company's activity, Registration, Resumes, Users, Skills and Their Training. Hence, the system comprises five modules, namely, User module, Company module, Admin module, Registration module and Training module.

Functionalities:
   Admin can

- Add a new company
- Delete/update a company
- Keeps track of students interested in placements
- Add a new training for students (which is demanded by many companies)
- Update/delete a training (which are not demanded by many companies), etc.

User (Job Seeking Student) can

- Register for a particular job
- Register for a particular company
- Undertake a training
- Submit resume
- Update resume, etc.

DOI: 10.1201/9781003287124-31

Company can

- Register in the placement office
- View Student resume
- Recruit a student with good resume and skills
- Recruit a student trained in a specific area, etc. (Figures 31.1–31.8).

31.2 UML Diagrams

1. **Admin** – Admin controls the Addition/Deletion/Updating of New Companies, Students & Training for students.
2. **Company Recruiters** – Company Recruiters focuses on recruiting the eligible students based on the job requirements and their resume and skills.
3. **Placement Managers** – Placement Managers act as a Connecting Bridge between the Students and the Companies by Managing the Job offers from Companies & Job Applications from students, collectively.
4. **Student** – Job seeking Students are the Ultimate users of this system where they can enrol themselves in a training, apply for jobs by submitting resumes, etc.

Usecase Specification

1. **Add New Training**
   Description: This usecase enables the Admin to add a New Training Course into the Placement Automation System that is meant to be used for students.
   Flow of Events
   Basic Flow: The students can enrol in a New Training.

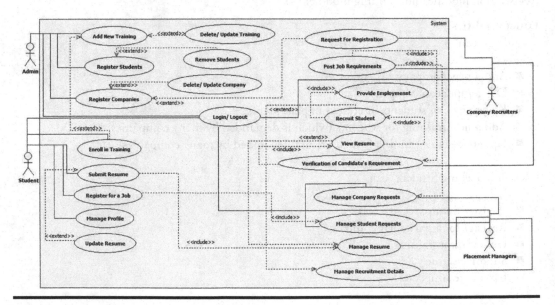

Figure 31.1 UML usecase diagram.

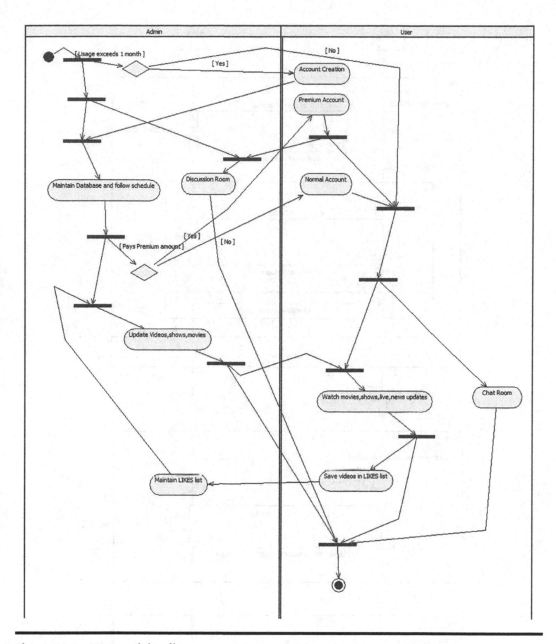

Figure 31.2   UML activity diagram.

Actor Specification

Alternative Flow: Nil.

Pre-Conditions: Admin Login should only be able to Add New Training.

Post-Conditions: Nil.

2. **Discussion Room**

Description: A chat room where only premium users can provide suggestions or complaints to the administrator directly.

Flow of Events

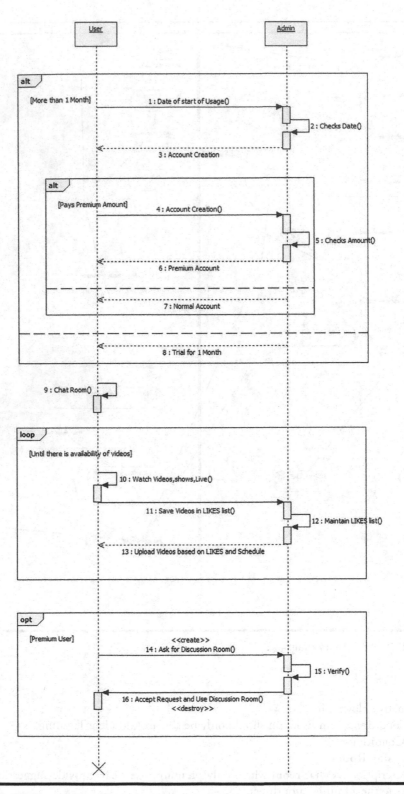

Figure 31.3   UML sequence diagram.

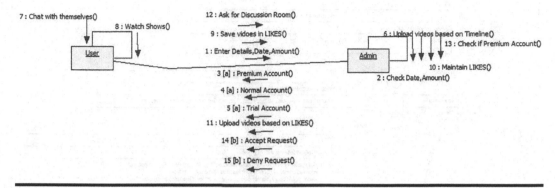

Figure 31.4   UML collaboration diagram.

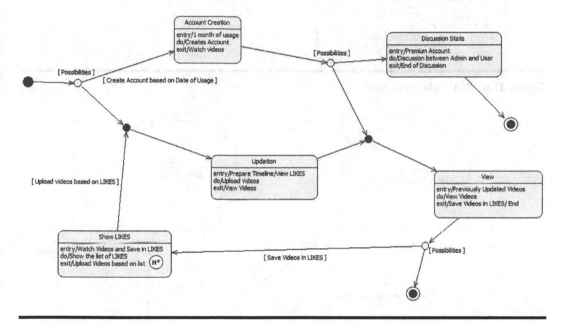

Figure 31.5   UML state chart diagram.

Basic Flow: Discussion Room.
Alternative Flow: Nil.
Pre-Conditions: Creation of Premium Account.
Post-Conditions: Nil.

3. **Update Shows, Movies, Live Stream and Recent News**
     Description: Update the shows, movies or news based on a schedule maintained so that users can watch it.
     Flow of Events
Basic Flow: Update of shows and movies.
Alternative Flow: Nil.
Pre-Conditions: Maintain a proper database and schedule the updates.
Post-Conditions: Users watch the updated shows, movies, news, etc.

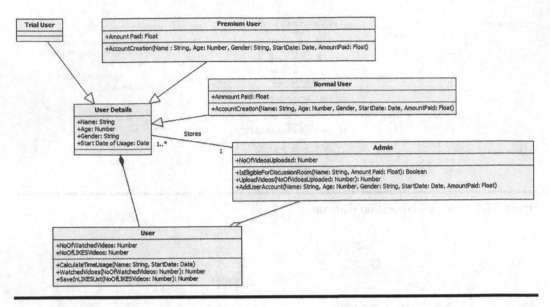

Figure 31.6   UML class diagram.

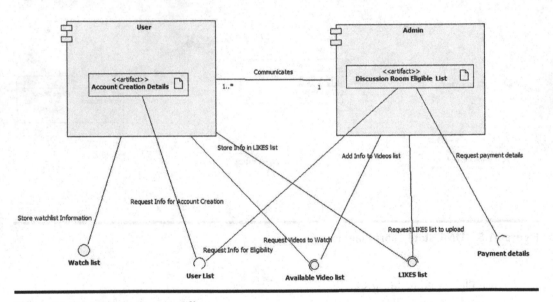

Figure 31.7   UML component diagram.

4. **Maintain LIKES List for Every User and Upload Videos Based on It**

   Description: Maintain a LIKES list for every user and upload videos based on it so that it would interest the users.

   Flow of Events

Basic Flow: Maintain LIKES list.

Alternative Flow: Normal update of shows, movies, etc.

Pre-Conditions: Users save videos in the LIKES list.

Post-Conditions: Update of videos.

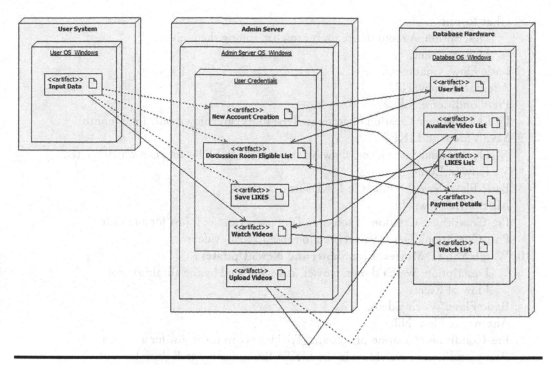

Figure 31.8   UML deployment diagram.

5. **Creation of Account**
    Description: Normal and premium users create an account by paying a specified amount and enjoy the services.
    Flow of Events
Basic Flow: Creation of account.
Alternative Flow: For 1 month, no account need to be created. Users can use the trial version.
Pre-Conditions: Nil.
Post-Conditions: Users can watch videos and use chat room.

6. **Premium Account Creation**
    Description: Creates an account for premium users by paying an amount higher than the normal user.
    Flow of Events
Basic Flow: Creation of Premium account.
Alternative Flow: Nil.
Pre-Conditions: Nil.
Post-Conditions: Watch videos and can use discussion rooms where they can discuss about
    suggestions and complaints.

7. **Normal Account Creation**
    Description: Creates an account for normal users by paying a specified amount.
    Flow of Events
Basic Flow: Normal account creation.
Alternative Flow: Nil.
Pre-Conditions: Nil.
Post-Conditions: Watch videos and use chat room to chat with other users.

8. **Chat Room**

    Description: A room where users can chat among themselves.

    Flow of Events

Basic Flow: Chat room.

Alternative Flow: Nil.

Pre-Conditions: Nil.

Post-Conditions: Creation of account. Trial users can enjoy it only for a month.

9. **Save Videos in LIKES**

    Description: Save videos, shows or movies in LIKES list and can watch it later.

    Flow of Events

Basic Flow: Save the videos in LIKES list.

Alternative Flow: Nil.

Pre-Conditions: Creation of account. Trial users can use it just for a month.

Post-Conditions: Get videos related to those LIKED videos.

10. **Watch Shows, Movies, Live Shows and News Updates**

    Description: Watch shows, movies, news updated by the administrator.

    Flow of Events

Basic Flow: Watch videos.

Alternative Flow: Nil.

Pre-Conditions: Creation of account. Trial users can use it just for a month.

Post-Conditions: Save videos in the LIKES list and can watch them later.

Chapter 32

Design of UML Diagrams for Farm Management System

32.1 Problem Statement

In India, 1 out of 4 farmers own a smartphone. But they don't use it optimally for insights on farming based on real-time data – such as weather, soil conditions, market conditions, labour availability etcetera, which can allow them to make data-driven decisions to get the best possible results. Current technologies that solve such issues are either paid services or inaccurate. They also tend to be more complex making it really hard for anyone to understand and interpret. An application if developed should primarily aim at reducing the risks, reducing the costs, improving yield, and most importantly, easy for anyone to interpret (Figures 32.1–32.8).

32.2 UML Diagrams

Actor Specification

1. **Admin** – The admin has control over the entire system. He/she is able to view, edit and delete records from the database and also alter the results for the queries the user selects. Also takes care of the Authentication of the users to provide user-specific details/results.
2. **User** – Users create an account and use the functionalities of the app to help them make data-driven decisions.

Usecase Specification

1. **Create Account**
   Description: User can create an account for himself/herself. Admin can also create an account for anyone.
   Flow of Events
   Basic Flow: Selects create account option and enter relevant details.

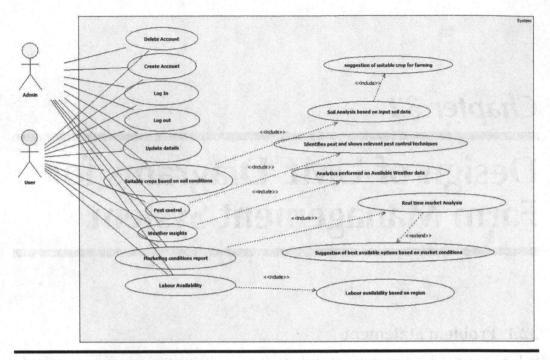

Figure 32.1   UML usecase diagram.

Alternative Flow: User can also create an account using his/her mail id.

Pre-Conditions: Account with current details must not exist in the database.

Post-Conditions: Nil.

2. **Delete Account**

Description: User can delete his/her account from the system. Admin can delete any account from the system database.

Flow of Events

Basic Flow: Admin/user selects delete account option and it deletes the account.

Alternative Flow: Nil.

Pre-Conditions: Account must exist/be created.

Post-Conditions: Accounts not in use, gets deleted eventually. Either by the user or by admin (after a specific time).

3. **Log In**

Description: User logs into the system.

Flow of Events

Basic Flow: Authenticates the user and grants access to the system.

Alternative Flow: Invalid login details, enter correct details again.

Pre-Conditions: User account must exist.

Post-Conditions: Nil.

4. **Log out**

Description: User logs out of the system.

Flow of Events

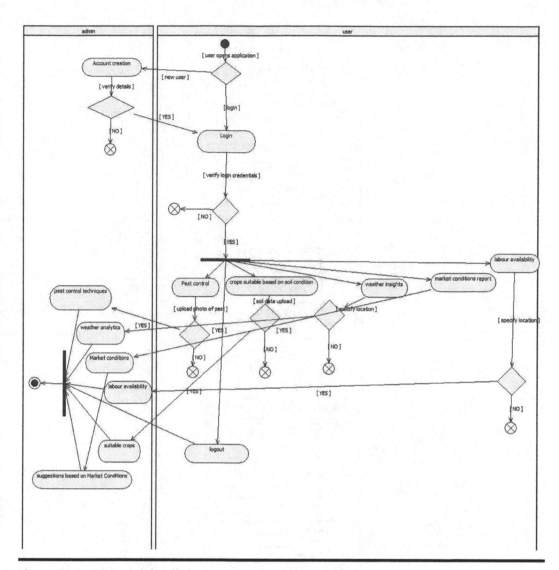

Figure 32.2   UML activity diagram.

Basic Flow: User clicks on the log-out option and his account session is terminated.
Alternative Flow: Nil.
Pre-Conditions: Must be logged in.
Post-Conditions: Nil.

5. **Update Details**
   Description: Updates/modifies the details of a user's account.
   Flow of Events
Basic Flow: All details are available to edit.
Alternative Nil.
Pre-Conditions: Must be logged in.
Post-Conditions: Details should be updated.

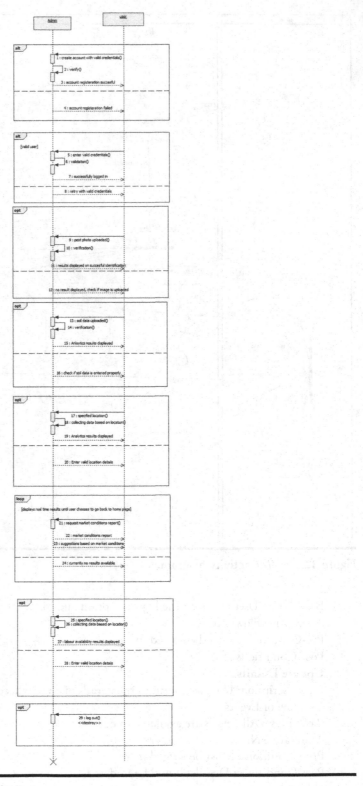

Figure 32.3   UML sequence diagram.

Figure 32.4   UML collaboration diagram.

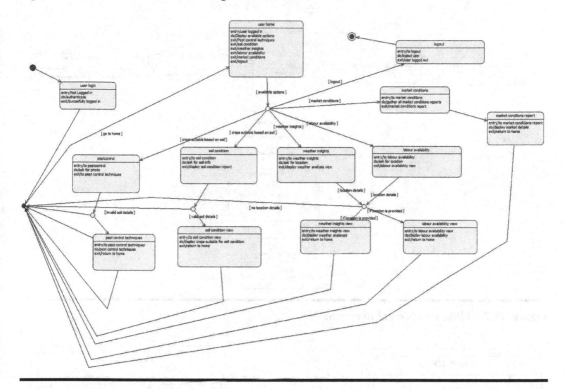

Figure 32.5   UML state chart diagram.

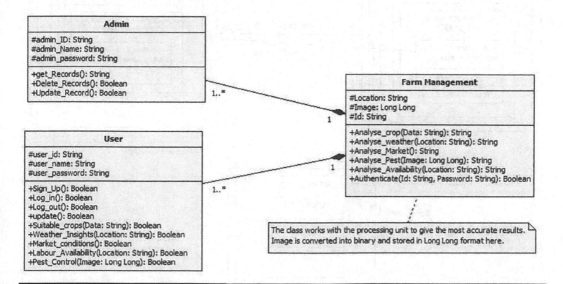

Figure 32.6   UML class diagram.

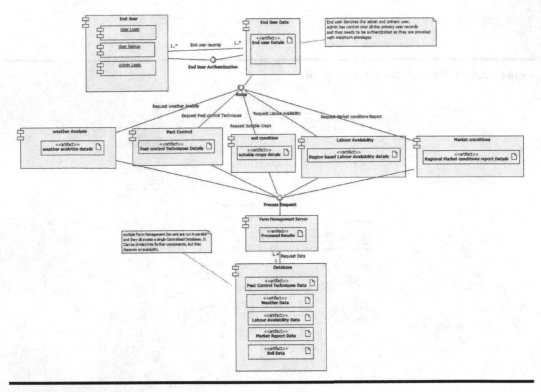

Figure 32.7   UML component diagram.

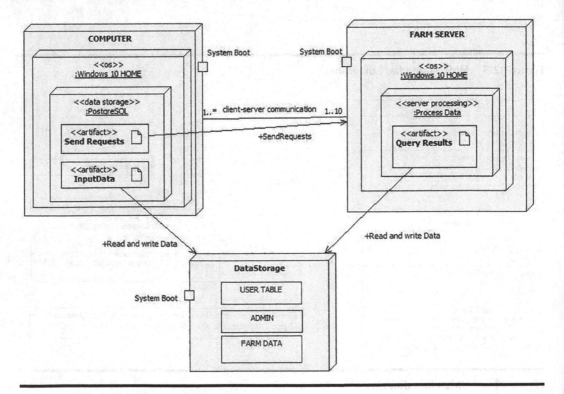

Figure 32.8   UML deployment diagram.

6. **Suitable Crops Based on Soil Conditions**

    Description: Suitable crops are suggested based on the input soil data.
    Flow of Events

    Basic Flow: Soil analysis based on input soil data.

    Alternative Flow: Not able to find any suitable crop.

    Pre-Conditions: User must give soil data to get the result of this query.

    Post-Conditions: Nil.

7. **Soil Analysis Based on Input Soil Data**

    Description: The soil data are analyzed to give meaningful insights.
    Flow of Events

    Basic Flow: Insights from soil analysis.

    Alternative Flow: If no data are given, no result is provided.

    Pre-Conditions: Soil data must be given as input.

    Post-Conditions: User uses these insights to make meaningful decisions.

8. **Pest Control**

    Description: Pest control techniques are suggested based on the type of pest.
    Flow of Events

    Basic Flow: User uploads photo of pest.

    Alternative Flow: No photo uploaded, upload a valid photo/image.

    Pre-Conditions: Photo of pest must be included.

    Post-Conditions: Pest control techniques are suggested to the user.

9. **Suggestion of Suitable Crop for Farming**

    Description: Suitable crop for farming is suggested.
    Flow of Events

    Basic Flow: Based on the soil analysis, suitable crops for farming are suggested.

    Alternative Flow: No suitable crops for current soil conditions.

    Pre-Conditions: Soil analysis is required.

    Post-Conditions: User has a variety of crop choices that will be suitable for the current soil
    condition.

10. **Weather Insights**

    Description: Insights based on weather data analysis.
    Flow of Events

    Basic Flow: Based on input weather data, analysis is performed.

    Alternative Flow: Relevant details must be filled to provide accurate results.

    Pre-Conditions: Weather data must be provided for analysis.

    Post-Conditions: Nil.

11. **Marketing Conditions Report**

    Description: User can check current market conditions.
    Flow of Events

    Basic Flow: Shows current market conditions report.

    Alternative Flow: Nil.

    Pre-Conditions: Location must be specified.

    Post-Conditions: The system makes suggestions based on real-time market analysis.

12. **Labour Availability**

    Description: Checks for labour availability.
    Flow of Events

    Basic Flow: User is required to specify the location to get accurate results.

Alternative Flow: User doesn't specify location, and shows most significant results of labour availability with its location.

Pre-Conditions: Nil.

Post-Conditions: Nil.

13. **Identifies Pest and Shows Relevant Pest Control Techniques**

Description: Based on the uploaded photo, the system identifies the pest and shows relevant pest control techniques.

Flow of Events

Basic Flow: User is shown pest control techniques.

Alternative Flow: When not able to recognize the pest, the system makes no suggestions to the user.

Pre-Conditions: Pest photo must be uploaded.

Post-Conditions: Relevant techniques must be shown as suggestions to the user.

14. **Real-Time Market Analysis**

Description: Market analysis is performed.

Flow of Events

Basic Flow: Based on current location and market trends, the system makes suggestions/recommendations.

Alternative Flow: If location isn't specified, it shows a global report.

Pre-Conditions: Location needs to be specified.

Post-Conditions: Nil.

15. **Analytics Performed on Available Weather Data**

Description: Analytics are performed based on the available weather data.

Flow of Events

Basic Flow: User is shown insights based on analysis.

Alternative Flow: Nil.

Pre-Conditions: Location must be specified by the user.

Post-Conditions: Nil.

16. **Suggestion of the Best Available Options Based on Market Conditions**

Description: Based on market analysis results, the system makes recommendations to the user.

Flow of Events

Basic Flow: User is suggested the best available options.

Alternative Flow: Nil.

Pre-Conditions: Location/region must be specified.

Post-Conditions: Nil.

17. **Labour Availability Based on Region**

Description: Shows the labour availability based on user location.

Flow of Events

Basic Flow: User must request for checking labour availability based on region.

Alternative Flow: No labour availability in the specified region.

Pre-Conditions: User must check labour availability by specifying the location.

Post-Conditions: Nil.

Chapter 33

Design of UML Diagrams for Green Rides

33.1 Problem Statement

This system is useful in the road transport and highways field (Ministry of Road Transport and Highways). Green rides is a technical solution for the general public to guide them to a less polluted path while travelling, to know about the traffic jam, identification of accident-prone spots, meals-on-wheel, the establishment of drive-mode applications. This app consists of a Google map view on the main screen. A user can select the source to destination path which then will be processed to give a number of routes to reach the destination from source with amount of traffic at various locations in that path along with current pollution status in that route (which updates overtime). If there exists a traffic jam, a user can blow a horn to all users within a specific radius. According to his current location in the form of a small notification which the persons in the specified radius will receive. The accidents that occurred at specific spots will be reported by the user to the concerned authority who will do the rescue operations and hence the accident-prone areas will be categorized based on the number of accidents taking place and a notification appears for the user to drive slow and safe when they are in that particular location. The road authority admin checks the system often. Meals-on-wheel provides information about hotels and restaurants which are available in the chosen route so that the user can place the order as per the available menu at a particular eating place including time of service so that one need not wait at the restaurant for placing the order. Drive-mode helps to minimize the risks of accidents while attending mobile phones during driving. This module would send an SMS to the caller that the particular person is driving when the geo-coordinates show the mobile shifting of the driver is beyond some specified speed limit (say, 20 kmph). Before start of the journey, this module can be turned on. The feedback feature allows the user to give feedbacks about the accuracy in the traffic and pollution levels in a given area (Figures 33.1–33.8).

DOI: 10.1201/9781003287124-33

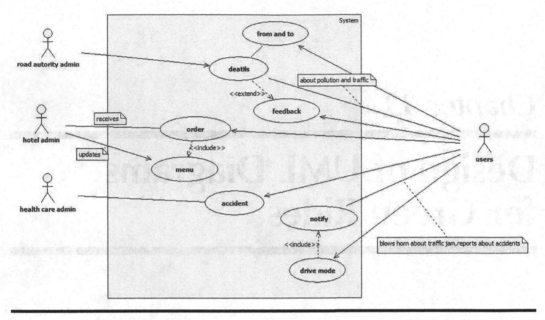

Figure 33.1   UML usecase diagram.

33.2 UML Diagrams

Actor Specification

1. **Road Authority Admin** – Updates details about everything that is reported and sorts the issue.
2. **Hotel Admin** – Updates the menu and receives orders.
3. **Health Care Admin** – Notices the accidents and provides help as soon as possible.
4. **Users** – Users can know details, can notify various activities, can drive safely and can order food.

Usecase Specification

1. **From and To**
   Description: Used to select the source and destination of the journey.
   Flow of Events
   Basic Flow: Selection of source and destination and can give feedback if interested.
   Alternative Flow: Nil.
   Pre-Conditions: User should login to the respective account.
   Post-Conditions: Once the selection is done, the user can get the details of traffic pollution levels and the best route to take.
2. **Details**
   Description: admin updates the details often and this contains all the necessary details.
   Flow of Events
   Basic Flow: User collects details and provides feedback if interested.
   Alternative Flow: Nil.

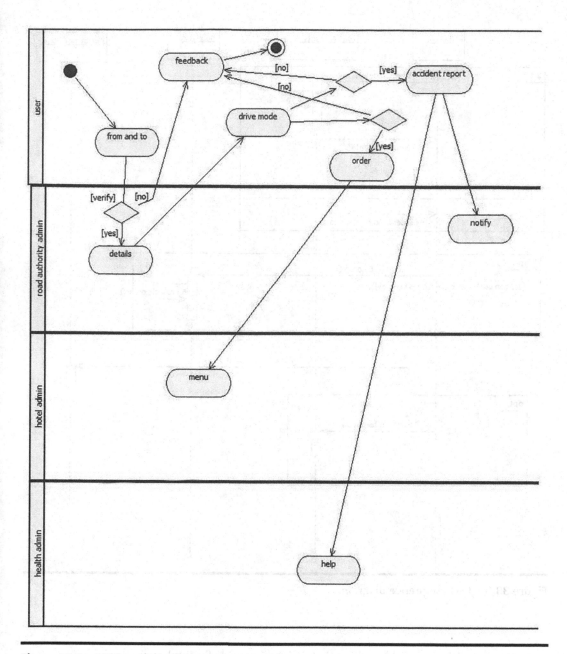

Figure 33.2   UML activity diagram.

Pre-Conditions: Should select source and destination.
Post-Conditions: Can provide feedback about detail correctness.
3. **Feedback**
   Description: Collects feedback.
   Flow of Events
Basic Flow: Collects feedback as a final step.
Alternative Flow: Nil.

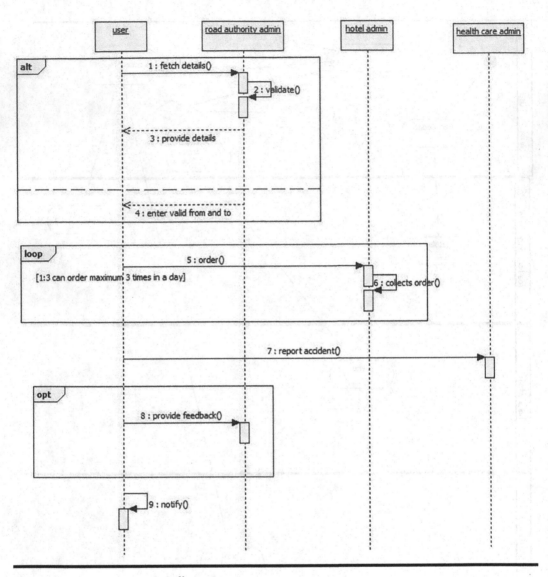

Figure 33.3   **UML sequence diagram.**

Pre-Conditions: Should go through details and provide feedback accordingly.
Post-Conditions: Nil.
4. **Order**
    Description: User orders for food and hotel admin collects orders.
    Flow of Events
Basic Flow: Go through the menu and select appropriately.
Alternative Flow: If the selected item isn't available, then select other or Nil.
Pre-Conditions: Should be logged in and should be on drive.
Post-Conditions: Arrive at the selected hotel and have lunch.

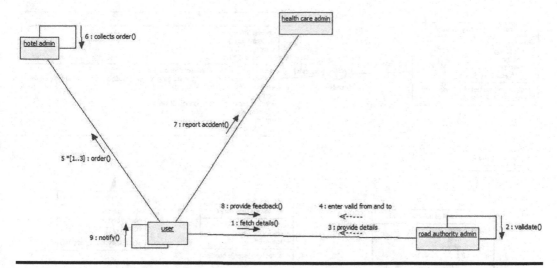

Figure 33.4   UML collaboration diagram.

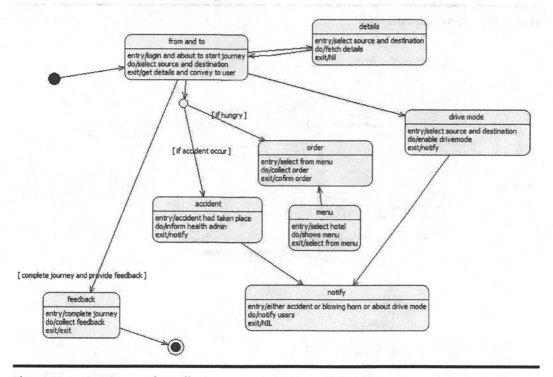

Figure 33.5   UML state chart diagram.

5. **Menu**

   Description: Has items from which users can select food.
   Flow of Events
   Basic Flow: Select food from menu and place order.
   Alternative Flow: Nil.

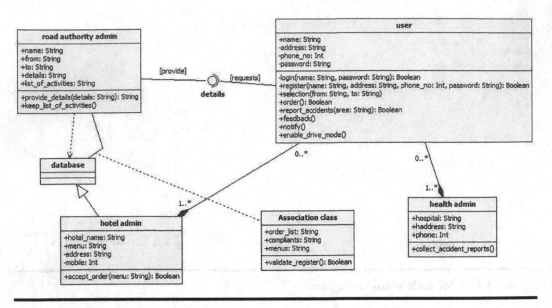

Figure 33.6   UML class diagram.

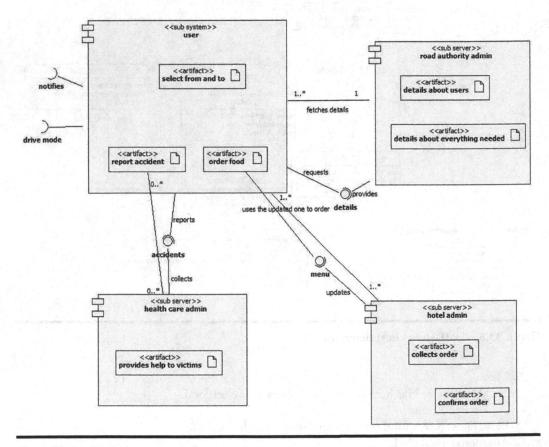

Figure 33.7   UML component diagram.

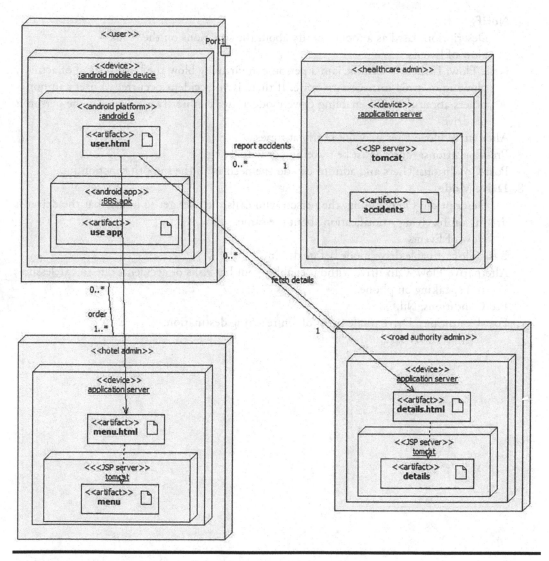

Figure 33.8 UML deployment diagram.

Pre-Conditions: Should be on a drive and the hotel should be on the way.

Post-Conditions: Should rate the hotel if requested.

6. **Accident**

Description: Users update accidents, if happened.

Flow of Events

Basic Flow: Details from the accident module are collected by road authority admin who updates the details module and the health care admin who offers immediate help.

Alternative Flow: Users notice accidents and avoid the route to stop traffic jam.

Pre-Conditions: User should come forward to notify.

Post-Conditions: Users can notify once more regarding the post-conditions after accident has taken place.

7. **Notify**

   Description: Used as a tool to notify about the situations on the roads.

   Flow of Events

   Basic Flow: If there is a traffic jam a person can virtually blow the horn instead of actually blowing to avoid unnecessary noise. If there is an accident occurred, a user can notify others about this. On enabling drive mode a user can notify a caller that the person is on drive.

   Alternative Flow: User may not notify at times.

   Pre-Conditions: A user must be travelling or witnessing.

   Post-Conditions: Users and admins can do the needful to the smooth functioning.

8. **Drive Mode**

   Description: On enabling, the person who calls the user get to know that the driver is driving on receiving a notification about the same.

   Flow of Events

   Basic Flow: Enable drive mode before driving.

   Alternative Flow: Can drive without enabling but has risks of accidents due to carelessness and speaking on phone.

   Pre-Conditions: Nil.

   Post-Conditions: Drive mode turns off on reaching destination.

Chapter 34

Design of UML Diagrams for Art Gallery Management System

34.1 Problem Statement

To provide an online platform to manage the buying, selling and storage of artistic creations provided by creators/other platforms or auctions and to organize events to exhibit these products. The system is a gallery having art pieces with its description, price and other information and the order activity, payment activity, order update activity and so on. The objective is to provide an online platform through which museums and art galleries can make use-off to exhibit their collections in times of unavailable street galleries. Like in times of pandemic also people need not bother not going to a museum or art gallery instead they can have online art shopping and art exhibits. The system should be immune to any chances of misuse and unauthorized reproduction of works of arts and designs. There will be two types of users accessing the system: Admin (Creators/authority of the art displayed) and Customer (One who looks to buy the art). The main features provided for the admin are that they will be able to update, add, delete, input price, description and information about an art (stock availability), generate report of gallery and that for the customers are that they will be able to order (Payment), delete order, view end-user projected art particulars (Figures 34.1–34.8).

34.2 UML Diagrams

Actor Specification

1. **Admin** – The person who has full access to the system and is responsible for all activities of the system.
2. **Customer** – People who use the system for either buying or referring.
3. **Delivery Person** – The person who takes out orders of the customers to them.
4. **System User** – The people who own the art that is put in the system.

DOI: 10.1201/9781003287124-34

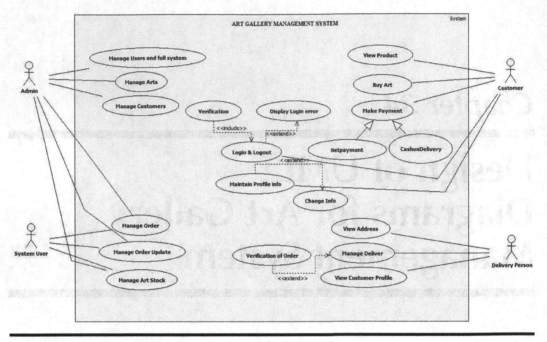

Figure 34.1   UML usecase diagram.

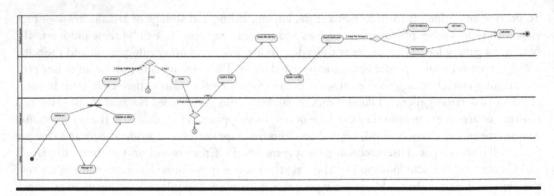

Figure 34.2   UML activity diagram.

Usecase Specification

1. **Buy Art**

   Description: Leads the customer to the process of buying the art they desire.
   Flow of Events

   Alternative Flow: Users can just make use of the system for viewing the items in the gallery and not necessarily buy anything.

   Pre-Conditions: The user should have properly logged in and should have checked for stock availability.

   Post-Conditions: Nil.

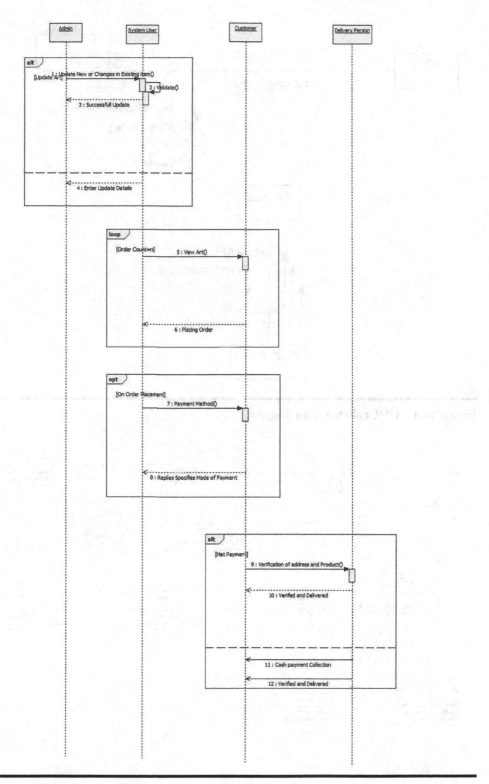

Figure 34.3   UML sequence diagram.

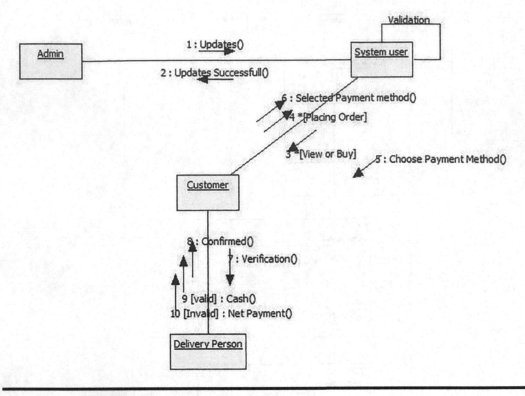

Figure 34.4 UML collaboration diagram.

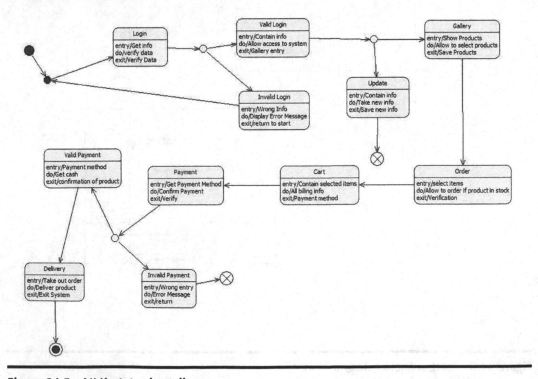

Figure 34.5 UML state chart diagram.

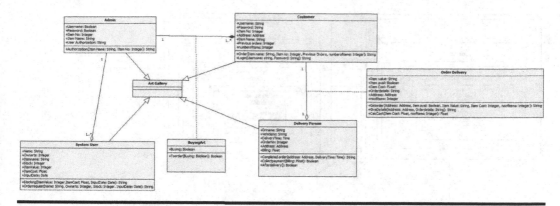

Figure 34.6   UML class diagram.

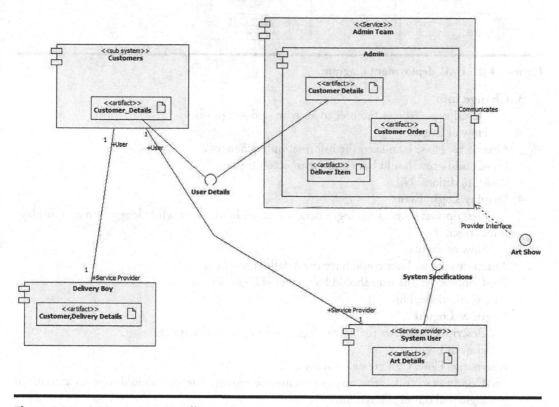

Figure 34.7   UML component diagram.

2. **Cash on Delivery**
      Description: Final stage of the system.
      Flow of Events
   Alternative Flow: Can make use of any online payment mode.
   Pre-Conditions: A person should have ordered for the delivery of an item.
   Post-Conditions: Nil.

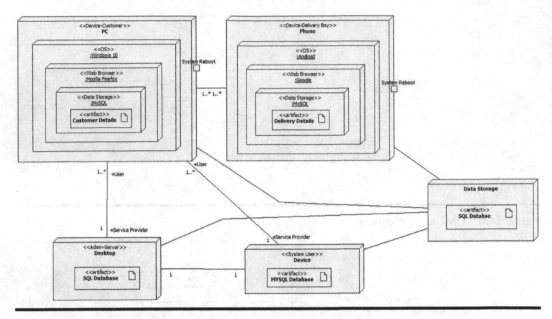

Figure 34.8   UML deployment diagram.

3. **Change Info**
    Description: Allows the user to keep an updated profile.
    Flow of Events
Alternative Flow: Can keep the information unchanged.
Pre-Conditions: Should have created an account prior.
Post-Conditions: Nil.
4. **Display Login Error**
    Description: Checks for login details entered by the user while logging in and displays if incorrect.
    Flow of Events
Alternative Flow: User could have the details entered correctly.
Pre-Conditions: The user should have entered login details.
Post-Conditions: Nil.
5. **Login & Logout**
    Description: Allows the user to login and logout of the system.
    Flow of Events
Alternative Flow: Can create an account.
Pre-Conditions: This is the first step to use the system. The user should have an account to login and out of the system.
Post-Conditions: Nil.
6. **Maintain Profile Info**
    Description: Allows the user to keep a profile.
    Flow of Events
Alternative Flow: Can keep the information unchanged.
Pre-Conditions: Should have created an account in prior.
Post-Conditions: Nil.

7. **Make Payment**

   Description: Allows the user to make payment in order to buy an item.

   Flow of Events

   Alternative Flow: User can opt for cash on delivery or net payment.

   Pre-Conditions: User should have selected an item from the system to buy.

   Post-Conditions: Nil.

8. **Manage Art Stock**

   Description: Keeps the system updated with new stocks.

   Flow of Events

   Alternative Flow: Nil.

   Pre-Conditions: Should be available to be put to display.

   Post-Conditions: Nil.

9. **Manage Arts**

   Description: Keeps the system updated with existing stocks (like the availability, quality, delivery time, etc.).

   Flow of Events

   Alternative Flow: Nil.

   Pre-Conditions: Should be already existing in the system.

   Post-Conditions: Nil.

10. **Manage Customers**

    Description: Maintains the records of the customers.

    Flow of Events

    Alternative Flow: Nil.

    Pre-Conditions: The customer should have logged in and out at least once.

    Post-Conditions: Nil.

11. **Manage Deliver**

    Description: Should assure that the correct order is delivered to the correct customer.

    Flow of Events

    Alternative Flow: Nil.

    Pre-Conditions: The customer should have ordered something.

    Post-Conditions: Nil.

12. **Manage Order**

    Description: Should be able to satisfy or complete an order.

    Flow of Events

    Alternative Flow: Nil.

    Pre-Conditions: An art should have its values.

    Post-Conditions: Nil.

13. **Manage Order Update**

    Description: Updates the order tracks.

    Flow of Events

    Alternative Flow: Order should be appropriately cancelled.

    Pre-Conditions: The order should be taken out for delivery.

    Post-Conditions: Nil.

14. **Manage Users and Full System**

    Description: Maintains complete system from end to end.

    Flow of Events

Alternative Flow: Nil.
Pre-Conditions: Should be given authority.
Post-Conditions: Nil.

15. **Net Payment**
    Description: Allows customers to pay online.
    Flow of Events
Alternative Flow: User can opt for cash on delivery.
Pre-Conditions: Customer should select an item to buy.
Post-Conditions: Nil.

16. **Verification of Order**
    Description: Makes sure that the correct order is delivered to the correct customer.
    Flow of Events
Alternative Flow: Nil.
Pre-Conditions: Someone must have made an order.
Post-Conditions: Nil.

17. **View Address**
    Description: Makes sure the order is delivered to the correct customer.
    Flow of Events
Alternative Flow: Nil.
Pre-Conditions: Someone must have made an order.
Post-Conditions: Nil.

18. **View Customer Profile**
    Description: Allows the delivery person to view customer profiles for any reference.
    Flow of Events
Alternative Flow: Nil.
Pre-Conditions: Someone must have made an order.
Post-Conditions: Nil.

19. **View Product**
    Description: Allows the user to view any product available in the system.
    Flow of Events
Alternative Flow: Nil.
Pre-Conditions: User should have logged in.
Post-Conditions: Nil.

Chapter 35

Design of UML Diagrams for GUIDE – Dropshipping Website

35.1 Problem Statement

The students in our college have a lot of unnecessary goods lying around, whereas many other people might be benefitted from those things. So I would like to put forward a website that can be used to sell or trade the goods with someone who needs them. It proves to be extremely useful in cases like buying and trading second-hand books or study materials among students and faculties. Initially, the website can exclusively only be accessed by the students within the PSG Tech College campus. Later on, if expected demands are met, it shall be expanded to other colleges. The sellers are given special accounts in which they are rated based on their previous records with which the buyers can choose their seller.

Functionalities:

1. The buyer can opt for the payment options with which they control the risk.
2. User-friendly website layout.
3. The buyer gets to inspect the product in front of the seller which ensures customer satisfaction (Figures 35.1–35.8).

35.2 UML Diagrams

Actor Specification

1. **Administrator** – Admin controls the organization of the products and reports the statistics about the movement of products and goods.
2. **Customer** – Customers get to view the products and can purchase the products if they want to. They will be asked to rate the product after a successful purchase.

DOI: 10.1201/9781003287124-35

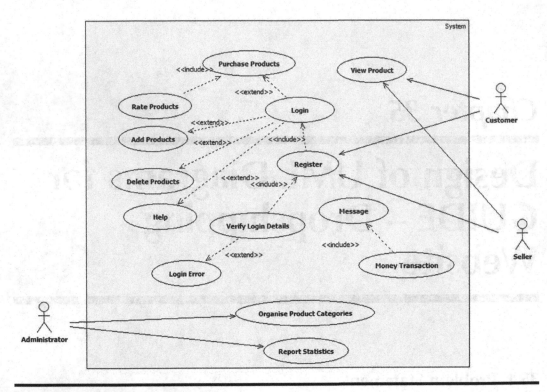

Figure 35.1 UML usecase diagram.

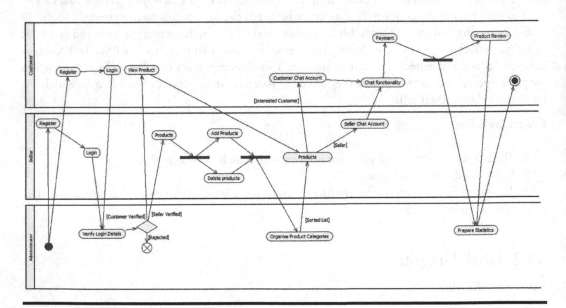

Figure 35.2 UML activity diagram.

3. **Seller** – Seller can add or delete the products he posted. This does not deny him from buyer products from other sellers with the same account.

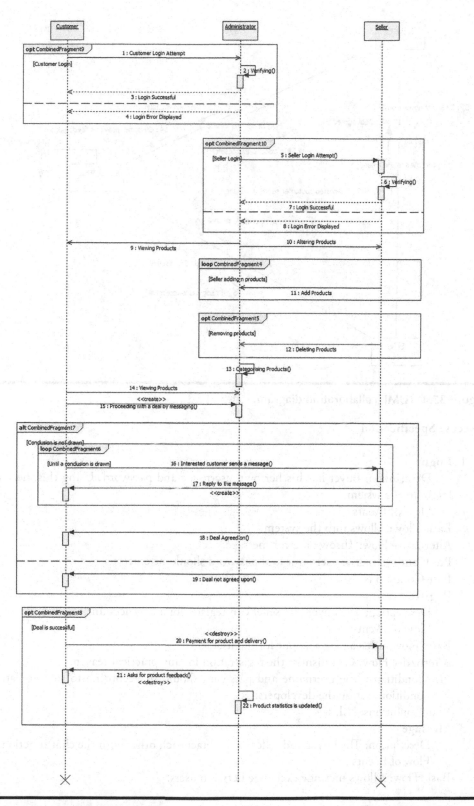

Figure 35.3   UML sequence diagram.

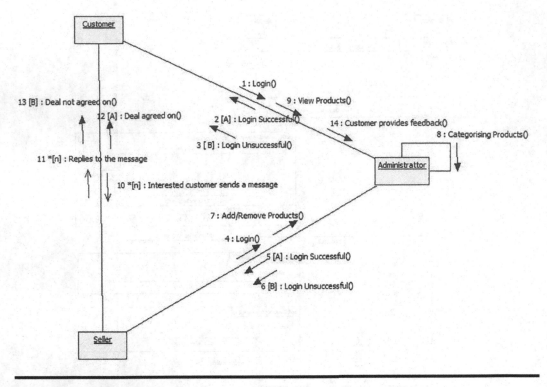

Figure 35.4   UML collaboration diagram.

Usecase Specification

1. **Login**

   Description: Buyer has his/her own username and password. Using this, he/she has to log in to the system.

   Flow of Events

   Basic Flow: Allows into the system.

   Alternative Flow: Throw an error message.

   Pre-Conditions: The username and password should be correct.

   Post-Conditions: Nil.

2. **Register**

   Description: The buyer and seller can register for a new account.

   Flow of Events

   Basic Flow: Adds a new account for the user.

   Alternative Flow: Can dismiss the registration for any practical reason.

   Pre-Conditions: The username and password should be according to the regulations and conditions set by the developers.

   Post-Conditions: Nil.

3. **Message**

   Description: The buyer and seller can contact each other with the chat functionality.

   Flow of Events

   Basic Flow: Allows message exchange between users.

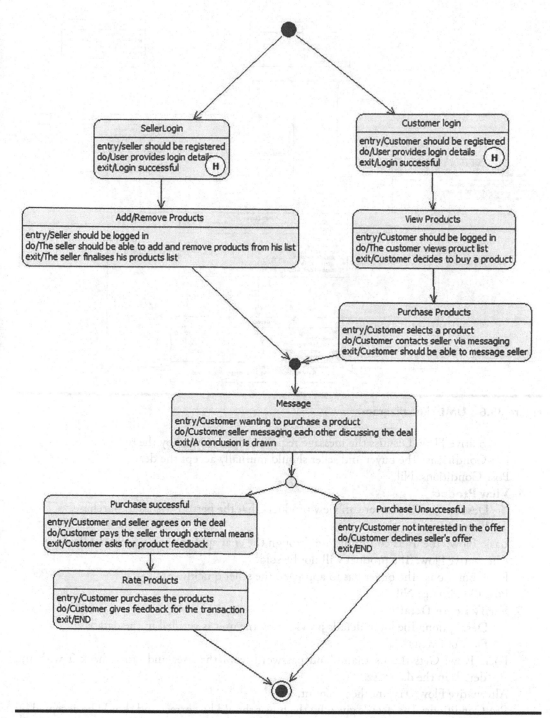

Figure 35.5   UML state chart diagram.

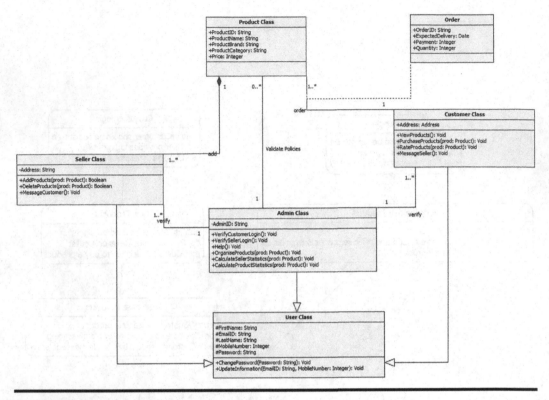

Figure 35.6   UML class diagram.

Alternative Flow: Dismiss the message request if not accepted by the seller.

Pre-Conditions: The buyer and seller should mutually accept the deal.

Post-Conditions: Nil.

4. **View Product**

   Description: The buyer can view products that the person wishes to purchase.

   Flow of Events

   Basic Flow: The users communicate through the chat application and seal the deal.

   Alternative Flow: The product will not be sold.

   Pre-Conditions: The buyer has to approach the seller quickly.

   Post-Conditions: Nil.

5. **Verify Login Details**

   Description: The login details provided by the user is verified in the database.

   Flow of Events

   Basic Flow: Gets the username and password from the user and cross-check it with the details in the database.

   Alternative Flow: Try another account.

   Pre-Conditions: The details given by the buyer should be correct and should be accepted by admin.

   Post-Conditions: Nil.

6. **Login Error**

   Description: If the details provided by the user does not match the details in the database, then this throws an error.

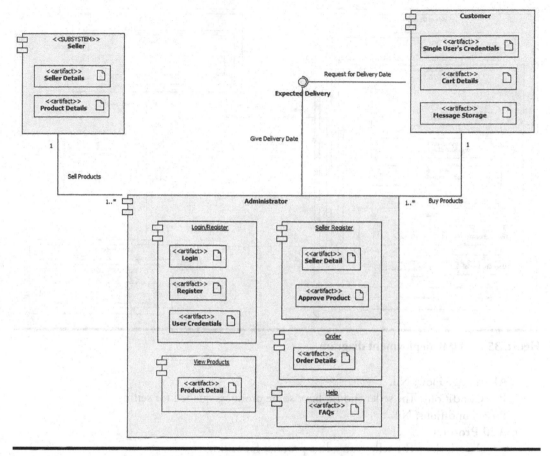

Figure 35.7   UML component diagram.

Flow of Events

Basic Flow: Verifies details and throws and errors if the provided conditions are not met.

Alternative Flow: Nil.

Pre-Conditions: Wrong information must be provided to invoke the error.

Post-Conditions: Nil.

7. **Help**

Description: The users can surf through FAQs and also post questions to which answers will be provided by our team.

Flow of Events

Basic Flow: The users can click on a link to visit the page to answer all their questions.

Alternative Flow: Nil.

Pre-Conditions: Nil.

Post-Conditions: Nil.

8. **Delete Products**

Description: The seller can delete the products they listed if they don't want to sell the product.

Flow of Events

Basic Flow: Sellers have the access to delete their uploaded products.

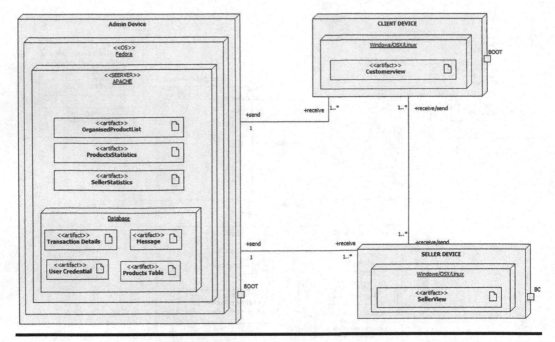

Figure 35.8   UML deployment diagram.

Alternative Flow: Nil.
Pre-Conditions: The seller should have some products queued for selling.
Post-Conditions: Nil.

9. **Add Product**
   Description: The seller can add a product for selling.
   Flow of Events
Basic Flow: Can add products for selling.
Alternative Flow: Nil.
Pre-Conditions: The seller should have an account. This avoids technical issues.
Post-Conditions: Nil.

10. **Purchasing Products**
    Description: The buyer can pay a fair price for the products.
    Flow of Events
Basic Flow: Paying the seller for their products.
Alternative Flow: Nil.
Pre-Conditions: The offer must be above the price set by the seller.
Post-Conditions: Nil.

11. **Rate Products**
    Description: The buyer can rate their experience of the purchase with respect to the product quality and seller response.
    Flow of Events
Basic Flow: Rating the seller interaction.
Alternative Flow: They can skip from rating the product.
Pre-Conditions: A successful purchase should be made.
Post-Conditions: Nil.

12. **Money Transaction**

    Description: The customer pays the seller through external means mediated by the chat application.

    Flow of Events

Basic Flow: Chat functionality can modulate the payment method both the users can agree
    upon.

Alternative Flow: Nil.

Pre-Conditions: The seller should be satisfied with the price.

Post-Conditions: Nil.

13. **Organize Product Categories**

    Description: The administrator organizes the product categories that may sometimes be included in the wrong categories by the seller.

    Flow of Events

Basic Flow: It allows the administrator to shift products from one category to another.

Alternative Flow: Nil.

Pre-Conditions: The product should be input in the wrong categories.

Post-Conditions: Nil.

14. **Report Statistics**

    Description: The administrator prepares statistics based on pre-defined criteria.

    Flow of Events

Basic Flow: The administrator prepares statistics.

Alternative Flow: Nil.

Pre-Conditions: Purchases of products should have been carried out.

Post-Conditions: Nil.

Chapter 36

Design of UML Diagrams for Online Quiz System

36.1 Problem Statement

Online learning is a part of many institution's course offerings around the world. The scope of online quiz systems increased in this pandemic situation. The objective of the system is to maintain and improve the education rate by conducting quizzes (exams). The system acts as a bridge between student and teacher to gain knowledge and monitor it by the institution (admin). This system provides teachers to know about the students in remote education. The delightful features of the system are online teachers, remote tests, auto evaluation and feedback from students. Admin is responsible for the registration of both teachers and students. Teachers define the number of questions, time of the quiz, schedule for the quiz and they can edit it. At the end of a quiz, students can see the correct answers and their performance (Figures 36.1–36.10).

36.2 UML Diagrams

Actor Specification

1. **Admin** – Admin is responsible for registering both teacher and student into the system.
2. **Student** – Students are opting for the courses and answering the quiz.
3. **Teacher** – Teachers create, conduct and evaluate the test.

Usecase Specification

1. **Registration**
    Description: It is the process of admitting students and teachers into the course by the admin.
    Flow of Events
    Basic Flow: Admitting students and teachers.
    Alternative Flow: Try again with valid details of student and teacher

DOI: 10.1201/9781003287124-36

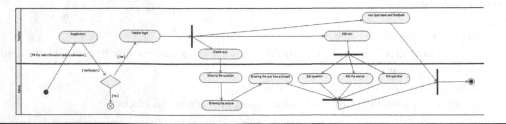

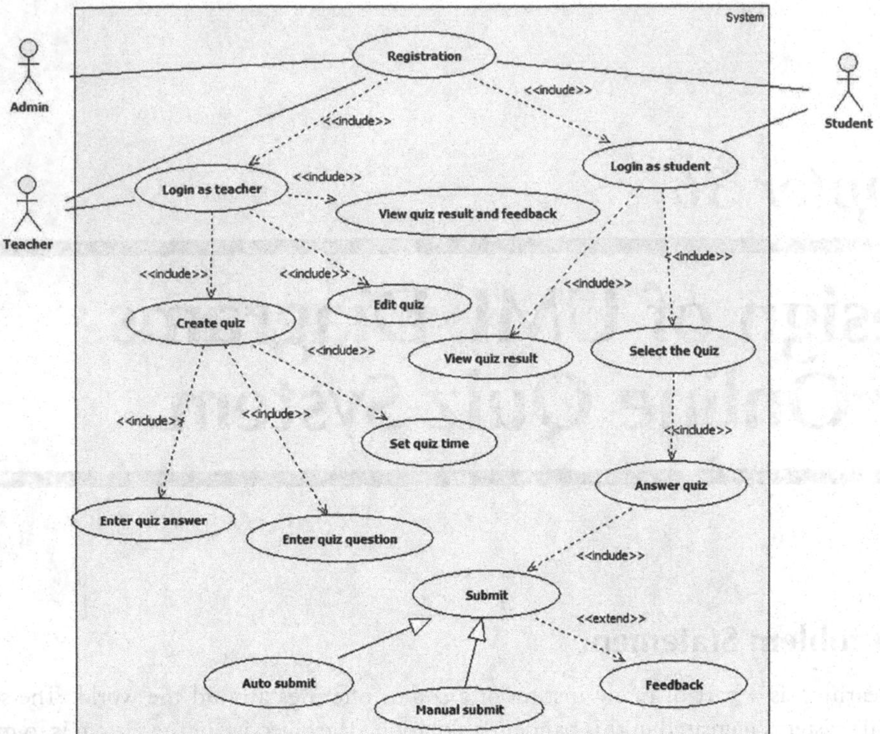

Figure 36.1   UML usecase diagram

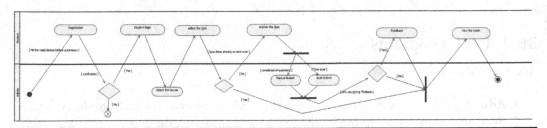

Figure 36.2   UML activity diagram – Scenario 1.

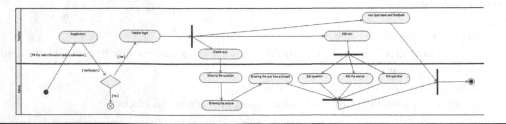

Figure 36.3   UML activity diagram – Scenario 2.

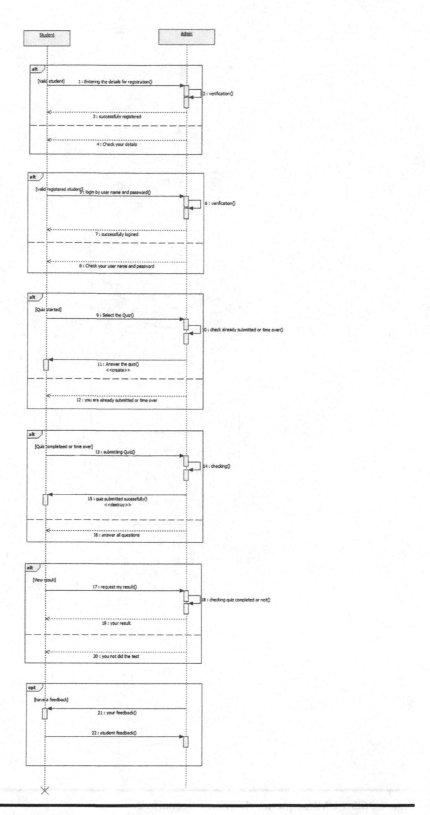

Figure 36.4 UML sequence diagram – Scenario 1.

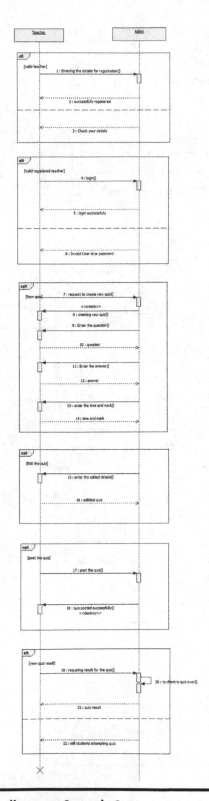

Figure 36.5 UML sequence diagram – Scenario 2.

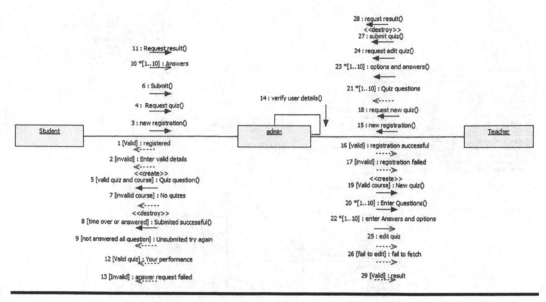

Figure 36.6   UML collaboration diagram.

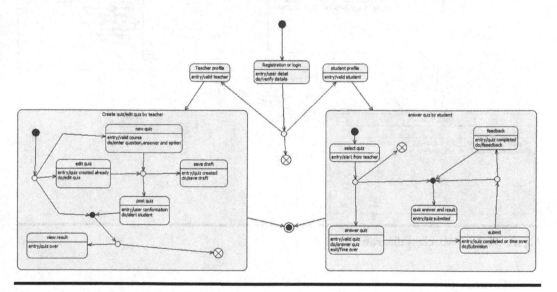

Figure 36.7   UML state chart diagram.

Pre-Conditions: Nil.
Post-Conditions: Nil.

2. **Login as Teacher**
   Description: Teacher login into his profile and prepare an analysis quiz.
   Flow of Events
   Basic Flow: Allowing into the system.
   Alternative Flow: Try again with valid data.
   Pre-Conditions: Teachers should be registered before login.
   Post-Conditions: Nil.

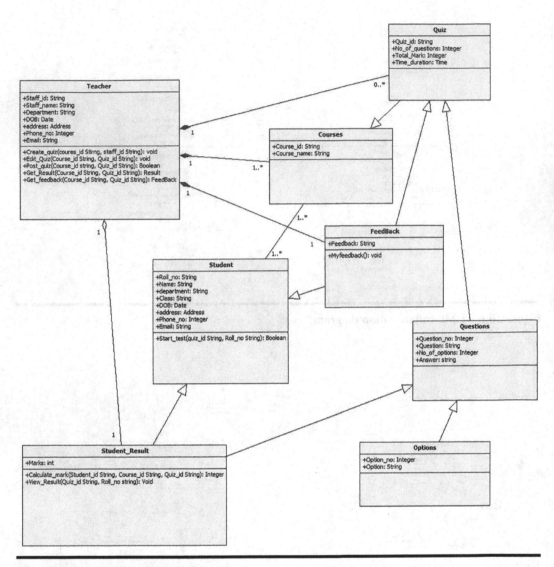

Figure 36.8   UML class diagram.

3. **Create Quiz**
>   Description: Preparing quiz questions and test schedule.
>   Flow of Events

Basic Flow: Allow to create a test.

Alternative Flow: Can delete the test.

Pre-Conditions: Teachers should be registered into the course.

Post-Conditions: Nil.

4. **Enter Quiz Question**
>   Description: Teachers can enter the quiz questions while creating the quiz.
>   Flow of Events

Basic Flow: Allow to create questions for the test.

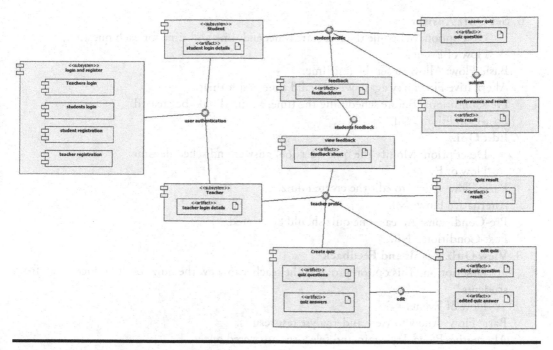

Figure 36.9   UML component diagram.

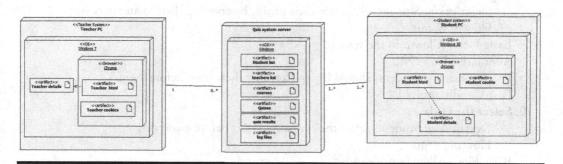

Figure 36.10   UML deployment diagram.

Alternative Flow: Can delete the question.
Pre-Conditions: Nil.
Post-Conditions: Nil.

5. **Enter Quiz Answer**

Description: Enter the quiz answers for the corresponding question for auto-correction.
Flow of Events

Basic Flow: Allow to enter the answer for the corresponding question.
Alternative Flow: Can delete answer and try again.
Pre-Conditions: Nil.
Post-Conditions: Nil.

6. **Set Quiz Answer**
   Description: Schedule the test start time, end time and time for each question.
   Flow of Events
   Basic Flow: Allow to set the test time.
   Alternative Flow: Try again with a valid time and format.
   Pre-Conditions: Before scheduling the time, a quiz should be created.
   Post-Conditions: Nil.

7. **Edit Quiz**
   Description: Modify the quiz question, answer and schedule time.
   Flow of Events
   Basic Flow: Allow to edit the created quiz.
   Alternative Flow: Nil.
   Pre-Conditions: At least one quiz should be created.
   Post-Conditions: Nil.

8. **View Quiz Result and Feedback**
   Description: This option provides the teacher to view the quiz result and feedback from students.
   Flow of Events
   Basic Flow: Allow to view and analyse test results.
   Alternative Flow: Try again and select the answered one.
   Pre-Conditions: Quiz should be answered by students.
   Post-Conditions: Nil.

9. **Login as Student**
   Description: Students enter into their profile by entering their id and password.
   Flow of Events
   Basic Flow: Allow into the system.
   Alternative Flow: Nil.
   Pre-Conditions: Students should be registered by the admin before login.
   Post-Conditions: Nil.

10. **Select the Quiz**
    Description: Students select the course and quiz before answering.
    Flow of Events
    Basic Flow: Allow into the quiz.
    Alternative Flow: Try again and select a valid quiz.
    Pre-Conditions: Students must be enrolled in the course.
    Post-Conditions: Nil.

11. **Answer the Quiz**
    Description: After selecting the quiz, the student starts answering the quiz.
    Flow of Events
    Basic Flow: Allow to answer the question.
    Alternative Flow: Quiz time over and contact your teacher.
    Pre-Conditions: Students start answering the quiz only in the scheduled time.
    Post-Conditions: Student finishes the quiz before its end time.

12. **Submit**
    Description: After answering the quiz or schedule time, quiz answers are submitted for evaluation.
    Flow of Events

Basic Flow: Allow to submit and leave the quiz.
Alternative Flow: Nil.
Pre-Conditions: Nil.
Post-Conditions: Nil.

13. **Auto Submit**

Description: Quiz answers are submitted automatically, after schedule time gets over.
Flow of Events

Basic Flow: Force to leave the quiz.
Alternative Flow: Nil.
Pre-Conditions: Auto submit, only if time is over.
Post-Conditions: Nil.

14. **Manual Submit**

Description: Students can submit answers before end time by manually.
Flow of Events

Basic Flow: Allow to leave the quiz.
Alternative Flow: Please answer all questions you have a time.
Pre-Conditions: Students should answer all questions before manual submission.
Post-Conditions: Nil.

15. **Feedback**

Description: After submitting the quiz, students can post the queries regarding the test.
Flow of Events

Basic Flow: Allow to send the queries to the teacher.
Alternative Flow: Ignore the feedback.
Pre-Conditions: Nil.
Post-Conditions: Nil.

16. **View Quiz Result**

Description: Students can view their performance and correct answers.
Flow of Events

Basic Flow: Allow to view the result and performance.
Alternative Flow: Try again or you did not attend the test.
Pre-Conditions: The quiz should be over.
Post-Conditions: Nil.

Chapter 37

Design of UML Diagrams for Book Bank Management System

37.1 Problem Statement

The book bank management is a software in which a member can register themselves and then he can borrow books from the book bank or the members can buy the books from the book bank.

A Book Bank lends books and magazines to member, who is registered in the system. It mainly concentrates on providing the book for authorized members only. A member can reserve a book or magazine that is not currently available in the book bank, so that when it is returned or purchased by the book bank, that person is notified. The book bank can easily create, replace and delete information about the titles, members and reservations from the system. The main issue of the system is that only registered members can lend the book from the book bank. In the case of lending, we should maintain the database for the status and issue of the book and also we have to calculate the fine amount with respect to the due date. We should maintain the book according to the department, generals, and year of study. Another main issue of the system is that if the user takes the book and misplace it on another shelf, then we have the chip of bar scanner to scan the books and indicate to the admin that the book has been replaced. All the above issues will be satisfied by developing the software as a user-friendly system. The main functionality of the system is that Sign in, Login, Log out, Book storing, Book retrieval, Book for buying, Stock Updating, Due fine, E-books, Payment, Book maintenance, Sales report, User records and Sorting. If the software is not developed, the members will affect based on criteria like the book is not in stock, the book is not arranged in order and maintenance will be more. The software is developed to satisfy the needs according to the members. The software will be very useful in the area of institutions, libraries and for general citizens. The software is developed to act as a useful interface for the users to easily access books.

DOI: 10.1201/9781003287124-37

37.2 Literature Review

Existing System: The present system is only some book banks are partially automated, that is by storing details in MS Excel Spreadsheets, whereas many other book banks are manual. A user has to visit the book bank personally at least thrice to get a set of the books that are needed. Also, only the user has to give the list of books needed along with the exact details of the ordered books, such as author's name, edition, name of the publication, etc. Only the list of users registered and the books available are stored in the database. Due to this the manual process and work involved in the existing system are more. A user has to visit the book bank personally to get registered, to request and also to receive books, and this is time-consuming. The book bank works only for a specific time within which the user should visit and complete all the procedures. The staff will have to manually search for the details of any particular user and the list of books ordered by the user.

Proposed System: In our proposed system, the user can register online in the system, enter his/her personal details, and can fill the registration form with a unique user Identifier. The user can complete all the procedures such as ordering books and confirming the booklist online and go to the book bank only for receiving the books. The system confirms the book list by means of automated email service. The books that would be needed by the user are predicted by the system according to the department and semester are chosen in the request books page. Hence the user is given a set of choices for selecting a book. Due to this all the processes such as registering, requesting books, etc. can be done online and automated. It saves a lot of time for the user and the book bank staff as well. There is no specific time for the user to register into the system and download the registration form. The user need not give the list of books needed, and can send only a confirmation for the same (Figures 37.1–37.8).

37.3 UML Diagrams

Actor Specification

1. **Admin** – Admin will manage the entire system periodically. The function of the admin extends in ways of adding new books, monitoring book issue and book order details and finally accepting payment of books.
2. **Librarian** – Librarian manages the books in the system making available the searched books by the members. He is the one who checks and accepts the return of books.
3. **User** – The user or member is the one who gets full access to books either buying or borrowing a book. A member is a registered user of the system who can search their required books.
4. **Visitor** – Visitor is an unregistered user of the system. A visitor must sign up in to order to view and search the books.

Usecase Specification

1. **Book Borrow**

    Description: This usecase is used to lend books to the user who wished to borrow.
    Flow of Events
    Basic Flow: The normal flow is that the member borrows a book from this system.
    Alternative Flow: The alternate flow is that if the required book is not available, then the
       member may search for the book with a different author.

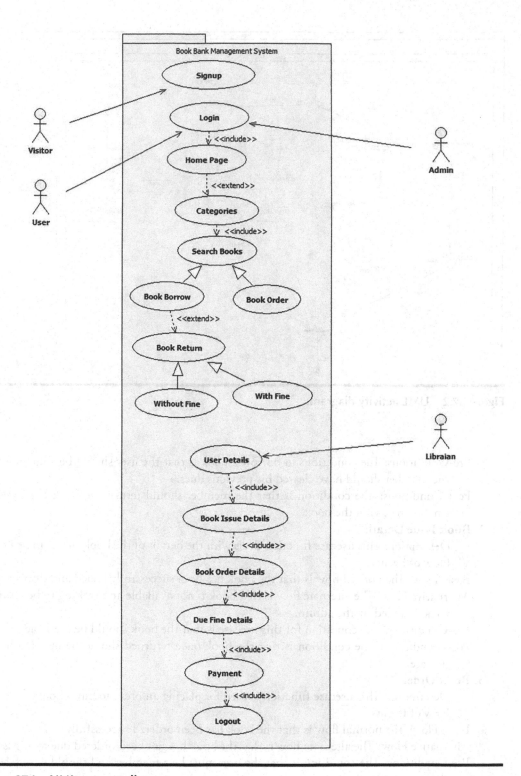

Figure 37.1   UML usecase diagram.

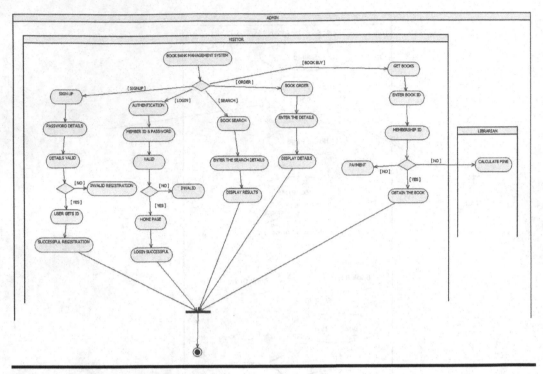

Figure 37.2   UML activity diagram.

Pre-Conditions: The conditions to borrow a book is that the user should be a member and the member should have cleared his previous dues.

Post-Conditions: The condition is that the member should return the book borrowed on time on receiving the book.

2. **Book Issue Details**

Description: This usecase function deals with the details of the book that is to be issued.
Flow of Events

Basic Flow: The normal flow is that the book has been successfully issued and displayed.

Alternative Flow: The alternate flow is that book is not available and waiting to be returned back or added by the admin.

Pre-Conditions: The condition for this usecase is that the book should be available.

Post-Conditions: The condition is that the book once returned should be updated in this usecase.

3. **Book Order**

Description: This usecase function is used for placing an order to buy a book.
Flow of Events

Basic Flow: The normal flow is that the book has been ordered successfully.

Alternative Flow: The alternate flow is that the book has not been ordered due to any issues.

Pre-Conditions: The condition is that the user must be a member and should have selected the required book.

Post-Conditions: The condition is the book should be returned within the specified time.

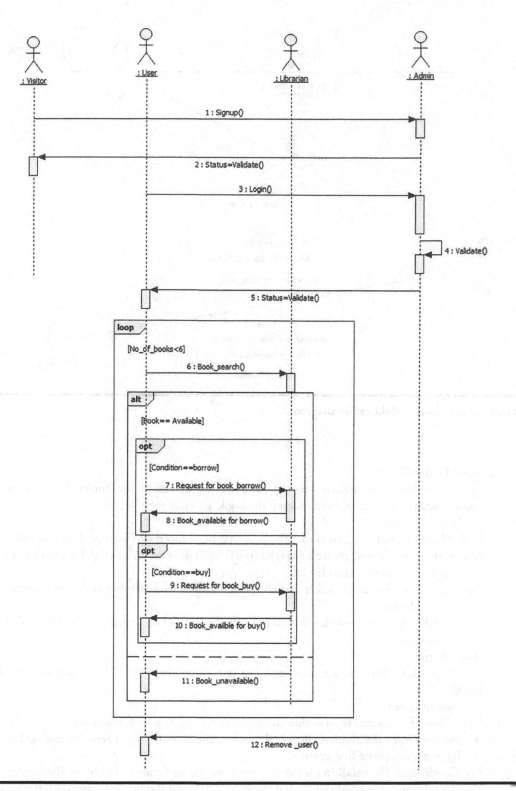

Figure 37.3   UML sequence diagram.

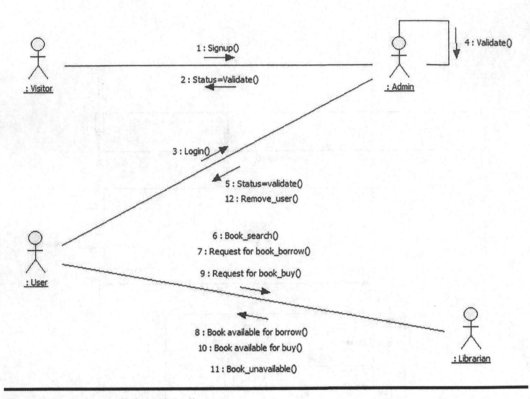

Figure 37.4   UML collaboration diagram.

4. **Book Order Details**

   Description: This usecase function displays the details of the books that have been ordered such as the person who ordered the book, its price etc.

   Flow of Events

   Basic Flow: The normal flow is that the book has been successfully ordered and detailed.

   Alternative Flow: The alternate way is that the book requested is not available then the alternate book is ordered and listed.

   Pre-Conditions: The condition is that the person should be a member and have selected his required book.

   Post-Conditions: The condition is that once the book has been returned the details should be removed.

5. **Book Return**

   Description: This usecase function is used for updating when the person returns the book.

   Flow of Events

   Basic Flow: The normal form is that the member returns the book borrowed.

   Alternative Flow: The alternate flow is that when the book has not been returned, calculating the appropriate fine amount.

   Pre-Conditions: The condition is that the book should be from the library or the system.

   Post-Conditions: The condition is that the book borrowed should be returned on time.

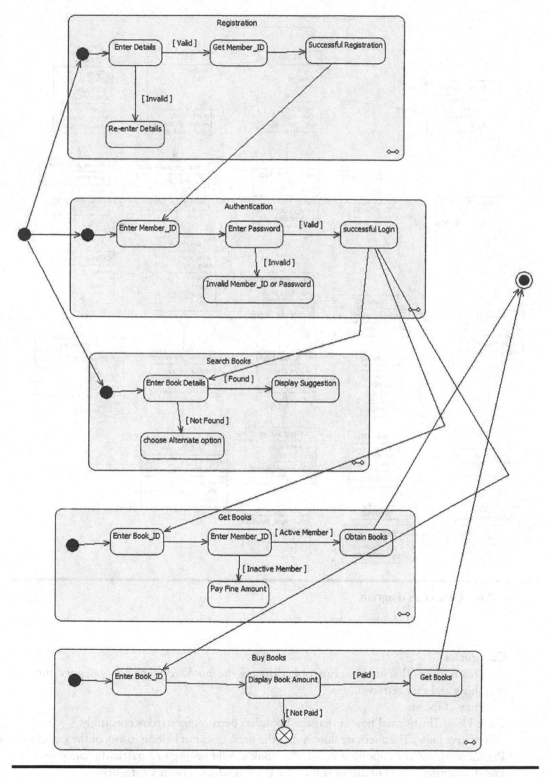

Figure 37.5   UML state chart diagram.

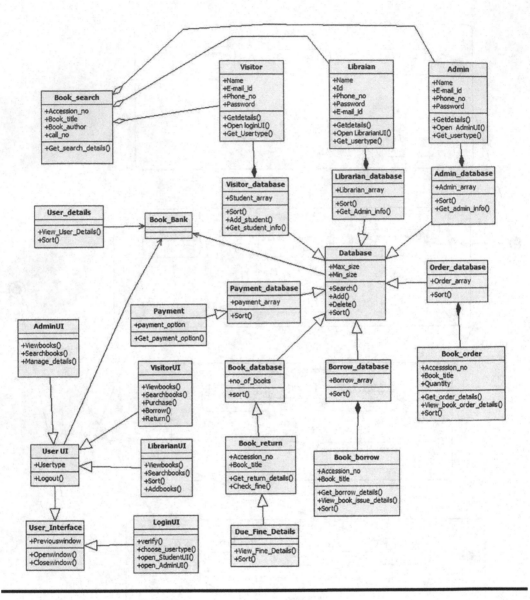

Figure 37.6   UML class diagram.

6. **Categories**

Description: This usecase function displays the books under each category for fast searching and easy retrieval.

Flow of Events

Basic Flow: The normal flow is that the book has been categorized accordingly.

Alternative Flow: The alternate flow is that the book does not belong to any of the categories.

Pre-Conditions: The condition is that the book should belong to a particular category.

Post-Conditions: The condition is that the book is selected from a category.

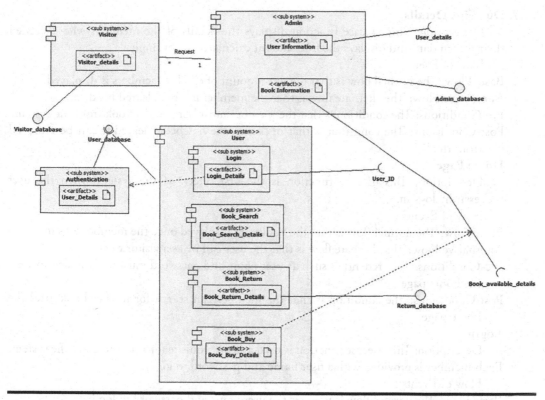

Figure 37.7   UML component diagram.

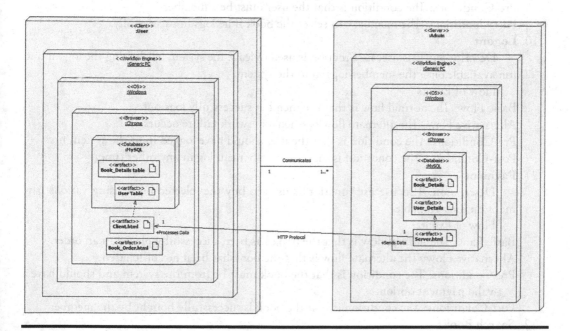

Figure 37.8   UML deployment diagram.

7. **Due Fine Details**

Description: This usecase function displays the details of the members who exceeded their return date and displays the fine amount calculated accordingly.

Flow of Events

Basic Flow: The normal flow is that the due amount of eligible members is displayed.

Alternative Flow: The alternate flow is that the member has not cleared his dues.

Pre-Conditions: The condition is that the member must borrowed a book from the system.

Post-Conditions: The condition is that once the due has been cleared it can be removed from the list.

8. **Home Page**

Description: This usecase function is the first screen of the system when the user successfully logs in.

Flow of Events

Basic Flow: The normal flow is that the books are displayed once the member logs in.

Alternative Flow: The alternate flow is that the user can be as a visitor to enter.

Pre-Conditions: The credentials such as user name and password must be provided to view the home page

Post-Conditions: The condition is that the member can search for his/her book after the home page.

9. **Login**

Description: This usecase function is used as a prerequisite for a user to enter the system. Each member is provided with a user name and password to log in.

Flow of Events

Basic Flow: The normal flow is to enter the user name and password to log in.

Alternative Flow: The alternate flow is that the user can be a visitor.

Pre-Conditions: The condition is that the user must be a member.

Post-Conditions: The member can select the book if he logs in successfully.

10. **Logout**

Description: This usecase function is used to leave the system by clicking the logout button available once the member logs in to the system.

Flow of Events

Basic Flow: The normal flow is that the member successfully logs out.

Alternative Flow: The alternate flow is when a network failure occurs.

Pre-Conditions: The condition is that the user should have logged in to the system first.

Post-Conditions: The condition is that the member can log in any other time.

11. **Payment**

Description: This usecase function is used to buy the selected book using various payment options available.

Flow of Events

Basic Flow: The normal flow is that the book has been successfully placed in an order.

Alternative Flow: The alternate flow is that the book has been not purchased.

Pre-Conditions: The condition is that the book must be from the system and should have a valid payment option.

Post-Conditions: The condition is that the book is successfully bought by the member.

12. **Search Books**

Description: This usecase function is used to search books based on author name, id, etc.

Flow of Events

Basic Flow: The normal flow is that the searched results of books are displayed.

Alternative Flow: The alternate flow is that browsing books through various categories.

Pre-Conditions: The condition is that the searched criteria must be a valid one.

Post-Conditions: The condition is that the book can be forwarded for buying or borrowing.

13. **Signup**

Description: This usecase function is used for the user to create a membership in the library.

Flow of Events

Basic Flow: It asks the user to input the username, password and email.

Alternative Flow: If the user doesn't provide correct details the user can visit the system as a user.

Pre-Conditions: The user must have a unique username, password and email.

Post-Conditions: The user can enter the system as a member.

14. **User Details**

Description: This functionality deals with the user details.it describes the total users who are accessing the systems.

Flow of Events

Basic Flow: When the user details are given the user is taken to the home page where he can access the books.

Alternative Flow: When the user is not registered the user can visit the system as a visitor.

Pre-Conditions: The user must be a member and he must give the perfect details.

Post-Conditions: Whenever the user logins he is taken to the home page where the user can access the books.

15. **With Fine**

Description: This functionality says when the user doesn't return the book ion the time the user has to pay the fine.

Flow of Events

Basic Flow: The members who exceeded the return date must be displayed with their fine amount.

Alternative Flow: The members of without fines are displayed.

Pre-Conditions: The user has to return the book with a fine when the user exceeds the due date.

Post-Conditions: The user must pay a fine in order to access the books.

16. **Without Fine**

Description: The functionality says that the user returns the book without any fine.

Flow of Events

Basic Flow: The system doesn't show any information about the fine details with respect to the users.

Alternative Flow: Fine amount is displayed if the user doesn't return the book with respect to time.

Pre-Conditions: The book must belong to the system and it should be returned within the given time.

Post-Conditions: The members can use the book till the due date.

Chapter 38

Design of UML Diagrams for Website Development

38.1 Problem Statement

Mega Associates is an evolving architectural firm that is facing a fierce competition. The competitors have a modern, well-built website that is pulling some of the firm's clients towards themselves. In order to avoid a situation like this and to retain all the firm's clients and to attract new ones, a refreshing website is needed. The website of the firm should include the major projects of the firm, a brief on all the available departments and collaborations, recent news with respect to the firm, the firm's insights, the history of the firm, mail or chat feature, and career opportunities with regard to the firm (Figures 38.1–38.8).

38.2 UML Diagrams

Actor Specification

1. **Customer** – Firm's customer who visits the website to know/contact the firm.
2. **Employee Candidate** – Any college graduate or other architects who look for job opportunities with the firm.
3. **Firm's Employee** – He/she is a firm's employee who is in charge of the updates with regards to the firm.

Usecase Specification

1. **Display Projects**
     Description: Functionality involves displaying all the major projects done by the firm.
     Flow of Events
     Basic Flow: Displays the projects of the firm.
     Alternative Flow: Nil.
     Pre-Conditions: Nil.
     Post-Conditions: Nil.

DOI: 10.1201/9781003287124-38

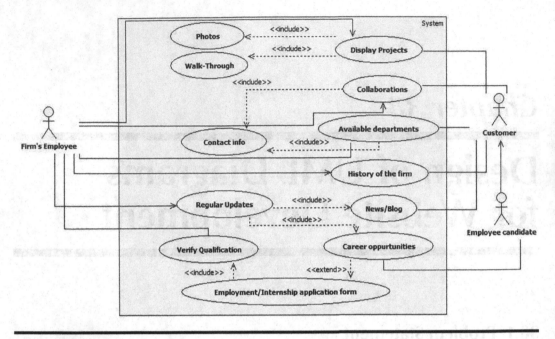

Figure 38.1   UML usecase diagram.

2. **Collaborations**

Description: This functionality tells about the various collaborations of the firm with other Companies/firms.

Flow of Events

Basic Flow: Explains about the various collaborations of the firm.

Alternative Flow: Nil.

Pre-Conditions: Nil.

Post-Conditions: If the customers want to contact the firm for a collaboration, they can use the contact the firm from the details given in the contact functionality.

3. **Available Departments**

Description: This functionality talks about the available departments in the firm and the services that they can offer.

Flow of Events

Basic Flow: Displays the departments and the services offered by the firm.

Alternative Flow: Nil.

Pre-Conditions: Nil.

Post-Conditions: If the customers want to contact the firm for a project, they can use the contact the firm from the details given in the contact functionality.

4. **History of the Firm**

Description: This functionality displays the history of the firm.

Flow of Events

Basic Flow: Displays the history of the firm.

Alternative Flow: Nil.

Pre-Conditions: Nil.

Post-Conditions: Nil.

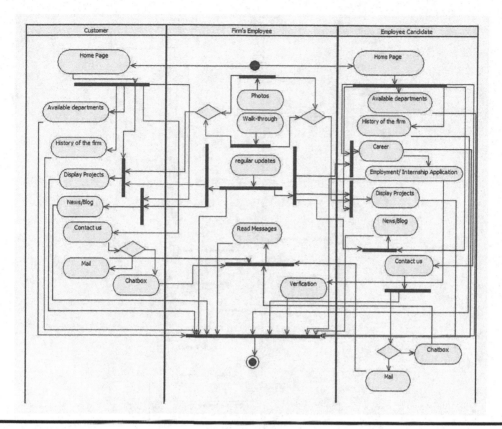

Figure 38.2   UML activity diagram.

5. **News/Blog**
    Description: This functionality gives the recent news with respect to the firm.
    Flow of Events
Basic Flow: Displays the recent news with respect to the firm.
Alternative Flow: Nil.
Pre-Conditions: Nil.
Post-Conditions: It is updated regularly by the update functionality.

6. **Career Opportunities**
    Description: This functionality displays all the available job opportunities with respect to the firm.
    Flow of Events
Basic Flow: Displays career opportunities.
Alternative Flow: Nil.
Pre-Conditions: Nil.
Post-Conditions: It is updated regularly by the update functionality.

7. **Photos**
    Description: This functionality displays the projects to the firm in the form of photos.
    Flow of Events
Basic Flow: Displays pictures of projects.

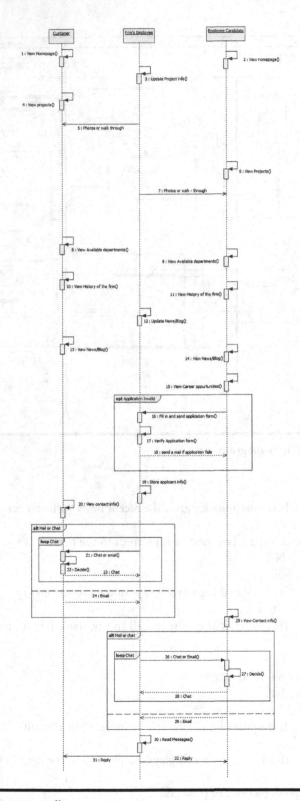

Figure 38.3   UML sequence diagram.

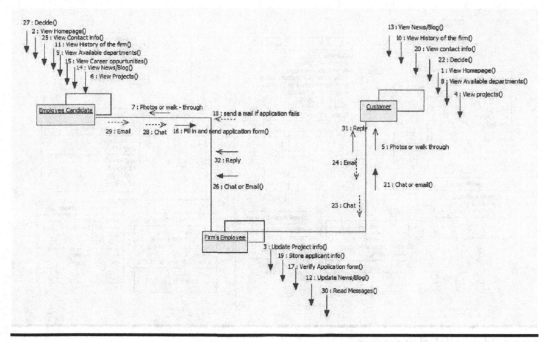

Figure 38.4   UML collaboration diagram.

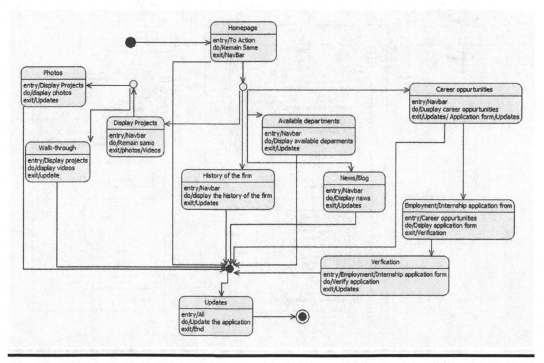

Figure 38.5   UML state chart diagram.

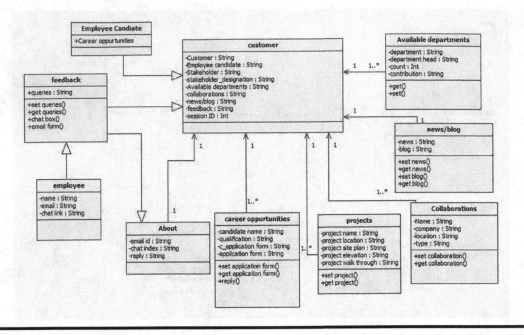

Figure 38.6   UML class diagram.

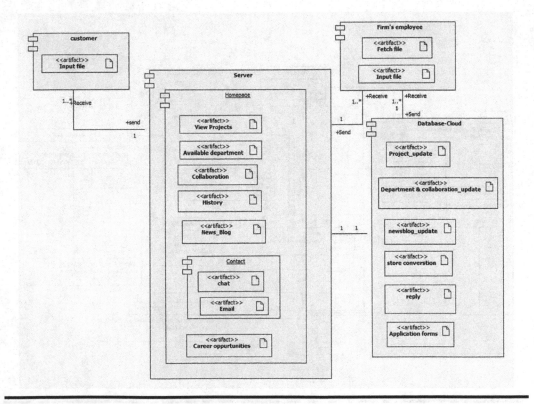

Figure 38.7   UML component diagram.

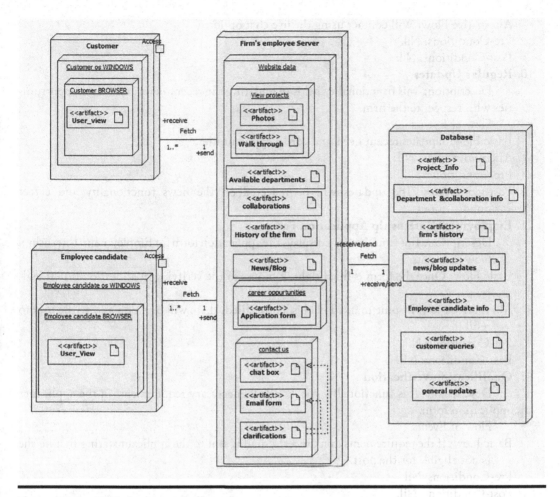

Figure 38.8   UML deployment diagram.

Alternative Flow: Displays walkthroughs of the projects.
Pre-Conditions: Nil.
Post-Conditions: Nil.

8. **Walk-Through**
    Description: This functionality displays the walk-through (animated/3D video of a building that is to be built) of the projects of the firm.
    Flow of Events
Basic Flow: Displays walkthroughs of the projects.
Alternative Flow: Displays pictures of projects.
Pre-Conditions: Nil.
Post-Conditions: Nil.

9. **Contact Info**
    Description: This functionality displays various forms of contact details/information with respect to the firm.
    Flow of Events
Basic Flow: Will contact using mail/mobile/address.

Alternative Flow: Will contact using the live chat option.

Pre-Conditions: Nil.

Post-Conditions: Nil.

10. **Regular Updates**

Description: This functionality helps in updating the recent news and career opportunities with respect to the firm.

Flow of Events

Basic Flow: Updates recent news and career opportunities.

Alternative Flow: Nil.

Pre-Conditions: Nil.

Post-Conditions: The updates will be reflected on the news functionality and career opportunities.

11. **Employment/Internship Application Form**

Description: This functionality displays the application form for Employment/Internship.

Flow of Events

Basic Flow: Once the form is filled right, it moves to the verifying qualification functionality part.

Alternative Flow: If some marked field is left unfilled, there will be a pop asking the user to refill it.

Pre-Conditions: Nil.

Post-Conditions: Nil.

12. **Qualification Verification**

Description: This functionality checks all the necessary requirements in the applicant's application form.

Flow of Events

Basic Flow: If the requirements don't meet, a mail is sent to the applicant stating that he/she is not eligible for the post.

Pre-Conditions: Nil.

Post-Conditions: Nil.

Chapter 39

Design of UML Diagrams for STARTUP MEET

39.1 Problem Statement

The policies and guidelines for startups vary from state to state. Also, startups related to a particular domain are emphasized in particular areas. The people with the startups ideas at different levels of implementation have to approach different firms or individuals for investment who are in their nearest business circles, if not in the same state. All of these will adversely impact the opportunities for the startups. Startup meet is a platform for people to privately approach firms or angel investors with their ideas implemented at different levels for funding and mentorship. Also, the government policies and loan schemes of different states can be known and applied. If people are interested in the idea a virtual presentation can be given about it to them. There will be profiles for investors and entrepreneurs (people with startup ideas) where they will be describing about what they are looking for. The entrepreneur has to request investors or mentors from different states for submitting his ideas. Once accepted he can send an abstract about it. If the investors like it, they can call for a presentation of it. The mentors also can give mentorship. The government loans and policies can be viewed and also be applied through the portal. So, startup meet is a comprehensive platform for people who are into startups (Figures 39.1–39.8).

39.2 UML Diagrams

Actor Specification

1. **Investors** – Investors will check startup ideas and either accept to invest or reject.
2. **Mentors/Consultants** – Mentors may/may not accept mentorship based on a startup idea.
3. **Entrepreneur** – He pitches the startup ideas to investors for investments and to mentors for mentorship.
4. **Admin** – He maintains all the records of the application users and their credentials.

DOI: 10.1201/9781003287124-39

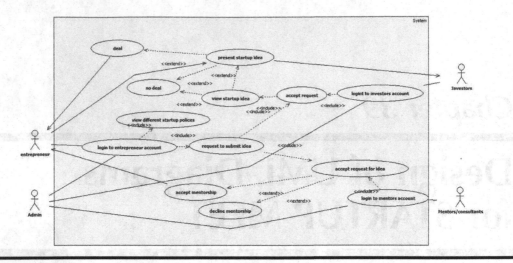

Figure 39.1   UML usecase diagram.

Usecase Specification

1. **Accept Mentorship**
    Description: If the mentor likes the startup idea, he accepts mentorship.
    Flow of Events
   Basic Flow: Accepts to give mentorship.
   Alternative Flow: Reject mentorship later.
   Pre-Conditions: Startup idea should be convincing.
   Post-Conditions: NIL.
2. **Accept Request**
    Description: Investors accept request to view startup ideas.
    Flow of Events
   Basic Flow: Views the startup idea.
   Alternative Flow: Reject request.
   Pre-Conditions: Login to the account.
   Post-Conditions: Has to view the idea.
3. **Accept Request for Idea**
    Description: Mentors accept request to view ideas.
    Flow of Events
   Basic Flow: Views the startup idea.
   Alternative Flow: Reject the request.
   Pre-Conditions: Login to the account.
   Post-Conditions: View the idea.
4. **Deal**
    Description: Investor accepts to invest in the venture.
    Flow of Events
   Basic Flow: Gives investment.
   Alternative Flow: No deal.

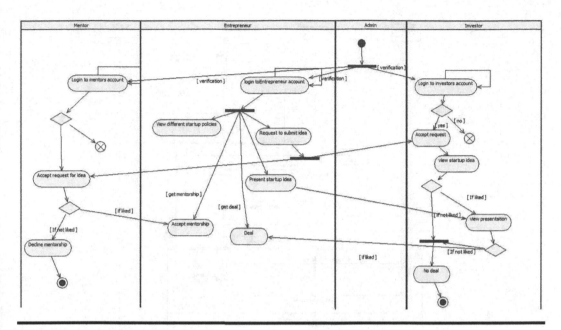

Figure 39.2   UML activity diagram.

Pre-Conditions: The presentation of idea has to be convincing.
Post-Conditions: NIL.

5. **Decline Mentorship**
    Description: Mentor rejects to give mentorship.
    Flow of Events
    Basic Flow: Not to give mentorship.
    Alternative Flow: Accept mentorship.
    Pre-Conditions: Didn't like the startup idea.
    Post-Conditions: NIL.

6. **Login to Entrepreneur Account**
    Description: Entrepreneur login into his account using his username and password.
    Flow of Events
    Basic Flow: Gives access to the account.
    Alternative Flow: Try again with the correct username/password.
    Pre-Conditions: The user should have an account.
    Post-Conditions: NIL.

7. **Login to Mentors Account**
    Description: Mentors login into their accounts using their username and password.
    Flow of Events
    Basic Flow: Gives access to the account.
    Alternative Flow: Try with the correct username/password.
    Pre-Conditions: His user should have an account.
    Post-Conditions: NIL.

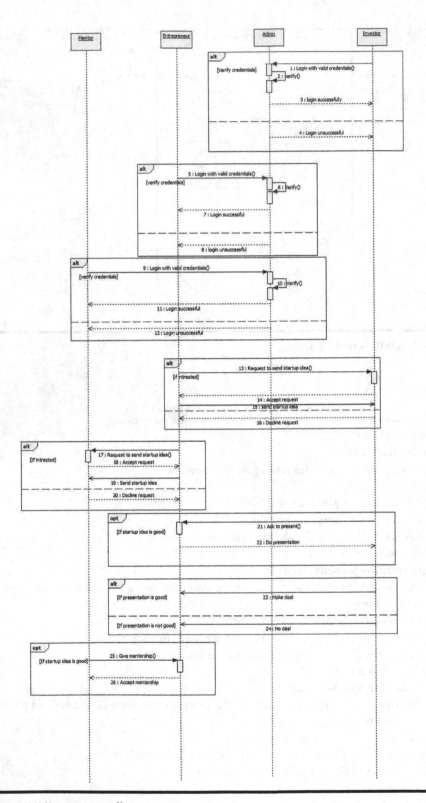

Figure 39.3   UML sequence diagram.

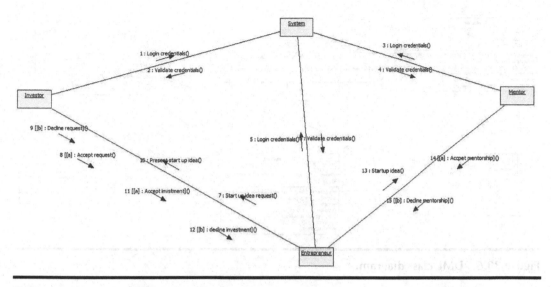

Figure 39.4   UML collaboration diagram.

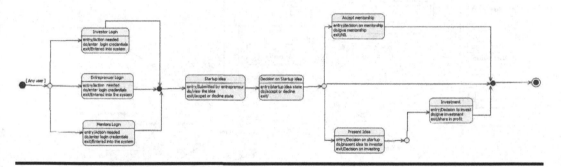

Figure 39.5   UML state chart diagram.

8. **Login to Investors Account**

Description: Investors login into their accounts using their username and password.

Flow of Events

Basic Flow: Gives access to the account.

Alternative Flow: Try with the correct username/password.

Pre-Conditions: The user should have an account.

Post-Conditions: NIL.

9. **No Deal**

Description: Investor declines to invest in the venture.

Flow of Events

Basic Flow: Doesn't give investment.

Alternative Flow: Deal.

Pre-Conditions: Doesn't like the presentation.

Post-Conditions: NIL.

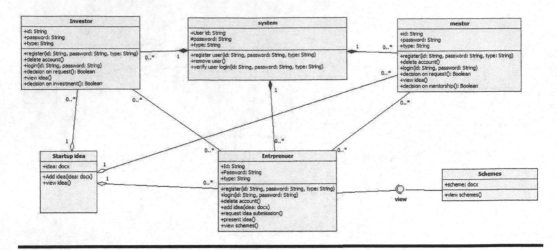

Figure 39.6   UML class diagram.

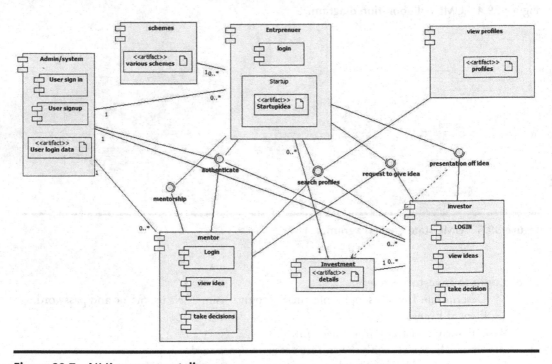

Figure 39.7   UML component diagram.

10. **Present Startup Idea**

Description: The entrepreneur tells everything about the startup to the investors.

Flow of Events

Basic Flow: Presenting the idea and making a deal.

Alternative Flow: Presenting the idea and making no deal.

Pre-Conditions: The investor should like the idea for allowing to present.

Post-Conditions: The investor should like the presentation to give investment.

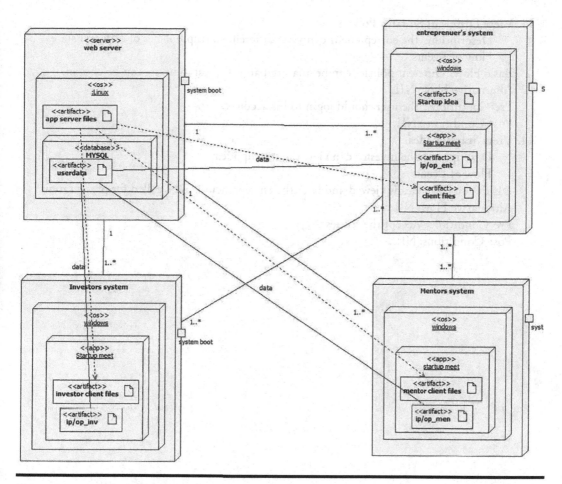

Figure 39.8   UML deployment diagram.

11. **Request to Submit Idea**
   Description: The entrepreneur requests to submit his startup idea to investors/mentors.
   Flow of Events
   Basic Flow: The request if accepted will show the idea to investors/mentors.
   Alternative Flow: The request is not accepted.
   Pre-Conditions: The entrepreneur should login to his account.
   Post-Conditions: NIL.

12. **View Different Startup Polices**
   Description: The entrepreneur can view different startup policies of different states.
   Flow of Events
   Basic Flow: Different policies can be analyzed and the best to invest can be chosen.
   Alternative Flow: NIL.
   Pre-Conditions: The user should login to his account.
   Post-Conditions: NIL.

13. **View Different Startup Polices**

Description: The entrepreneur can view different startup policies of different states.

Flow of Events

Basic Flow: Different policies can be analyzed and the best to invest can be chosen.

Alternative Flow: NIL.

Pre-Conditions: The user should login to his account.

Post-Conditions: NIL.

14. **View Startup Idea**

Description: The investor can view the startup idea.

Flow of Events

Basic Flow: The idea is viewed and later the entrepreneur can be called for presentation.

Alternative Flow: NIL.

Pre-Conditions: Accept the request.

Post-Conditions: NIL.

Chapter 40

Design of UML Diagrams for Video Suggestion System

40.1 Problem Statement

The Video Suggestion System is used in social networking platforms such as YouTube and Facebook. The ultimate aim of this system is to suggest the videos to the users based on the factors such as trending, similar views of the people and their search results. The Video Suggestion System will be found helpful in place of searching a video based on the preference and taste of the user and it also found that it can play a role in the entertainment sector. The system begins with the collection of the history or activities of the users, processing the collected data, creating dataset for suggesting videos and finally when people refresh for the suggestion, it loads videos based on the dataset (Figures 40.1–40.14).

40.2 UML Diagrams

Actor Specification

1. **Administrator** – Administrator is the superuser who has the access to edit and view all the records in the database.
2. **Normal User** – Normal user who will be surfing the videos on the internet, get suggested videos and whose history and recorded will be recorded for further suggestions.

Usecase Specification

1. **Store Personal Information**
   Description: This function stores the personal information of the normal user in the database.
   Flow of Events
   Basic Flow: This function stores the personal information of the normal user in the database.
   Alternative Flow: NIL.

DOI: 10.1201/9781003287124-40

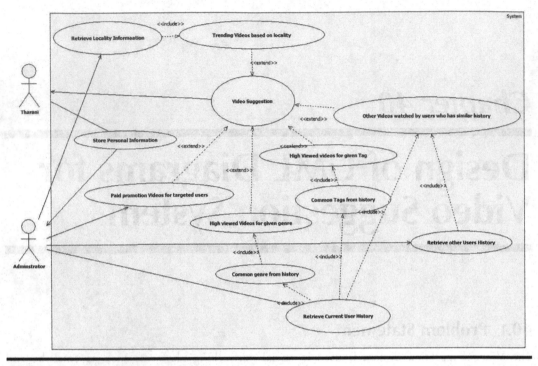

Figure 40.1   UML usecase diagram.

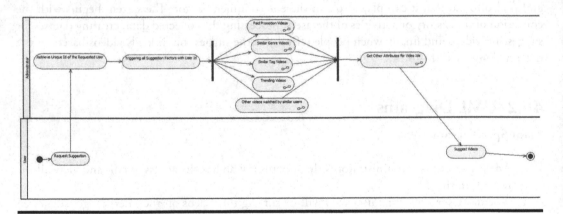

Figure 40.2   UML activity diagram – Main scenario.

Pre-Conditions: Gets write access for the user's personal information in the database.

Post-Conditions: Check whether the record is stored in the database.

2. **Retrieve Locality Information**

Description: This function retrieve the locality information from the personal of the current user.

Flow of Events

Basic Flow: Retrieves the location information of the given user.

Alternative Flow: NIL.

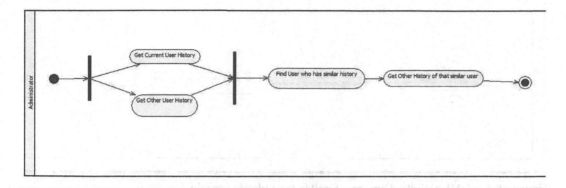

Figure 40.3   UML activity diagram – Other videos watched by similar user scenario.

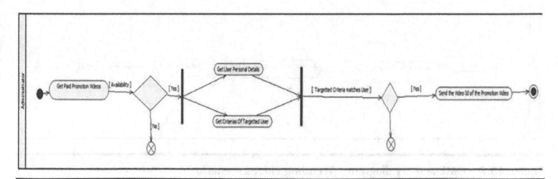

Figure 40.4   UML activity diagram – Paid promotion videos scenario.

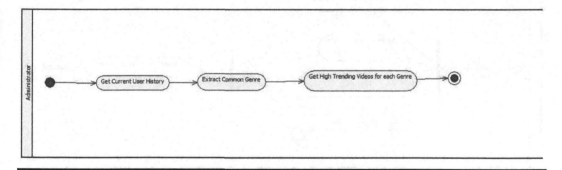

Figure 40.5   UML activity diagram – Similar genre videos scenario.

Pre-Conditions: Gets the read access to the user location in the database.

Post-Conditions: Return the location of the current user.

3. **Display Login Error**

Description: Functionality involves throwing an error if the username or password doesn't match.

Flow of Events

Basic Flow: It calculates the trending videos for the given locality based on the views of the users in that location.

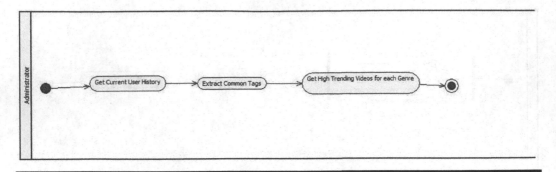

Figure 40.6   UML activity diagram – Similar tag videos scenario.

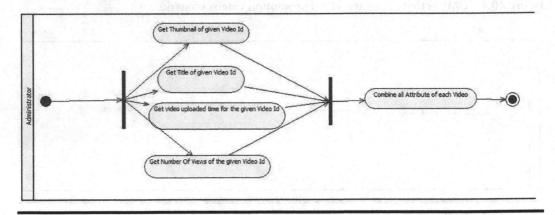

Figure 40.7   UML activity diagram – Trending videos scenario.

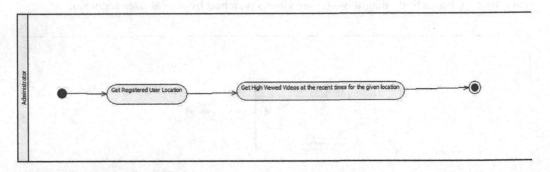

Figure 40.8   UML Activity diagram – Video attributes scenario.

Alternative Flow: NIL.
Pre-Conditions: Get the input as the location of the current user.
Post-Conditions: Returns the video ids of trending videos.

4. **Retrieve Current User History**
Description: This function retrieves the history details of the current user.
Flow of Events
Basic Flow: It retrieves the recent history of the given user.
Alternative Flow: NIL.

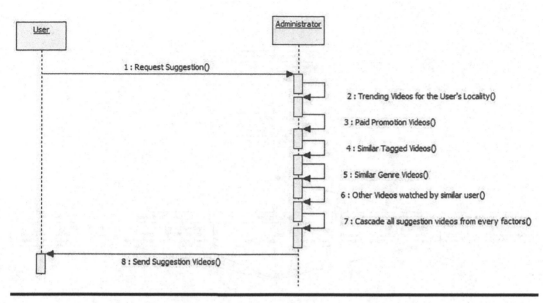

Figure 40.9   UML sequence diagram.

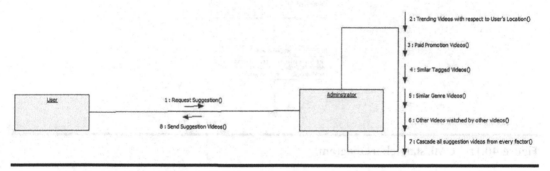

Figure 40.10   UML collaboration diagram.

Pre-Conditions: Check the connection of the database and gets access to read user history in the database.

Post-Conditions: Returns the video ids of the recent history.

5. **Common Genre from History**

Description: This function returns common genres from the users' history.

Flow of Events

Basic Flow: It extracts the common genre from the user history.

Alternative Flow: NIL.

Pre-Conditions: The student should have an account in a bank.

Post-Conditions: NIL.

6. **High Viewed of Given Genre**

Description: This function returns highly viewed videos for the given genre.

Flow of Events

Basic Flow: It fetches the highly viewed videos for the given genre.

Alternative Flow: NIL.

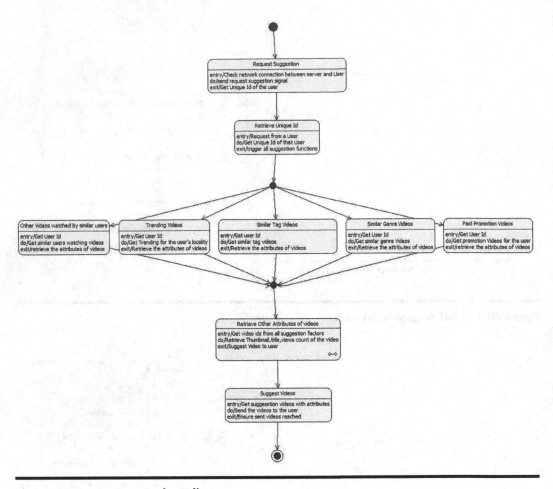

Figure 40.11   UML state chart diagram.

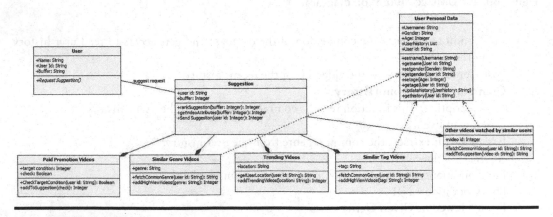

Figure 40.12   UML class diagram.

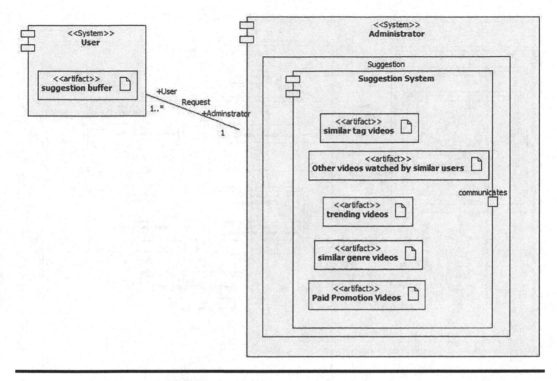

Figure 40.13   UML component diagram.

Pre-Conditions: Gets the read access for the videos and their attributes in the database and also receive the genre as input.

Post-Conditions: Returns the high viewed video id for the given genre.

7. **Paid Promotion Videos for the Targeted User**

Description: This function returns the video ids of specially promoted by the administrator.
Flow of Events

Basic Flow: It checks whether the targeted attributes match with the current user (such as locality and gender) and if matches, pass the video to the suggestion.

Alternative Flow: NIL.

Pre-Conditions: Check whether the administrator posted promotion videos.

Post-Conditions: Return the video id of the promoted videos.

8. **Common Tags from the History**

Description: This function returns common tags using the recent history of the user.
Flow of Events

Basic Flow: It extracts the common tags from the user history.

Alternative Flow: NIL.

Pre-Conditions: Gets the inputs from user history.

Post-Conditions: Returns list of common tags.

9. **High Viewed Videos of the Given Tags**

Description: This function returns highly viewed videos for the given tag.
Flow of Events

Basic Flow: It fetches the current highly viewed videos for the given tags.

Alternative Flow: NIL.

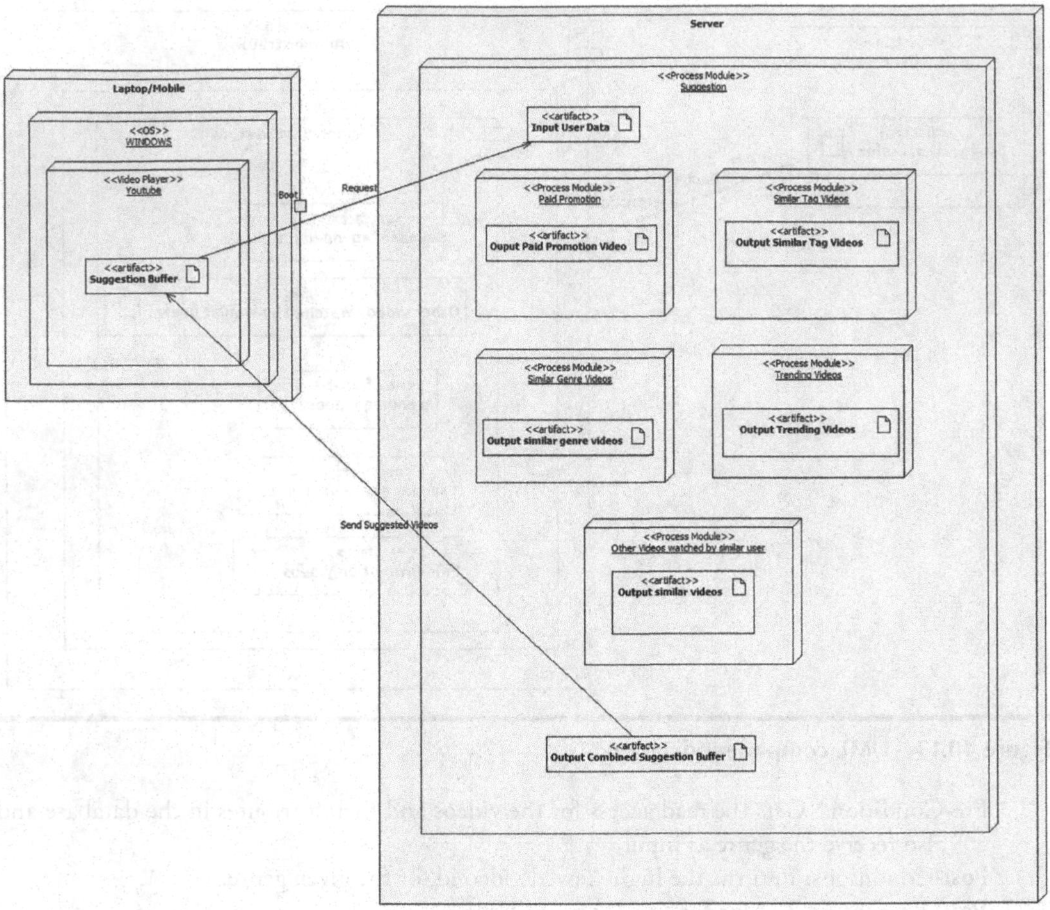

Figure 40.14 UML deployment diagram.

Pre-Conditions: Gets the read access for the videos and their attributes in the database and also receive the tags as input.

Post-Conditions: Returns video ids for the given tags.

10. **Retrieve Other Users History**

Description: This function retrieves the other similar users' history from the database.

Flow of Events

Basic Flow: It fetches the videos from the database based on the user history.

Alternative Flow: NIL.

Pre-Conditions: Checks the database connection and gets access to read other common user history.

Post-Conditions: Return the videos of the other similar user.

11. **Other Videos Watched by Users Who Has Similar Videos**

Description: This function returns the similarly viewed videos ids using the history of other users.

Flow of Events

Basic Flow: It matches the current user history with other user history and retrieves the similar videos watched by the other users.

Alternative Flow: NIL.

Pre-Conditions: Gets the current user history and other common users history as input.

Post-Conditions: Returns the videos id of a similarly viewed video.

12. **Video Suggestion**

Description: This function suggests the video with the related attributes such as thumb-nail, upload time, channel, views using the video id as input.

Flow of Events

Basic Flow: It prioritize the video Ids received as input and sends the video and its related attributes, when the user request for the suggestion of videos.

Alternative Flow: NIL.

Pre-Conditions: Gets read access to the videos and related attributes in the database and also receives the list of video Id for the suggestion.

Post-Conditions: Returns the video and its related attributes.

Index

Printed in the United States
by Baker & Taylor Publisher Services